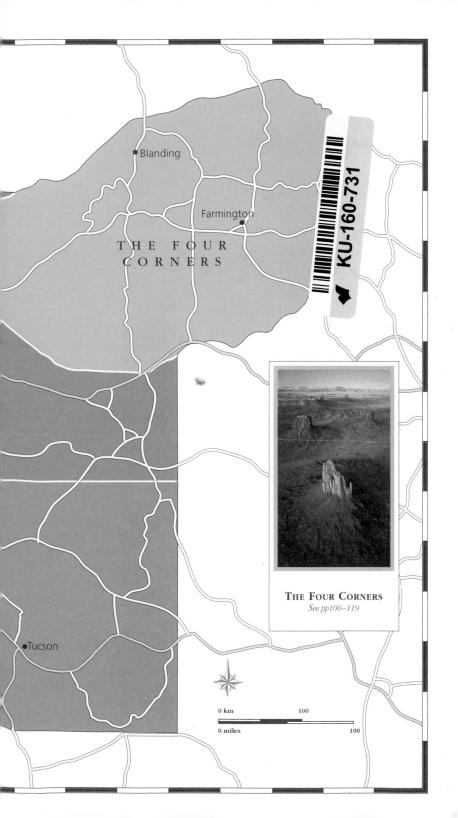

Blanding

Farmington

THE FOUR
CORNERS

THE FOUR CORNERS
*See pp100–119*

Tucson

0 km          100

0 miles        100

EYEWITNESS TRAVEL GUIDES

# ARIZONA & THE GRAND CANYON

# EYEWITNESS TRAVEL GUIDES

# ARIZONA & THE GRAND CANYON

## DK

LONDON, NEW YORK,
MELBOURNE, MUNICH AND DELHI
www.dk.com

MANAGING EDITOR Aruna Ghose
ART EDITOR Benu Joshi
SENIOR EDITOR Rimli Borooah
EDITOR Bhavna Seth Ranjan
DESIGNER Mathew Kurien
PICTURE RESEARCH Taiyaba Khatoon
DTP COORDINATOR Shailesh Sharma
DTP DESIGNER Vinod Harish

MAIN CONTRIBUTOR
Paul Franklin
PHOTOGRAPHERS
Demetrio Carrasco, Alan Keohane, Francesca Yorke
ILLUSTRATORS
P. Arun, Gary Cross, Eugene Fleurey, Claire Littlejohn,
Chris Orr & Associates, Mel Pickering,
Robbie Polley, John Woodcock

Reproduced by Colourscan (Singapore)
Printed and bound in China by L. Rex Printing Co. Ltd

First published in Great Britain in 2005
by Dorling Kindersley Limited
80 Strand, London WC2R 0RL

**Reprinted with revisions 2006**

◁ **Tall saguaro cacti in the Sonoran Desert, Southern Arizona**

**Relaxing in the rose-colored
sandstone of Antelope Canyon**

# CONTENTS

## INTRODUCING
## ARIZONA

**Wupatki National Monument with ruins
of a 12th-century pueblo building**

World famous Monument Valley in the Four Corners region

# ARIZONA & THE FOUR CORNERS AREA BY AREA

Hispanic pottery

# TRAVELERS' NEEDS

# SURVIVAL GUIDE

Visitors enjoying a trail ride at a dude ranch in Southern Arizona

Contemporary glass skyscrapers in downtown Phoenix

San Xavier del Bac Mission in Tucson, Southern Arizona

# INTRODUCING
# ARIZONA

# Putting Arizona on the Map

A RIZONA AND THE FOUR CORNERS AREA, which also takes in parts of Utah, Colorado, and New Mexico, lie in the southwest corner of the United States. Bordered by Mexico in the south, California in the west, and Texas in the east, the region covers around 113,000 sq miles (292,000 sq km). It is sparsely populated, with 60 percent of its population of around 5.3 million living in the cities. Arizona's most famous sight is the magnificent Grand Canyon.

◁ *The Southwest*, oil on canvas by Walter Ufe (1876–1936)

Satellite picture of the Colorado River winding through Grand Canyon

# A PORTRAIT OF ARIZONA

A T THE HEART OF ALL THINGS ARIZONAN *lies its landscape – stark and stunning, vast and magnificent. There is little in Arizona that is "normal" – from towering red rock buttes and deserts that secretly hoard explosions of life, to deep canyons that are encyclopedias of the planet's history. Everywhere there is a sense of grandeur, drama, and contrast.*

Native American tribes have lived in this region for thousands of years. They had flourishing civilizations that subsequently vanished, leaving mysterious and haunting ruins, which are today just a stone's throw from modern cities of glass and steel, towering above the ancient desert.

**Skull of a buffalo**

The Spanish, too, had a thriving culture here, a century before English colonists turned westward toward Arizona and the Southwest. When the Anglos finally reached the Southwest, their deeds and misdeeds gave rise to the legends of the Wild West.

### CLIMATE & ENVIRONMENT

Elevation, to a great extent, controls the environment in Arizona. For every 1,000 ft (300 m) in altitude, temperatures fall 3–5°F (1–2°C), and different flora and fauna dominate.

In Arizona's southwest corner, the Sonoran Desert is often little more than a 100 ft (30.5 m) above sea level. Here, days are searingly hot, nights are cold, and vegetation is sparse. Heading east, the land rises around 1,000 to 3,000 ft (300–1,000 m), and the desert often bursts into vibrant bloom after spring showers. The northern half of the state is dominated by the Colorado Plateau – a rock tableland covering a vast area of around 130,000 sq miles (336,700 sq km) and rising as high as 12,000 ft (3,660 m).

In southeastern Arizona, some mountains higher than 10,000 ft (3,048 m) are surrounded by desert, which has blocked the migration of plants and animals for millions of years, creating unique ecosystems called

Cacti and dried chilis adorn this flower shop in Tucson's historic El Presidio district

◁ Spring flowers, such as sand verbena and dune primrose, cover the desert landscape

"Sky Islands." Here are found animals such as the Mount Graham red squirrel that exist nowhere else.

In this land of contrasts, an hour's drive can lead from arid, barren lands of near-mystical silence, to mountains blanketed in lush and verdant forests fed by sparkling snow-melt streams.

Most parts of Arizona enjoy more than 300 days of sunshine a year, yet around 90 percent of the land receives as little as 2 in (5 cm) and no more than 20 in (50 cm) of annual rainfall. Sudden summer rainstorms on the Colorado Plateau cause flash floods. Summer temperatures in the desert often reach more than 100°F (38°C), but can drop by up to 50°F (10°C) after sunset.

**Mount Graham red squirrel in the Sky Islands**

### A CULTURAL CROSSROADS

Modern Arizona has been forged by the same three great cultures that have helped shape much of America: Native American, Hispanic, and Anglo-American. Spanish is the second language in Arizona, and throughout the Southwest. Everyday English is peppered with a range of Spanish phrases, reflecting a regional heritage stretching back to the 16th century. While US history usually focuses on developments in the east coast British colonies, Spanish explorers were in the Southwest in 1539 *(see p38)*, 80 years before the Pilgrims landed at Plymouth Rock. Native Americans have a far older relationship with Arizona. The Hopis and Pueblos trace their ancestry to the ancient peoples *(see pp22–3)* who built the elaborate cliff dwellings at the sites of Mesa Verde, Canyon de Chelly, and Chaco Canyon. Today's Native populations have a hand in the government of their own lands and have employed a variety of ways to regenerate their economies – through casinos, tourism, coal production, and crafts such as pottery, basketry, and Hopi *kachina* dolls. Native American spiritual beliefs are complex, as each tribe has different practices, which are often tied to ancestors and the land. Most Native festivals and dances are open to visitors, although some are private affairs for spiritual reasons.

### POLITICS & ECONOMY

Today, Arizona is the country's fifth-largest state. Despite the fact that its population is increasing, Arizona remains one of the least populated in the United States, with an average density of just 45 people per square mile. However, there is intense urbanization in certain areas – Phoenix, Tucson, and Flagstaff account for around 40 percent of the state's

**Native Americans performing a traditional dance during the Navajo Nation Fair at Window Rock**

Downtown Tucson – the city's historical and cultural heart – at night

population. This has put an immense pressure on the region's resources, particularly water, which has become one of the most pressing issues facing Arizona. In the 1930s, dam-building projects were initiated, starting with the Hoover Dam. The controversial Glen Canyon Dam, opened in 1963, flooded a vast area of natural beauty, as well as many sacred sites of the Native Americans. Today, many tribes have asserted ownership of the water on their lands. Water has also been channeled increasingly toward urban use as farmers in need of cash sell or lease their water rights.

Manufacturing, high technology, and the tourism industry have taken over from mining and ranching as the region's principal employers. However, mining and agriculture remain important elements of the economy.

Saxophone player, downtown Phoenix

### ENTERTAINMENT & THE ARTS

Arizona's canyons, deserts, mountains, rivers, and man-made lakes offer a plethora of hiking, watersports, skiing, and golfing opportunities. One of the best ways to experience the landscape is on a trail ride, while armchair cowboys can attend that great Southwestern event – the rodeo. The state's federally-protected national parks, recreation areas, and monuments – such as Grand Canyon National Park, Glen Canyon National Recreation Area, and Saguaro National Park – are favorite haunts for hikers, rock climbers, and 4WD enthusiasts.

Beside outdoor sport and activities, Arizona's red rock landscapes and light have always inspired artists, many of whom have settled in Sedona, Flagstaff, and Prescott. For culture lovers, there are orchestras, theaters, operas, and dance companies, who perform regularly in Phoenix and Tucson. Both cities also have a vibrant nightclub scene, featuring country, jazz, and alternate sounds. A flourishing Hispanic music scene livens up nightclubs, while Native American musicians such as Carlos R. Nakai mix traditional sounds with classical music and jazz.

The attractions of the stunning landscape and a romantic sense of the past combine to conjure up the legends of the "Wild West." For many, the Southwest offers the chance to indulge that bit of cowboy in their souls.

# Landscapes of Arizona

ARIZONA'S COLORFUL, beautiful, and varied landscape has been shaped by millions of years of volcanic eruption, uplift, and wind and water erosion. For much of the Paleozoic Era (between about 570 and 225 million years ago), the state was mostly covered by a vast inland sea that deposited over 10,000 ft (3,048 m) of sediment, which hardened into rock. Following the formation of the Rocky Mountains, some 80 million years ago, rivers and rainfall eroded the rock layers and formed the deep canyons and arches that distinguish Arizona's landscape.

The central geological feature of the region is the Colorado Plateau, which covers some 13,000 sq miles (34,000 sq km). It is cut through by many canyons, including the Grand Canyon *(see pp48–55)*.

***Coral Pink Sand Dunes State Park's*** *shimmering pink sand dunes cover more than 50 percent of this 3,700-acre (1,500-ha) park.*

**The butte formations** of Monument Valley *(see pp102–103)* are the result of erosion and their tops mark the level of an ancient plain.

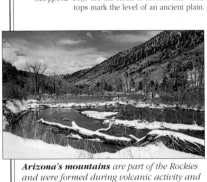

***Arizona's mountains*** *are part of the Rockies and were formed during volcanic activity and continental plate movement some 65 million years ago. Snow-covered peaks, forests of pine, juniper, spruce, and fir, and streams and small lakes fed by snowmelt, as well as alpine meadows are all found in this area.*

## GEOGRAPHICAL REGIONS

Arizona's prominent features are the Colorado Plateau and the Sonoran Desert, which is divided into Colorado Desert and Arizona Upland. The High Country mountain ranges are surrounded by desert, creating the "Sky Islands" *(see p16).*

### KEY

- Colorado Desert
- Arizona Upland
- Colorado Plateau
- High Country
- Sky Islands

Grand Canyon

*Lake Powell* (see pp62–3) *was formed by the damming of Glen Canyon in 1963. The creation of the 185-mile (300-km) long lake was reviled by environmentalists, and celebrated by watersport enthusiasts and parched farmers and city dwellers.*

*Antelope Canyon, in the Glen Canyon area, is the most famous of Arizona's narrow "slot" canyons. The canyon's rose-colored sandstone chambers, sculpted into sensual curves by centuries of flash floodwaters and desert winds, are a favorite subject for photographers.*

**The orange sand** of Monument Valley's desert floor is dotted with plants such as sagebrush and cacti.

## MESAS, BUTTES & SPIRES

Like canyons, mesas come in many sizes. Some large ones measure over 100 miles (160 km) across, and are often the result of land being forced up by geological forces. Other mesas, buttes, and spires are hard-rock remains left behind as a large plain cracked, and then eroded away.

*The Colorado Plateau is crossed by river-forged canyons. Elevations here range from 2,000 ft (600 m) above sea level to around 13,000 ft (3,900 m). Dramatic variations in the landscape include desert, verdant river valleys, thickly forested peaks, and eroded bizarre sandstone formations.*

# Flora & Fauna

D ESPITE THE fact that over 70 percent of Arizona is occupied by desert, it is not an arid, lifeless wasteland. Here, elevation, more than any other factor, determines the flora and fauna of a location.

The Sonoran Desert in the south is divided into the low elevation, arid Colorado Desert, and the comparatively higher and more verdant Arizona Upland. Covering much of the state's northern third is the 13,000 sq mile (34,000 sq km) Colorado Plateau. Above 7,000 ft (2,134 m) is High Country, where green pine forests, alpine meadows, and sparkling rivers abound. In the extreme southeast of the state, where the Sonoran Desert gives way to a part of the Chihuahuan Desert, the green-topped mountains of the High Country are surrounded by arid desert, creating special eco-zones called Sky Islands, where unique species have developed over the millennia.

*The mountain lion, also known as cougar or puma, is found in remote desert and mountain areas in Arizona. The males may be up to 8 ft (2.4 m) long and weigh 150 lbs (68 kg).*

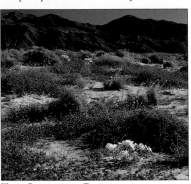

## THE COLORADO DESERT
Dry for most of the year, this vast, arid portion of the Sonoran Desert gets a small amount of winter rain that results in a display of wildflowers in spring. Other flora and fauna found here include creosote bush, cacti, yucca, jackrabbits, desert tortoises, and bighorn sheep.

## THE ARIZONA UPLAND
The summer "monsoon" and winter storms make the upland region – in the northeast of Arizona's Sonoran Desert – the greenest of the deserts. It is famous for its tall saguaro cactus *(see p90)*, some of which attain heights of 50 ft (15 m), and provide a home for animals such as the gila woodpecker and the elf owl.

*The blacktailed jackrabbit is born with a full coat of muted fur to camouflage it from predators such as the coyote.*

*Prickly pear cacti flower in spring and are among the largest of the many types of cacti that flourish in the Sonoran Desert.*

*The Joshua tree was named by Mormons who pictured the upraised arms of Joshua in its branches.*

*The desert tortoise can live for more than 50 years. It is now a protected species and is increasingly difficult to spot.*

## DANGERS IN THE DESERT

The danger of poisonous desert creatures has often been exaggerated. Although some desert creatures do, on rare occasions, bite or sting people, the bites are seldom fatal unless the victims are small children or have serious health problems. To avoid being hurt, never reach into dark spaces or overhead ledges where you can't see. Watch where you place your feet, and shake out clothes and shoes before putting them on. Never harass or handle a poisonous creature. If you are bitten, stay calm and seek medical help immediately.

*The Arizona bark scorpion is golden in color. America's most venomous scorpion, it has a sting that requires prompt medical help.*

*The diamondback rattlesnake is found in Arizona's deserts and mountains. Its bite is venomous, but seldom deadly if treated. It usually strikes only when surprised.*

## THE COLORADO PLATEAU

Classically Western with canyons, cliffs, mesas, and buttes, the Colorado Plateau is dotted with cacti, sage, and mesquite in its lower reaches. At higher altitudes, the flora changes to piñon pines and junipers. Rattlesnakes, cougars, and coyotes are among the wildlife found on the plateau.

## THE HIGH COUNTRY

At higher elevations, Arizona's plants and animals are similar to those of Canada. Black bears, mule deer, and elk are some of the fauna. Ponderosa pines are found at 6,000–9,000 ft (1,829–2,743 m), aspen forests at 8,000–11,000 ft (2,438–3,353 m), and alpine meadows at 11,000–13,000 ft (3,353–3,962 m).

*Piñon pines are ball-shaped, less than 30 ft (9.1 m) tall, and are found between 4,000 and 6,000 ft (1,829 m).*

*Black bears inhabit Arizona's mountainous areas. Their diet consists of nuts, insects, and small mammals. They are shy, but may approach humans out of curiosity or if they smell food.*

*The coyote is a small, highly intelligent member of the dog family. It hunts both solo and in packs, and can often be heard howling at night.*

*Aspen trees are common at elevations over 8,000 ft (2,438 m). Their leaves turn a rich golden color in fall.*

# Art of Arizona

**Ancient pottery bowl**

ARIZONA'S QUALITIES of light, open spaces, and colorful landscapes have inspired art and craft for centuries – from intricate baskets and pottery of the Native Americans to the religious art of the early Spanish missions. In the 1800s, Frederic Remington and Charles Russell painted romantic images of the Wild West. Later, in the 20th century, Ansel Adams photographed the beauty and physical drama of the land. Today, Arizona is a dynamic center for the arts, with vibrant art museums, busy galleries, and a lively community of artists.

**Basketwork** *is associated with most Native tribes. Braided, twined or coiled from willow or yucca leaves, the baskets are decorated differently by each tribe.*

**Anglo art** *developed as European settlers moved westward. Works by Frederic Remington (see p24), such as* Cowboy on a Horse *seen above, and by Thomas Moran captured cowboy life and the stunning landscapes of the West. Today, this tradition continues with artists portraying traditional and contemporary life in the West.*

## TRADITIONAL NATIVE ART

Five hundred years before Columbus arrived in the New World, Native tribes in Arizona were producing baskets, pottery, and jewelry of stunning delicacy and beauty. Thousands of artifacts recovered from Ancient Puebloan, Hohokam, and Mogollon sites are on display at major institutions. The Heard Museum *(see pp78–9)* has one of the world's most comprehensive collections of both ancient and contemporary Native art, and the Arizona State Museum *(see p89)* has a significant display that covers 2,000 years of Native history. The Museum of Northern Arizona in Flagstaff *(see p66)* features superb examples of Sinagua pottery and artifacts from early Navajo, Hopi, and Zuni tribal life. Native tribes still produce traditional art and crafts, and trading posts are an excellent place to see and purchase them *(see pp146–7).*

**Pottery**
*One of the oldest of all Native art forms, exceptional pottery collections can be seen at the Edge of Cedars State Park (see p117).*

## CONTEMPORARY SCULPTURE

One of the most popular art forms in Arizona today, excellent examples of contemporary sculpture, such as the piece featured here – *Dineh* (1981) – can be seen in galleries throughout the state. *Dineh*, meaning "the people," is the word the Navajo use to describe themselves. This bronze displays clean lines and smooth surfaces that evoke the strength and dignity of the subjects.

## MODERN NATIVE ARTISTS

Native artists often blend traditional themes with modern styles. The *Red-Tailed Hawk* (1986) by Daniel Namhinga reflects his Hopi-Tewa heritage in the stylized *kachina* and birdwing forms, boldly rendered in bright desert colors. It is part of the Native art collection at Heard Museum *(see p79)*.

*Latin art first appeared in Arizona during the Spanish Colonial period, usually representing religious themes. Today, it depicts the Hispanic cultures of the American Southwest and Mexico. Exhibits featuring the works of renowned contemporary Latin artists can be found at major art museums.*

**Silver Jewelry**
*Made from silver and turquoise, jewelry is a relatively new art form developed by the Navajo and Zuni tribes in the late 1800s.*

**Rugs**
*Weaving began in the mid-1800s. Today, a fine Navajo rug can sell for thousands of dollars.*

**Carvings**
Kachina *represent Hopi spirits. They can be traced to the tribe's early history, and ancient* kachinas *are valued collector's items.*

# Architecture of Arizona

ARIZONA'S DISTINCTIVE ARCHITECTURE traces its influences to the Ancient Puebloan master-builders, whose stone and adobe cliff dwellings, such as Canyon de Chelly's Antelope House *(see p108)*, were suited to the region's harsh climate. Historic architecture can be seen in many old town districts, where adobes are arranged around a central plaza. But there are also other styles, from the Spanish Colonial of the 18th century to those of the 19th and early 20th century. Wooden storefronts, Victorian mansions, and miners' cottages all lend a rustic charm to the region's many mountain towns. Scottsdale *(see p80)* has an architecture school that was set up by Frank Lloyd Wright, one of the 20th century's most famous architects.

**Immaculate Conception Church, Ajo** *(see p96)*

## TRADITIONAL ADOBE

**Adobe ovens such as these were once used for baking**

The traditional building material of the Southwest is adobe, a mixture of mud or clay and sand, with straw or grass as a binder. This is formed into bricks, which harden in the sun, then built into walls, cemented with a similar material, and plastered over with more mud. Adobe deteriorates quickly and must be replastered every few years. Modern adobe-style buildings are often made of cement and covered with lime cement stucco painted to look like adobe. Original dwellings had dirt floors and wooden beams *(vigas)* as ceiling supports. These structures also had adobe ovens that were used for baking.

*Canale* (water pipe)     Adobe bricks

*A traditional adobe rancho or ranch house has a flat roof with pipes* (canales) *to drain away water.*

## SPANISH COLONIAL

In the 17th and 18th centuries, Spanish Colonial missions combined the Baroque style of Mexican and European religious architecture with Native design, using local materials and craftsmen. This style underwent a resurgence as Spanish Colonial Revival, from 1915 to the 1930s, and was incorporated into private homes and public buildings. Red-tiled roofs, ornamental terra-cotta, and stone or iron grille work were combined with white stucco walls. A fine example is Tucson's Pima County Courthouse *(see p88)*, with its dome adorned with colored tiles.

Moorish-style dome

**Domes and towers of San Xavier del Bac Mission**

Ornate wooden carvings

Iron grille work

*San Xavier del Bac Mission* (see pp92–3) *exemplifies the Baroque tradition of the Spanish Colonial churches.*

## MISSION REVIVAL

Similar in spirit to Spanish Colonial trends, the early 20th-century Mission Revival style is characterized by stucco walls made of white lime cement, often with graceful arches, flat roofs, and courtyards, but with less ornamentation. A fine example of a Mission Revival-style bungalow is the J. Knox Corbett House in Tucson's Historic District *(see p88)*. Built of brick but plastered over in white to simulate adobe, it has a red-tile roof and a big screen porch at the back.

Façade of J. Knox Corbett House

Red-tiled roof          White plaster

*J. Knox Corbett House in Tuscon was designed in the popular Mission Revival style by the Chicago architect David Holmes in 1906.*

## CONTEMPORARY ARCHITECTURE

Arizona has inspired three of the 20th century's most prominent American architects. Frank Lloyd Wright (1867–1959) advocated "Organic Architecture" – the use of local materials and the importance of creating structures that blended with their settings. The architectural complex he built at Taliesin West in Scottsdale includes a school, offices, and his home. Constructed from desert stone and sand, the expansive proportions of the complex reflect the vastness of the Arizona Desert.

**Interiors of the Frank Lloyd Wright-designed Taliesin West in Scottsdale, Phoenix**

Mary Elizabeth Jane Colter (1870–1958) was one of the most influential architects in America at a time when women architects were virtually unknown. At the turn of the 20th century, the Santa Fe Railroad hired Colter to design several buildings in the Grand Canyon area. Colter was fascinated by Native American building styles and is credited with starting the architectural style called National Park Service Rustic. Her masterpiece is Hopi House *(see p54)*, completed in 1904.

In the 1940s, Italian Paolo Soleri (b. 1919) studied at Taliesin. In 1956, he established the Cosanti Foundation *(see p81)* devoted to what he termed "arcology." This synthesis of architecture and ecology minimizes energy waste, which is endemic in modern buildings and towns.

**The visitor building at Arcosanti, designed by Paolo Soleri**

**Desert View's stone watchtower designed by Mary Colter, at Grand Canyon South Rim**

# Native Cultures of Arizona

**Hopi wicker plaque**

THE NATIVE PEOPLES of Arizona have maintained many of their traditions, in spite of more than 400 years of armed conflict and brutal attempts at cultural assimilation since the arrival of the Spanish in 1539. Such hardships have forged their determination to retain cultural identities, though some have chosen to move between two worlds – living and working in the modern world while taking part in tribal life and traditional ceremonies. Since the mid-20th century, Native groups have led political campaigns for the restoration of homelands and compensation for past losses.

Today, there are 23 Native reservations in Arizona, the Navajo Reservation being the largest. Tourism and gambling have brought much-needed revenue, but battles over land rights and environmental issues continue.

**Rodeo in session at the Apache reservation in Whiteriver, Arizona**

## THE APACHE

DESPITE THEIR reputation as fierce warriors, reinforced by their legendary leaders Cochise and Geronimo *(see p38)*, traditionally the Apache were mainly hunter-gatherers. They are thought to have roamed south from their Athabascan-speaking homelands in northern Canada during the 15th century.

The largest Apache reservations are the adjoining San Carlos and Fort Apache reservations in the east-central part of Arizona. Over 12,000 Apaches live on them, with the primary industries being cattle ranching, timber, and tourism. Successful management of their natural resources has ensured a degree of economic stability.

Visitors are welcome at the Apache reservations to watch rituals such as the *nah'ib'es* or Sunrise Ceremony, which marks a girl's transition to womanhood. Dances, festivals, and rodeos are also held on the reservations *(see pp30–33)*.

## THE NAVAJO

WITH A POPULATION of more than 200,000, the Navajo Nation is the largest reservation in southwestern USA, covering more than 25,000 sq miles (64,750 sq km) in Arizona, New Mexico, and southern Utah. The spiritual center of the Navajo Nation is Canyon de Chelly *(see pp106–9)*, where Navajo farmers still live, tend to their sheep, and make rugs using the sheep wool. The Navajo

are generally welcoming to visitors, and act as guides in Monument Valley and other sites on their land *(see pp102–3)*. They have resisted building casinos to raise money, basing their economy on tourism and the sale of natural resources such as oil, coal, and uranium. However, many Navajo are opposed to the pollution that strip-mining and other industrial enterprises have brought.

While many Navajo now live off the reservation in cities and towns, the traditional dwelling, the *hogan*, remains an important focus of their cultural life. Today's *hogan* is an octagonal wood cabin, often fitted with electricity and other modern amenities, where family gatherings take place.

Navajo religious beliefs are still bound up with daily life, with farmers singing corn-growing songs and weavers incorporating a spirit thread into their rugs. Colorful and intricate sand paintings still play a part in healing ceremonies, which aim to restore *hozho*, or harmony, to ill or troubled individuals.

**Navajo Indian woman shearing wool from a sheep**

## THE HOPI

THE PREDOMINANT Pueblo tribe in Arizona is the Hopi, whose reservation is located in the center of the Navajo Reservation. They are one of 20 Pueblo tribes in the Southwest. Pueblo tribes share many of the same religious and cultural beliefs, though there are linguistic differences from tribe to

## Hopi Spirituality

Religion is a fundamental element of Hopi lifestyle. Their ceremonies focus on *kachina* (or *katsina*) – spirit figures that symbolize nature in all its forms. Familiar to visitors as the painted, carved wooden dolls available in many gift stores, the *kachina* lie at the heart of Hopi spirituality. During the growing season (December to July), these spirit figures are represented by *kachina* dancers who visit Hopi villages. During the rest of the year, the spirits are believed to reside in a shrine in the high San Francisco Peaks, north of Flagstaff. Hopi religious ceremonies are often held in the *kiva*, a round underground chamber, usually closed to visitors. Most celebrations are closed to non-Hopis, but some are open to the public. Photography of Pueblo villages and ceremonies is forbidden.

**Young Hopi Rainbow dancer**

## The Havasupai & Hualapai

These two tribes occupy two reservations that stretch along the southern rim of the Grand Canyon. They trace their ancestry to the ancient Hohokam people and share similar languages. The only town on the Havasupai reservation is Supai, 8 miles (13 km) from the nearest road. The reservation is the gateway to the beautiful Havasu Canyon and emerald green Havasu Falls *(see p48)*, a popular destination for hikers.

## The Ute

This tribe once reigned over a vast territory, covering 85 percent of Colorado until as late as the 1850s. Steady encroachment by settlers and mining interests eventually forced them to resettle. Today, the Ute welcome visitors to their two reservations along the southern Colorado border. The Ute Mountain Reservation is home to the little known but spectacular Ancestral Puebloan ruins of Ute Mountain Tribal Park *(see p110)*, and the southern Ute Reservation attracts thousands of visitors each year to the popular Sky Ute Casino, Lodge, and Museum. The southern Utes also hold a colorful Bear Dance on Memorial Day weekend.

tribe. Most Pueblo tribes trace their ancestry to the Ancestral Puebloan people *(see pp36–7)*, who spread across the area from around 300–200 BC. The town of Walpi on the Hopi Reservation has been continuously occupied since AD 1100.

The oldest Hopi villages are on three mesa-tops, called First, Second, and Third mesas. The groups on each mesa are distinct, exceling at different crafts – pottery on First Mesa, jewelry on Second Mesa, and basketry on Third Mesa. All the settlements produce colorful *kachinas*.

The land occupied by the Hopi is among the starkest and most barren in all America. However, using the ancient irrigation techniques of their ancestors, the Hopi grow corn, beans, and squash. Each village holds sacred dances and ceremonies throughout the year.

## The Tohono O'odham

Along with their close relatives, the Pima people, the Tohono O'odham live in South Arizona's Sonoran Desert. Due to the harsh environment here, neither tribe has ever been moved off its ancestral lands. These

**Young dancer at an Ute powwow, a gathering of Native Indians**

tribes are among the most anglicized in the region. The Tohono O'odham are mainly Christian. However, they still practice traditional ceremonies, such as the Saguaro Wine Festival and the Tcirkwena Dance, and are known for their fine basketwork.

**Ute woman sewing moccasins with Mount Ute in the background**

# The Wild West

Romanticized in a thousand cowboy movies, the "Wild West" conjures up images of tough men herding cattle across the country before living it up in a saloon. But frontier life was far from romantic. Settlers arriving in this wilderness were caught up in a first-come-first-serve battle for land and wealth, fighting Native Americans and each other for land.

The rugged life of the prospectors and ranch cowboys helped to create the idea of the American West. Visitors can still see mining ghost towns such as Chloride (see p73) or enjoy re-enacted gunfights on the streets of Tombstone. In the late 19th century, however, such survival skills as good shooting often co-existed with a kill-or-be-killed ethos.

**Women in the** *Wild West often had to step into the traditional roles of men. Calamity Jane, a woman scout, was known to be an excellent shot and horse rider.*

**A reward poster** *for William Bonney (better known as Billy the Kid), who was one of the Wild West's most notorious outlaws. He was eventually tracked and killed by Sheriff Pat Garrett at Fort Sumner, New Mexico, on July 14, 1881.*

## REWARD

### ($5,000.00)

Reward for the capture, dead or alive, of one Wm. Wright, better known as

## "BILLY THE KID"

Age, 18. Height, 5 feet, 3 inches. Weight, 125 lbs. Light hair, blue eyes and even features. He is the leader of the worst band of desperadoes the Territory has ever had to deal with. The above reward will be paid for his capture or positive proof of his death.

JIM DALTON, Sheriff.

## DEAD OR ALIVE!
## BILLY THE KID

*Deadwood Dick was the nickname of cowboy Nat Love, famed for his cattle-roping skills. Although there were around 5,000 black cowboys, there are no sights or museums commemorating them in the Southwest today.*

**Cowboys** were famous for their horsemanship and sense of camaraderie. The painting shows two friends attempting to save another.

**The Conversation, or Dubious Company** *(1902) by Frederic Remington highlights the tensions between Natives and the US army, which had played a central role in removing tribes from their ancestral lands.*

*Cowboy fashion* began to appear in advertisements in around 1900. The ever popular Levi Strauss denim clothing can be bought across the region (see p142).

*Guided trail rides* are a great way to explore the Wild West and are part of the package of activities available at dude ranches (see p152). These ranches offer visitors the opportunity to experience the contemporary cowboy lifestyle.

**Horses** were vividly depicted in Remington's dramatic action scenes. They were painted with astonishing realism, revealing a profound knowledge of their behavior and physique.

## THE GUNFIGHT AT THE OK CORRAL

One of the most famous tales of the Wild West is the Gunfight at the OK Corral in Tombstone, Arizona (*see p98*). This struggle pitted two clans against each other, the Clantons and the Earps. The usual, often disputed, version features the Clantons as no-good outlaws and the Earps as the forces of law and order. In 1881 Virgil Earp was the town marshal, and his brothers Morgan and Wyatt were temporary deputies. The showdown on October 26 had the Earps and their ally Doc Holliday on one side and Billy Clanton and the McLaury brothers, Tom and Frank, on the other. Of the seven combatants, only Wyatt Earp emerged untouched by a bullet. Billy, Tom, and Frank were all killed. Wyatt Earp moved to Los Angeles, where he died in 1929.

**Scene from the 1957 film, *Gunfight at the OK Corral*, with Burt Lancaster and Kirk Douglas**

## SOUTHWESTERN COWBOYS

New York-born artist Frederic Sackrider Remington (1861–1909) became well known for his epic portraits of cowboys, horses, soldiers, and Native Americans in the late 19th century. Featured above is *Aiding a Comrade* (1890), one of his works which celebrates the bravery and loyalty of the cowboy, at a time when they and small-scale ranchers were being superceded by powerful mining companies and ranching corporations. Remington lamented the passing of these heroes: "Cowboys! There are no cowboys anymore!"

# Mines & Mineral Collecting

Arizona's tremendous mineral wealth, which has shaped much of the state's history, is a result of its unique geology. People have sought and used Arizona's mineral riches for centuries. Early Native jewelry was made of turquoise and raw copper. In the 1800s, gold and silver deposits were discovered, and towns grew up overnight to house the swelling populations of miners. It was copper, though, that provided Arizona its greatest mineral boom, with mines at Jerome, Bisbee, and Globe producing high-grade ore for over a century. Today, rockhounds from around the world collect beautiful crystals and rare minerals. Souvenirs can also be found in rock shops, or at any of the gem and mineral shows that Arizona hosts (see p142).

**Mine tours** are conducted by historic mines, and offer an insight into the everyday life of early miners.

## MINERAL COLLECTING SAFETY TIPS

- Practice prudent desert safety (see pp160–61).
- Never venture out alone.
- Always try to explore new areas with a qualified guide.
- Contact local rock shops or mineral clubs for up-to-date information on collecting sites.
- Always obtain permission before collecting on private property.
- Never enter an open mine shaft; beware of hidden shafts in the desert floor.
- Wear safety gear, particularly goggles, when using tools.

**Rock and gem shows** are hosted across Arizona every year. They are a good place to see world-class rocks, minerals and gems, and learn about mineralogy and rock collecting.

## MINERAL COLLECTING

Rockhounding with other collectors can be both exciting and educational. Visitors will find a number of excellent rock collecting sites throughout Arizona, particularly in the state's central and southern regions. Some of these sites are easily accessible, and visitors only require to know which area of the desert floor, canyon, or dry wash to search. Other sites, particularly mine sites and private property, require special permission to explore. The accessibility of sites may vary – local rock shops and mineral clubs are excellent sources of up-to-date information for newcomers.

*Gold panning is a fascinating pastime that can be enjoyed at many of Arizona's streams. Guided tours to sites that yield precious gold flakes cater to both newcomers and skilled panners.*

## RESOURCES

### ROCK & MINERAL CLUBS

**Mineralogical Society of Arizona**
W www.azminerals.com

**Sedona/Oak Creek Gem & Mineral Society**
W www.sedonagemandmineral.org

**Tucson Gem & Mineral Society**
C (520) 322-5773.

**Tucson Old Pueblo Lapidary Club**
C (520) 323-9154.

### MINE TOURS

**Gold Mine Tours**
Oatman, AZ 86433.
W www.goldroadmine.com

**Queen Mine Tour**
Bisbee, AZ.
C (520) 432-2071.

### GOLD PANNING TOUR

**Arrowhead Desert Tours**
W www.azdeserttours.com

### SHOPS

**Arizona Gems & Minerals**
C (928) 772-6443.

**Copper City Rock Shop**
W www.coppercityrockshop.com

**Discount Agate House**
C (520) 323-0781.

## ARIZONA MINERALS

Arizona's mines yield exquisite minerals such as the brilliant blue-green azurite and chrysocolla, rich green malachite, darker-than-emerald dioptase, rust-red wulfenite, and turquoise, which has been revered for centuries. Most regions in the state produce beautiful quartz; crystals as small as sand grains or as big as cucumbers, royal purple amethyst, translucent rose quartz, agates of every hue, and stunning geodes – rocks whose hollow centers are filled with glittering crystals.

Azurite     Malachite     Rose quartz

Quartz     Amethyst     Polished quartz

# Route 66 in Arizona

**Route 66 Flagstaff sign**

ROUTE 66 is America's most famous road. Stretching for 2,448 miles (3,941 km) from Chicago to Los Angeles, it is part of the country's folklore, symbolizing the freedom of the open road and inextricably linked to the growth of automobile travel. Known also as "The Mother Road" and "America's Main Street," Route 66 was officially opened in 1926 after a 12-year construction process linked the main streets of hundreds of small towns that had been previously isolated. In the 1930s, a prolonged drought in Oklahoma deprived more than 200,000 farmers of their livelihoods and prompted their trek to California along Route 66. This was movingly depicted in John Steinbeck's novel *The Grapes of Wrath* (1939).

*Seligman features several Route 66 stores and diners. Set among Arizona's Upland mountains, the road here passes through scenery that evokes the days of the westward pioneers.*

*Route 66 in Arizona passes through long stretches of wilderness bearing none of the trappings of the modern world. The state has the longest remaining stretch of the original road.*

**KEY**

━━ Route 66

══ Other roads

- - State boundary

```
0 km          40
0 miles       40
```

*Oatman, a former gold-mining boomtown (see p73), has 19th-century buildings and boardwalks lining its historic main street. Mock gunfights are regularly staged here.*

*The Grand Canyon Caverns, discovered in 1927, are around 0.75 miles (1.2 km) below ground level. On a 45-minute guided tour visitors are led through football field-sized caverns adorned with stalagmites and seams of sparkling crystals.*

## ROUTE 66 IN POPULAR CULTURE

In the 1940s and 1950s, as America's love affair with the car grew and more people moved west than ever before, hundreds of motels, restaurants, and tourist attractions appeared along Route 66, sporting a vibrant new style of architecture. The road's end as a major thoroughfare came in the 1970s with the building of a national network of multilane highways. Today, the road is a popular tourist destination in itself, and along the Arizona section, enthusiasts and conservationists have helped to ensure the preservation of many of its most evocative buildings and signs.

### LOCATOR MAP

— Route 66

☐ Map area

**Bobby Troup, composer of the popular song, *Route 66*, in a 1948 Buick convertible**

*Holbrook was founded in 1882 and is another Route 66 landmark. It is famous for Wigwam Village Motel (see p126), a restored 1950s motel, where visitors can stay in rooms that resemble Indian teepees.*

Parks

Winona

Winslow

Joseph City

Chambers

Navajo

*Flagstaff is home to the famous Museum Club roadhouse (see p149). It became a nightclub nicknamed "The Zoo," which was favored by country musicians traveling the road, including such stars as Willie Nelson.*

*Williams is known for its many nostalgic diners and motels. Twisters Soda Fountain (see p137), also known as The Route 66 Place, is crammed with road memorabilia, including the original 1950s soda fountain and bar stools.*

# ARIZONA THROUGH THE YEAR

Stringing *ristras* of hot chili peppers

HE WEATHER in the state of Arizona is well known for its extremes, ranging from the heat of the desert to the ice and snow of the mountains. Temperatures vary according to altitude, and so the higher the elevation of the land, the cooler the area will be. Because the climate can be unbearably hot during the summer months, particularly in the southern parts of the state, many people prefer to travel to Arizona during spring and fall. This part of the world is particularly beautiful in fall, with an astounding array of golds, reds, and yellows in the forests and national parks. Besides Arizona's natural beauty, visitors can experience many different kinds of festivals and celebrations, which are unique to the state and reflect its diverse mix of the three main Southwestern cultures – Native American, Hispanic, and European.

## SPRING

EVERYONE ENJOYS being outdoors in spring, and many festivals and celebrations are held at this time throughout Arizona.

## MARCH

**Cactus League Spring Training** *(month long)* Phoenix and Tucson. Major league baseball teams play in pre-season practice and exhibition games.
**Guild Indian Fair & Market** *(first weekend)* Phoenix. Held at the Heard Museum, the fair features Indian dancing, arts, crafts, and Native American food.
**Sedona International Film Festival** *(first weekend)* Sedona. Film fans gather to view films and attend the workshop at the festival.

Native dancer at the Guild Indian Fair and Market, Phoenix

Rides at the Maricopa County fair held in Phoenix

**Midnight at the Oasis Festival** *(early Mar)* Yuma. Cars and nostalgia, with over 800 restored and unusual cars on display.
**Fourth Avenue Street Fair** *(mid-Mar)* Tucson. Artists from all over the United States, food vendors, live music performances, sidewalk performers, kids' entertainment, and fun activities for all.
**St. Patrick's Day Parade** *(mid-Mar)* Sedona. Annual parade celebrates the green, preceded by a 3.1-mile (5-km) race.

## APRIL

**Sunday on Central** *(early Apr)* Phoenix. Vibrant street fair with music and dancing on a number of stages.
**Arizona Book Festival** *(first Sat)* Phoenix. Event sees 200 local and national authors, and hundreds of exhibitors with new and used books.

**Easter Pageant** *(week preceding Easter)* Mesa. Large annual outdoor theatrical production held every night at the Mormon Temple with a cast of hundreds in historical costumes.
**Maricopa County Fair** *(mid-Apr)* Phoenix. Carnival, entertainment, competitions, education, and fun times for all ages.
**Tucson International Mariachi Conference** *(mid–late Apr)* Tucson. Annual celebration of Mexican *mariachi* music and dancing.
**Pima County Fair** *(late Apr)* Tucson. Horses and cattle, gems and minerals, concerts, exhibits, rides, and food provide great family fun.
**La Vuelta de Bisbee** *(late Apr)* Bisbee. A professional 80-mile (129-km) bicycle race in the Bisbee area.

## SUMMER

SUMMER IS WARM and is the time for many open-air events, from carnivals and rodeos to cultural events. The weather in July and August, however, can be extreme, especially in Southern Arizona, which has very high temperatures and violent summer storms.

## MAY

**El Cinco de Mayo** *(May 5)* Many Arizona towns. Festivities to mark the 1862 Mexican victory over the French include parades, dancing, and Mexican food.
**Wyatt Earp Days** *(Memorial Day weekend)* Tombstone. Mock gunfights, chili cook-off, "hangings," 1880s fashion show, street entertainment, and barbecue.
**Bill Williams Rendezvous** *(Memorial Day weekend)* Williams. Enthusiasts from all over the US gather for a black-powder shoot, carnival, street parade, and pioneer arts and crafts.
**Phippen Western Art Show & Sale** *(Memorial Day weekend)* Prescott. Western art and sculpture buyers, sellers, and admirers come for the juried fine arts show.

## JUNE

**Sharlot Hall Museum Folk Arts Fair** *(first weekend)* Prescott. Demonstrations of the arts, skills, and entertainments of the territorial years.

Folk arts fair at Sharlot Hall Museum, Prescott

**Sedona Taste** *(Sunday before Father's Day)* Sedona. Chef's from top restaurants prepare food samples and serve fine wines.
**Pine Country Pro Rodeo** *(third weekend)* Flagstaff. Competitors take part in bronc and bull riding, roping, and barrel racing.
**Summer Rodeo Series** *(June–mid-Aug)* Williams. Watch cowboys in rodeo events, including bareback, team roping, calf roping, bull riding, and more.

## JULY

**Fourth of July** *(4 July)* Most Arizona towns. Celebrations include parades, fireworks, rodeos, sports, music festivals, and Indian dances.
**Flagstaff Festival of the Arts** *(early July–mid-Aug)* Flagstaff. A celebration of the arts, featuring films, concerts, plays, and operas.
**Frontier Days** *(first week)* Prescott. The oldest professional rodeo in the world, featuring calf roping and wild horse racing.

**Arizona Highland Celtic Festival** *(third Saturday)* Flagstaff. Entertainment and activities for all ages with bagpipers, dances, athletic demonstrations, and food.
**White Mountain Native American Art Festival & Indian Market** *(third weekend)* Pinetop-Lakeside. Features the region's finest Native artists, demonstrations, performances, and foods.
**Arizona Cardinals Training Camp** *(late July–mid-Aug)* Flagstaff. Most practice sessions of this NFL team are open to the public.
**Shakespeare Sedona** *(month long)* Sedona. Theatrical productions of Shakespearean selections.

## AUGUST

**Summerfest** *(first weekend)* Flagstaff. Juried artists and craftspeople, musicians, an array of fine foods, and activities for children.
**White Mountain Bluegrass Music Festival** *(second weekend)* Pinetop-Lakeside. The region's finest bluegrass and gospel music, arts and crafts fair featuring children's crafts, music workshops, and food.
**Payson Rodeo** *(third weekend)* Payson. Sanctioned by the Professional Rodeo Cowboy Association (PRCA), the best of the best compete for sizeable prize money.
**Arizona Cowboy Poets Gathering** *(third weekend)* Prescott. Blend of traditional and contemporary poems, songs and stories about the lives of working cowboys on the Arizona range, held at the Sharlot Hall Museum.

Hispanic musicians or *mariachis* play at a Cinco de Mayo celebration

## FALL

THE AUTUMNAL forests and mountains of Arizona are striking, ablaze with brilliant yellows, reds, and golds. Fall is one of the best seasons for touring and sightseeing because the temperature is cooler and more comfortable.

### SEPTEMBER

**Navajo Nation Fair & Rodeo** (*early Sep*) Window Rock. Largest Native American fair in the US with a parade, a rodeo, traditional song and dance, and arts and crafts.
**Rendezvous of the Gunfighters** (*Labor Day weekend*) Tombstone. Includes a parade, stage-coach rides, chili cook-offs, and mock shootouts.
**Coconino County Fair** (*Labor Day weekend*) Flagstaff. Carnival rides, food, local arts and crafts exhibits, demolition derby and car shows, and live music.

**Grand Canyon Music Festival** (*mid-Sep*) Grand Canyon Village. Fine chamber music, from Baroque to classical, jazz, fusion, and cross over.
**Andy Devine Days** (*mid-Sep*) Kingman. PRCA rodeo, parade and activities honor the town of Kingman and actor Andy Devine.
**Apache County Fair** (*mid-Sep*) St. Johns. Horse racing, entertainment, and livestock shows and exhibits.
**Jazz on the Rocks Festival** (*third weekend*) Sedona. Great names in jazz perform for thousands of visitors.
**Flagstaff Festival of Science** (*late Sep*) Flagstaff. Ten days of events, including field trips, interactive exhibits, and open-houses at museums and observatories.

### OCTOBER

**Air Affaire** (*first weekend*) Page. Air-show pilots entertain and thrill with aerobatics, showmanship, speed, and fun.
**Kingman Air & Auto Show** (*first weekend*) Kingman. Air show with acrobatics and an auto show with drag racing.
**Fort Verde Days** (*second weekend*) Camp Verde. Annual event with parade, horse events, barbecue, cavalry drills, and art show.
**Helldorado Days** (*third weekend*) Tombstone. Features re-enactments, parades, a carnival, and music and street entertainment.

**Calf roping at a Southwest rodeo**

### GRAND CANYON (NORTH RIM)

| °F/°C | | | |
|---|---|---|---|
| | 77/25 | | |
| 53/12 | | 59/15 | |
| | 46/8 | | 37/3 |
| 32°F 0°C | | | |
| 29/–2 | | 31/–1 | 16/–9 |

| | | | |
|---|---|---|---|
| ☀ | 10 hrs | 12 hrs | 10 hrs | 6 hrs |
| ☂ | 1.7 in | 2.9 in | 1.3 in | 3.1 in |
| month | Apr | Jul | Oct | Jan |

### PHOENIX

| °F/°C | | | |
|---|---|---|---|
| | | 104/40 | |
| 82/28 | 77/25 | 86/30 | |
| 54/12 | | 55/13 | 64/18 |
| 32°F 0°C | | | 39/4 |

| | | | |
|---|---|---|---|
| ☀ | 12 hrs | 13 hrs | 10 hrs | 8 hrs |
| ☂ | 0.3 in | 1 in | 0.3 in | 0.8 in |
| month | Apr | Jul | Oct | Jan |

- Average daily maximum temperature
- Average daily minimum temperature
- Average daily hours of sunshine
- Average monthly rainfall

**Climate**
*The climate varies across the state. Phoenix and the southern areas have hot and dry summers and mild, sunny winters, whereas towns, such as Flagstaff, in the northern areas have snowy winters. These areas are colder due to their higher elevation.*

### GRAND CANYON (SOUTH RIM)

| °F/°C | | | |
|---|---|---|---|
| | 84/29 | | |
| 61/16 | 54/12 | 64/18 | |
| | | 37/3 | 41/5 |
| 32°F 0°C | | | |
| 30/–1 | | 19/–7 | |

| | | | |
|---|---|---|---|
| ☀ | 11 hrs | 11 hrs | 9 hrs | 8 hrs |
| ☂ | 1.02 in | 1.8 in | 1.06 in | 1.3 in |
| month | Apr | Jul | Oct | Jan |

### FLAGSTAFF

| °F/°C | | | |
|---|---|---|---|
| | | 82/28 | |
| 58/14 | | 64/18 | |
| | 50/10 | | 42/6 |
| 32°F 0°C | | | |
| 27/–3 | | 31/–1 | 15/–9 |

| | | | |
|---|---|---|---|
| ☀ | 11 hrs | 12 hrs | 9 hrs | 7 hrs |
| ☂ | 1.5 in | 2.8 in | 1.6 in | 2 in |
| month | Apr | Jul | Oct | Jan |

### TUCSON

| °F/°C | | | |
|---|---|---|---|
| | 99/37 | | |
| 81/27 | 74/23 | 84/29 | |
| 51/11 | | 57/14 | 64/18 |
| 32°F 0°C | | | 39/4 |

| | | | |
|---|---|---|---|
| ☀ | 12 hrs | 12 hrs | 10 hrs | 9 hrs |
| ☂ | 0.3 in | 2.4 in | 1.1 in | 0.9 in |
| month | Apr | Jul | Oct | Jan |

**London Bridge Days**
*(late Oct)* Lake Havasu City. Annual celebration commemorates the dedication of the bridge with a parade, concerts, and a Renaissance Festival.

## WINTER

Christmas in Arizona is celebrated in traditional American style, with lights decorating almost every building and tree. Much of the state – the low elevation areas – experiences mild, sunny winters. In areas above 7,000 ft (2,130 m), the ski season stretches from mid-December to early April.

### NOVEMBER

**Yuma Colorado River Crossing Balloon Festival**
*(late Nov)* Yuma. More than 50 hot air balloons fill the sky. Food, entertainment, and fireworks are part of the evening celebrations.
**Wahweap Festival of Lights** *(last Saturday)* Page. Decorated boats and houseboats are paraded after sundown, illuminating the waters of Lake Powell.

### DECEMBER

**La Fiesta de Tumacacori**
*(first weekend)* Tumacacori. Festival held on mission grounds to celebrate the Native American heritage of the upper Santa Cruz Valley.
**Christmas City** *(late Nov–Dec)* Prescott. Parades, musical events, open houses, and shopping opportunities abound in Arizona's official "Christmas City."
**Fourth Avenue Street Fair**
*(early Dec)* Tucson. Artists, food vendors, live music, sidewalk performers, kids' entertainment, and fun activities for all.
**Festival of Lights** *(second Sat)* Sedona. Take part in the lighting of 6,000 luminarias in Tlaquepaque's courtyards, and enjoy carolers, musicians and dancers in this Spanish shopping center.

**Saguaro cactus illuminated by Christmas lights**

## JANUARY

**Fiesta Bowl Festival & Parade** *(Dec 31 and New Year's Day)* Phoenix. Parade, street party, and college football at the Arizona State University Sun Devil Stadium.
**Southern Arizona Square and Round Dance & Clogging Festival** *(mid-Jan)* Tucson. The festival attracts thousands of dancers.
**FBR Open Golf Tournament** *(late Jan–early Feb)* Scottsdale. PGA's annual golf tournament.
**Pow Wow – Gem & Mineral Show** *(late Jan–early Feb)* Quartzsite. Largest and oldest of eight gem and mineral shows held during January and February.
**Scottsdale Celebration of Fine Art** *(mid-Jan–late Mar)* Scottsdale. Watch art being created as over 100 artists work in studios set up for the event.
**Chrysler Classic** *(Jan or Feb)* Tucson. This PGA tournament attracts top players.

## FEBRUARY

**Tubac Festival of the Arts** *(early Feb)* Tubac. An important arts and crafts festival.
**Silver Spur Rodeo** *(first weekend)* Yuma. Features arts and crafts, rodeo, and Yuma's biggest parade.
**Tucson Gem & Mineral Show** *(mid-Feb)* Tucson. Open to visitors. One of the biggest gem and mineral shows in the US.
**La Fiesta de los Vaqueros** *(late Feb)* Tucson. Rodeo and other cowboy events, plus the world's largest non-motorized parade.
**Flagstaff Winterfest** *(month long)* Flagstaff. Competitive Nordic and Alpine skiing, dog sled races, stargazing and concerts, and family activities.

**Skiers riding a chair lift outside Flagstaff**

# THE HISTORY OF ARIZONA

T HE STORY OF ARIZONA'S *human history has been played out against a dramatic and hostile landscape. Despite the arid conditions, Native civilizations have lived here for thousands of years. Over the centuries, they have adjusted to the Hispanic colonizers of the 17th and 18th centuries, and the Anglo-Americans of the 19th and 20th. Each of these has molded the state's history.*

Long before the appearance of the Spanish in the 1500s, the Southwest was inhabited by a variety of Native populations. Groups of hunters are believed to have walked to the region by crossing the Bering Straits over a land bridge that once joined Asia with North America around 25,000–35,000 years ago.

The first Native American peoples of this region are known as Paleo-Indians. Skilled hunters of mammoths and other large Pleistocene animals, the Paleo-Indians roamed the area in small groups between 10,000 and 8,000 BC. As the large mammals died out, they turned to hunting small game and gathering roots and berries. These hunter-gatherers are called the Archaic Indians. Anthropologists believe settled farming societies appeared gradually as the population grew, and that new crops and farming techniques were introduced by migrants and traders from Mexico around 800 BC, when corn first began to be cultivated in the region. Among the early farmers were the Basket-makers, named for the finely wrought

*Kachina doll*

baskets they wove. Part of the early Ancestral Puebloan, or Anasazi, culture, these people are thought to have lived in extended family groups, in pithouse dwellings. By around AD 500, large villages, or pueblos, began to develop in the area. These usually centered around a big pithouse that was used for communal or religious purposes – the forerunner of the ceremonial *kiva (see pp36–7),* which is still used today by the descendants of the Ancestral Puebloans to hold religious ceremonies.

By AD 700, there were three main cultures in the region: the Hohokam, Mogollon, and the Ancestral Puebloan. These were sophisticated agricultural societies that developed efficient and innovative techniques to utilize the desert's limited resources. The Mogollon were known for their pottery, and were one of the first groups to adjust to an agrarian lifestyle. The Hohokam farmed Central and Southern Arizona between 300 BC and AD 1350, and their irrigation systems enabled them to grow two crops a year.

## TIMELINE

*Stone spear point*

**6,000 BC** Appearance of Archaic Indians, skilled small-game hunters and tool makers

**600 BC** Corn arrives from Mexico. Start of agriculture, although the semi-nomadic quest for food predominates

**200 BC** Basket-makers in Four Corners region

| 10,000 BC | 5,000 BC | 1,000 BC | AD 1 |
|---|---|---|---|

**10,000 BC** Arrival of Paleo-Indians. A nomadic people, they hunted big game across the relatively temperate grasslands of Arizona

**500 BC** Beans and squash are grown, agriculture expands

**300 BC** Hohokam civilization in Central and Southern Arizona

◁ **Papago Indian woman from Pima County, Arizona, 1903**

# The Ancestral Puebloans

THE HAUNTINGLY BEAUTIFUL and elaborate ruins left behind by the Ancestral Puebloan people are a key factor in the hold that this prehistoric culture has over the public imagination. Also known as "Anasazi," a name coined by the Navajo meaning "Ancient Enemy Ancestor," today they are more accurately known as the Ancestral Puebloans, and are seen as the ancestors of today's Pueblo peoples.

The first Ancestral Puebloans are thought to have settled at Mesa Verde *(see pp118–19)* in around AD 550, where they lived in pithouses. By around AD 800 they had developed masonry skills and began building housing complexes using sandstone. From AD 1100 to 1300, impressive levels of craftsmanship were reached in weaving, pottery, jewelry, and tool-making.

*Ceramics*, such as this bowl, show the artistry of the Ancestral Puebloans. Pottery is just one of many ancient artifacts on show in museums in the region.

*Kivas* are round pit-like rooms dug into the ground and roofed with beams and earth.

*Jackson Stairway* in Chaco Canyon is evidence of the engineering skills of the Ancestral Puebloans. They also built networks of roads between their communities and extensive irrigation systems.

Bone awl

Needle

*Tools* of various types were skillfully shaped from stone, wood, and bone. The Ancestral Puebloans did not work metal, yet they managed to produce such beautiful artifacts as baskets, pottery, and jewelry.

Drills

*The blue corn* growing on this Hopi Reservation today is a similar plant to that grown by Ancestral Puebloans. They were also skilled at utilizing the medicinal properties of plants, including cottonwood bark, which contains a painkiller.

*The **kiva** was the religious and ceremonial center of Ancestral Puebloan life. Still used by modern Pueblo Indians, a kiva usually had no windows and the only access was through a hole in the roof. Small kivas were used by a single family unit, while large kivas were designed to accommodate the whole community.*

## WHERE TO FIND ANCESTRAL PUEBLOAN RUINS

Navajo National Monument *(see p104)*; Canyon de Chelly National Monument *(see pp106–9)*; Hovenweep National Monument *(see p110)*; Chaco Culture National Historical Park *(see pp112–13)*; Mesa Verde National Park *(see pp118–19)*.

*Petroglyphs were often used by Ancestral Puebloans as astronomical markers for the different seasons. This one was found at the Petrified Forest National Park (see p67).*

Pueblo Bonito features many examples of the masonry skills used by the Puebloan peoples.

## THE PUEBLO PEOPLE

By AD 1300 the Ancestral Puebloans had abandoned many of their cities and migrated to areas where new centers emerged. Theories on why this occurred include a 50-year drought; the strain that a larger population placed on the desert's limited resources; and a lengthy period of social upheaval, perhaps stimulated by increasing trade with tribes as far away as central Mexico. Most archeologists agree that the Ancestral Puebloans did not disappear but live on today in Puebloan descendants who trace their origins to Mesa Verde, Chaco, and other sacred ancestral sites.

## CHACO CANYON'S PUEBLO BONITO

At Chaco Canyon *(see pp112–13)* the largest "great house" ever built was Pueblo Bonito with more than 600 rooms and 40 *kivas*. One current theory is that these structures did not house populations but were, in fact, public buildings for commerce and ceremonial gatherings. The lives of the Ancestral Puebloans were short, barely 35 years, and as harsh as the environment in which they lived. Their diet was poor, and arthritis and dental problems were common. Women often showed signs of osteoporosis or brittle bones as early as their first childbirth.

**Painstaking excavation at an Ancestral Puebloan *kiva* in Chaco Canyon**

## ANCIENT CULTURES

By around AD 800, the Ancestral Puebloans began to build elaborate ceremonial centers, such as Chaco Canyon *(see pp112–13)*, and to move pueblos off open mesa tops to cliff recesses in canyons such as Mesa Verde *(see pp118–19)*. Their numbers started diminishing around 1250. Chaco Canyon was abandoned about 1275, and Mesa Verde by 1300. By 1350, there was virtually no trace of the Ancestral Puebloans on the Colorado Plateau. Soon after, the Hohokams and the Mogollons became extinct. Experts theorize that a combination of a long drought and social unrest caused them to break up into smaller groups that were easier to sustain. However, these groups may not have vanished entirely. It is believed that the Hopi are the descendants of the Ancestral Puebloans, and that the Pima and Tohono O'odham trace their ancestry to the Hohokam *(see pp22–3)*.

## THE NAVAJO & THE APACHE

The Navajo and Apache originated in the Athabascan culture of Canada and Alaska. The Navajo moved south between 1200 and 1400, while the Apache are thought to have arrived in the late 15th century. The Navajo were hunters who took to herding sheep brought by the Spanish. The Apache groups – Jicarilla, Mescalero, Chiricahua, and Western Apache – continued their nomadic lifestyle. They were skillful warriors, especially the Chiricahua of Southern Arizona, whose leaders Cochise and Geronimo fought Hispanic and Anglo settlers to deter them from colonization in the late 19th century.

## THE ARRIVAL OF THE SPANISH

In 1539, the Franciscan priest Fray Marcos de Niza led the first Spanish expedition into the Southwest. He was inspired by hopes of finding gold, and the desire to convert the Native inhabitants to Christianity. A year later, Francisco Vasquez de Coronado arrived with 330 soldiers, 1,000 Indian allies, and more than 1,000 heads of livestock. He conquered Zuni Pueblo, and spent two years traversing Arizona, New Mexico, Texas, and Kansas in search of the legendary city of gold, Cibola. His brutal treatment of the Pueblo people sowed the seeds for the Pueblo Revolt 140 years later.

Engraving by Norman Price of Coronado setting out to discover a legendary kingdom of gold in 1540

## TIMELINE

| | | | |
|---|---|---|---|
| **600** Earliest date for settlement of Acoma and Hopi mesas | **1020** Chaco Canyon is at its height as a trading and cultural center | **1300** Mesa Verde abandoned | **1539** Fray Marcos de Niza heads first expedition to the Southwest |
| **800** | **1000** | **1200** | **1400** | **1600** |
| **800** Large pueblos such as Chaco Canyon under construction | **1250** Ancient sites are mysteriously abandoned; new smaller pueblos are established along the Rio Grande | **1400** Navajo and Apache migrate from Canada to the Southwest | **1598** Juan de Oñate founds permanent colony in New Mexico |

**Illustration of the 1680 Pueblo Indian Revolt**

## THE COLONY OF NEW MEXICO

In 1598, Juan de Oñate arrived in the Southwest with 400 settlers, and set up a permanent colony called New Mexico. The colony included all of the present-day states of New Mexico and Arizona, as well as parts of Colorado, Utah, Nevada, and California.

Spanish attempts to conquer the Indian Pueblos led to hard and bloody battles but, despite the harsh conditions, more settlers, priests, and soldiers began to arrive in the area, determined to subdue the Natives, and to suppress their religious practices.

As the Spanish colonists spread out, they seized Pueblo farmlands and created huge ranches for themselves. A Pueblo uprising began on August 9, 1680, resulting in the deaths of 375 colonists and 21 priests, with the remaining 2,000 settlers driven south across the Rio Grande. In 1692, however, Don Diego de Vargas reclaimed Santa Fe, re-establishing Spanish control of the land. By the late 18th century, the Spanish were attempting to extend their power westward to California. Their first Arizona settlement was at Tubac, near Tucson, in 1752.

The beginning of the end of Spanish control came with the Louisiana Purchase of 1803. The French emperor, Napoleon, sold Louisiana, an enormous area of about 828,000 sq miles (2.2 million sq km) of land, to the recently formed United States. Land-hungry Americans began a rapid westward expansion toward the borders of Spanish-controlled Mexico. Compounding Spain's problems, Mexico's fight for independence began in 1810, but it was not until 1821 that independence was finally declared. The newly independent Mexicans were glad to do business with their Anglo-American neighbors, who brought much-needed trade.

### THE MISSIONS

In the late 17th century, Jesuit missionary Father Eusebio Kino lived alongside and established a rapport with the Pima people of Southern Arizona. He initiated the Jesuit practice of bringing gifts of livestock and seeds for new crops, including wheat. Those Natives involved in the missionary program escaped forced labor. Kino inspired the Natives living south of Tucson, at a place called Bac, to begin work on the first mission there, which later became the Southwest's most beautiful mission church, San Xavier del Bac (see pp92–3). When Kino died in 1711, there were around 20 missions across the region.

**Father Eusebio Kino**

Juan de Oñate

**1680** Pueblo Revolt drives Spanish out of the Southwest

**1691** Father Kino establishes first mission at Tumacacori, Arizona

**1692** Diego de Vargas retakes Santa Fe

**1711** Death of Father Kino; 20 missions in Southern Arizona

*Anza*

**1752** First European settlement in Arizona set up at Tubac

**1775** Tucson founded. Juan Batista de Anza reaches San Francisco

**1776** Two Franciscan priests are first to travel the Old Spanish Trail

**1783** Construction begins on Mission San Xavier del Bac

**1803** Louisana Purchase extends US boundary to New Mexico border

| 1650 | 1700 | 1750 | 1800 |
|---|---|---|---|

A group of cowboys roping a steer, painted by C. M. Russell (1897)

**THE ARRIVAL OF ANGLO-AMERICANS**
The first non-Spanish people of
European descent, or Anglo-Americans,
to arrive in the Southwest were
"mountain men" and fur trappers in the
early 1800s. They learned survival skills
from Native tribes, married Native
women, and usually spoke more than
one Native language as well as Spanish.

While the Hispanic and the Natives
were happy to trade with the Anglos,
they were, at the same time, angered
by the new settlers who built ranches
and even towns on lands to which they
had no legal right.

**LAND DISPUTES & THE INDIAN WARS**
After the Civil War (1861–65), reports of
land and mineral wealth in the west fil-
tered back east, and Anglo settlement
in the west increased rapidly. By the
1840s, the US government had
embarked on a vigorous expansion
westward, with settlers accompanied by
United States' soldiers. The primary
problem they encountered were the
constant raids by Natives, dubbed "the
Indian problem." The US cavalry
countered with raids and massacres of

its own. In 1864, more than 8,000
Navajo were forced off their land, and
made to march "The Long Walk" of 370
miles (595 km) east to a reservation at
Bosque Redondo in New Mexico. Many
died during harsh weather en route,
and many more from disease at the
reservation. In 1868, the Navajo were
given 20,000 sq miles (51,800 sq km)
across Arizona, New Mexico, and
southern Utah.

In 1845, the US acquired Texas and,
when Mexico resisted further moves, it
set off the Mexican War. The Treaty of
Guadalupe-Hidalgo ended the conflict
in 1848, and gave the US the Mexican
Cession (comprising California, Utah,
Nevada, Northern Arizona, and parts of
New Mexico, Wyoming, and Colorado)
for $18.25 million. In 1854, the United
States bought Southern Arizona through
the Gadsden Purchase for $10 million.
Finally, in 1863, the US government recognized Arizona as a separate territory,
and drew the state line that exists
between it and New Mexico today.

In the 1870s, vast areas of Arizona
became huge cattle and sheep ranches,
and by the 1880s, four major railroads

## TIMELINE

| | | | | | |
|---|---|---|---|---|---|
| **1821** Mexico declares independence from Spain | **1846–48** US expansionism leads to war with Mexico | **1869** John Wesley Powell leads first US expedition through the Grand Canyon | **1881** Gunfight at OK Corral | **1901** Grand Canyon Railway brings tourists to the region | **1912** Arizona admitted to Union, becomes the 48th state |
| **1825** | | **1850** | **1875** | | **1900** |
| **1824** Republic of Mexico established | | **1854** The US gets Southern Arizona with the Gadsden Purchase | **1864** Colonel Kit Carson conducts a campaign against the Navajo at Canyon de Chelly. The survivors are forcibly marched to New Mexico on "The Long Walk" | **1886** Indian Wars end with the surrender of Geronimo | |
| | **1848** Mexican territory ceded to US under Treaty of Guadalupe-Hidalgo | | | *Geronimo* | |

## APACHE WARRIORS

The nomadic Apache lived in small communities in southeastern Arizona, and southern and northwestern New Mexico. Seeing them as a threat to the settlement of these territories, the US military was determined to wipe them out. The hanging of one of Chief Cochise's relatives in 1861 instigated a war that lasted more than a decade until Apache reservations were established in 1872. In 1877, a new leader, Victorio, launched a three-year guerrilla war against the settlers that ended only with his death. The most famous Apache leader, Geronimo, led a campaign against the Mexicans and Anglos from 1851 until he surrendered in 1886. He was sent to a reservation in Florida.

**Apache leader Geronimo, in a fierce pose in this picture from 1886**

crossed the region. These became a catalyst for new industries in the region. Arizona was granted statehood in 1912, and in the years leading up to and following World War I, the state experienced an economic boom because of its rich mineral resources.

### THE DEMAND FOR WATER

As the region's population expanded, the supply of water became one of the most pressing issues, and a series of enormous dams were constructed. Dam- and road-building projects, in turn, benefited the region's economy and attracted even more settlers.

**Mining boom prospector**

The Hoover Dam was constructed between 1931 and 1936, but by the 1960s even that proved inadequate. Soon after, Glen Canyon Dam was completed in 1963, flooding an area of great beauty. The dam created the huge reservoir of Lake Powell, destroying a number of ancient Native ruins.

The issue of water continues to be a serious problem in the Southwest, and projects to harness water from available sources are under debate.

### THE SOUTHWEST TODAY

Arizona's economy continues to prosper, and its population is still growing, augmented by thousands of winter residents from the north, or "snowbirds." An ever-increasing number of tourists visit the state's scenic and historic wonders, preserved in national parks, monuments, and recreational areas. Set up in the early 20th century, the parks highlight conservation issues and Native cultures, all of which will help guard Arizona's precious heritage for generations to come.

**1931–36** Hoover Dam constructed

**1974** Central Arizona Project initiated to harvest water from the Colorado River for thirsty Phoenix

**2000–2003** Forest fires devastate large tracts of timber in Eastern and Northern Arizona

| 1925 | 1950 | 1975 | 2000 |
|------|------|------|------|

*Glen Canyon Dam*

**1963** Opening of the Glen Canyon Dam

**1996** Bill Clinton signs Navajo-Hopi Land Dispute Settlement Act, ending violent conflicts between tribes

# ARIZONA & THE
# FOUR CORNERS
# AREA BY AREA

# Introducing Arizona & the Four Corners

THIS IS A REGION of vast expanses and stunning natural beauty. In Arizona's southwest corner lies the hostile, but eerily beautiful, Sonoran Desert. Its boundaries are marked by the important cities of Tucson and Phoenix. To the north the landscape rises through the red rock canyonlands around Sedona to green mountain towns such as Flagstaff and Payson. Beyond lies the enormous Colorado Plateau, cut by the almost unimaginable depth and beauty of the Grand Canyon *(see pp48–55)*. In the

**One of the Mittens in Monument Valley**

east, the Four Corners area is the only place in the USA where four states – Utah, Colorado, Arizona, and New Mexico – meet at a single point. It is dominated by dramatic canyonlands such as Monument Valley and ancient ruins that stand as haunting epitaphs in a lonely but captivating landscape.

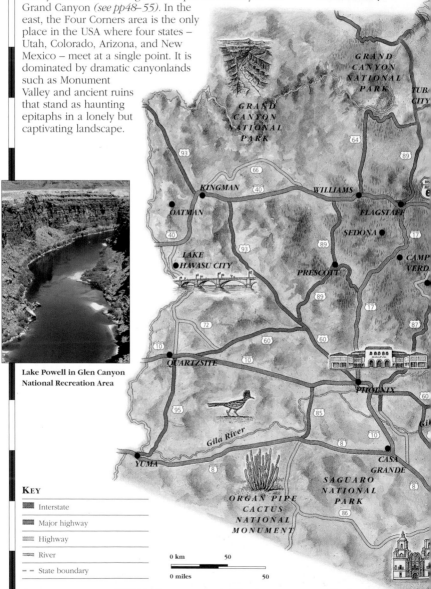

**Lake Powell in Glen Canyon National Recreation Area**

*OURAY*

*TELLURIDE*

**COLORADO**

*BLANDING*

191

145

550

**UTAH**

*CORTEZ*

*DURANGO*

**FOUR CORNERS MONUMENT NAVAJO TRIBAL PARK**

160

**MESA VERDE NATIONAL PARK**

160

*MONUMENT VALLEY*

163

160

150

550

*BLOOMFIELD*

64

*SHIPROCK*

64

64

*FARMINGTON*

64

*KAYENTA*

160

191

**CANYON DE CHELLY NATIONAL MONUMENT**

666

371

44

160

**NEW MEXICO**

**NAVAJO INDIAN RESERVATION**

264

**CHACO CULTURE NATIONAL HISTORICAL PARK**

264

*GANADO*

264

**HOPI INDIAN RESERVATION**

87

6

*WINDOW ROCK*

191

## GETTING AROUND

Phoenix is a major hub for international and domestic flights, but many airlines fly directly to Tucson as well. The region is serviced by Amtrak train services and regular Greyhound buses. Driving, however, is the preferred option and the area has a network of well-maintained highways. Northern Arizona is bisected by I-40 and I-10 cuts across the south; I-17 is the main north–south artery. A private car is essential for getting around the Four Corners; a high-clearance 4WD vehicle is recommended for traveling many interesting, unpaved regional roads.

40

40

*WINSLOW*

*HOLBROOK*

191

**RIZONA**

77

180

191

*SHOW LOW*

60

60

*PINETOP-LAKESIDE*

*FORT APACHE*

191

*GLOBE*

70

191

10

*UCSON*

10

*TOMBSTONE*

80

80

82

*BISBEE*

*NOGALES*

**Skyscrapers dominating the skyline of downtown Phoenix**

### SEE ALSO

• *Where to stay* pp124–31

• *Where to eat* pp134–41

# GRAND CANYON & NORTHERN ARIZONA

OR MOST PEOPLE, Northern Arizona is famous as the location of Grand Canyon, a gorge of breath-taking proportions carved out of rock by the Colorado River. Northern Arizona's other attractions include the high desert landscape of the Colorado Plateau, with its sagebrush and yucca, punc-tuated by the forested foothills of the San Francisco Peaks. The Kaibab, Prescott, and Coconino National Forests cover large areas, and provide the set-ting for the lively city of Flagstaff as well as for the charming towns of Sedona and Jerome. The region is dot-ted with fascinating mining ghost towns such as Oatman, a reminder that Arizona won its nickname, the Copper State, from the mineral mining boom of the first half of the 20th century. More than 25 percent of Arizona is Native American reservation land. The state is also home to several centuries-old Puebloan ruins, most notably the hilltop village of Tuzigoot and the hill-side remains of Montezuma Castle.

## SIGHTS AT A GLANCE

**Historic Towns & Sights**
Camp Verde ⑮
Flagstaff ③
Hoover Dam ⑰
Jerome ⑫
Kingman ⑲
Lake Havasu City ㉑
Oatman ⑳
Prescott ⑯
Quartzsite ㉒
Sedona ⑧
Williams ⑩

**National Parks & Monuments**
*Grand Canyon* ①
Montezuma Castle National Monument ⑭
Petrified Forest National Park ⑦
Sunset Crater Volcano National Monument ⑤
Tuzigoot National Monument ⑪
Walnut Canyon National Monument ⑥

Wupatki National Monument ④

**Areas of Natural Beauty**
*Heart of Arizona Tour* ⑬
Lake Mead National Recreation Area ⑱
*Lake Powell & Glen Canyon National Recreation Area* ②
Oak Creek Canyon ⑨

**KEY**

✈ International airport
═ Interstate
═ Major highway
─ Highway
─ Railroad

# Grand Canyon ❶

G RAND CANYON is one of the world's great natural
wonders and an instantly recognizable symbol of the
Southwest. The canyon runs through Grand Canyon
National Park *(see pp50–51)*, and is 277 miles (446 km)
long, an average of 10 miles (16 km) wide, and around
5,000 ft (1,500 m) deep. It was formed over a period of six
million years by the Colorado River, whose fast-flowing
waters sliced their way through the Colorado Plateau
*(see p15)*, which includes the gorge and most of Northern
Arizona and the Four Corners region. The plateau's
geological vagaries have defined the river's twisted course,
and exposed vast cliffs and pinnacles that are ringed by
rocks of different colors, variegated hues of limestone,
sandstone, and shale *(see pp52–3)*. The canyon is spectacular by any standard, but its beauty is in the ever-shifting
light patterns, and the colors that the rocks take on –
bleached white at midday, but red and ocher at sunset.

**Mule Trip Convoy**
*A mule ride is a popular
method of exploring the
canyon's narrow trails.*

**Havasu Canyon**
*The 10-mile (16-km) trail to the
beautiful Havasu Falls is a
popular hike. The land is owned
by the Havasupai tribe, who
offer horseback rides and guided
tours into the canyon.*

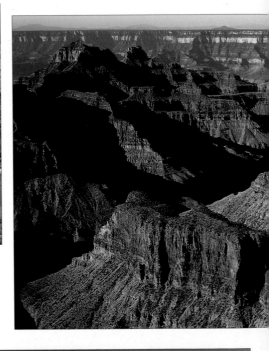

**Grandview Point**
*At 7,400 ft (2,250 m),
Grandview Point is one of the
highest places on the South
Rim, the canyon's southern
edge. It is one of the stops
along Desert View Drive (see
p51). The point is thought to
be the spot from where the
Spanish had their first glimpse
of the canyon in 1540.*

### North Rim

*The North Rim receives roughly one-tenth the number of visitors of the South Rim. While less accessible, it is a more peaceful destination offering a sense of unexplored wilderness. It has a range of hikes, such as the North Kaibab Trail, a steep descent down to Phantom Ranch on the canyon floor.*

**VISITORS' CHECKLIST**

**Road map** B2. ✈ *Grand Canyon Airport, Tusayan.* 🚆 *Grand Canyon Railway from Williams.* 🚌 *From Flagstaff.* ℹ️ *Visitor Center, Canyon View Information Plaza, south of Mather Point, AZ, (928) 638-7888.* ⓦ *www.nps.gov/grca* ◐ *South Rim: year round. North Rim: summer only.* ● *North Rim: mid-Oct–mid-May: closed by snow.* 🎟 🚻 *partial.* 🅿 🛍 🚻 🍴

### Phantom Ranch

*This lodging (see p125) offers the only roofed accommodation on the canyon floor. It is reserved for guests taking the overnight mule trip, but hikers and rafters can dine there and stay at the nearby campground.*

### YAVAPAI POINT AT THE SOUTH RIM

Situated 5 miles (8 km) north of the canyon's South Entrance, along a stretch of the Rim Trail, is Yavapai Point. Its observation station offers spectacular views of the canyon, and a viewing panel identifies several of the central canyon's landmarks.

### Bright Angel Trail

*Used by both Native Americans and early settlers, the Bright Angel Trail follows a natural route along one of the canyon's enormous fault lines. It is an appealing option for day hikers because, unlike some other trails in the area, it offers some shade and several seasonal water sources.*

# Grand Canyon National Park

A WORLD HERITAGE SITE, Grand Canyon National Park is located entirely within the state of Arizona. The park covers 1,904 sq miles (4,930 sq km), and is made up of the canyon itself, which starts where the Paria River empties into the Colorado, and stretches from Lees Ferry to Lake Mead *(see p72)* and adjoining lands. The area won protective status as a National Monument in 1908 after Theodore Roosevelt visited in 1903, observing that it should be kept intact for future generations as "... the one great sight which every American ... should see." The National Park was created in 1919.

The park has two main entrances, on the North and South Rims of the canyon. However, the southern section of the park receives the most visitors and can become very congested during the summer season *(see pp54–5)*.

**North Kaibab Trail** follows Bright Angel Creek bed, past Roaring Springs, and descends to Phantom Ranch.

North Rim Entrance Station

Point Sublime

Crystal Creek

Bright Angel Point

Shiva Temple

Colorado River

Isis Temple

**Grand Canyon Lodge**
*Perched above the canyon at Bright Angel Point, the Grand Canyon Lodge has rooms and a number of dining options* (see pp55, 125 & 134).

HAVASU CANYON

Diana Temple

**Bright Angel Trail** starts from the South Rim. It is well maintained but demanding. It descends into the canyon and connects with the North Kaibab Trail up on the North Rim.

Hopi Point

Yavapai Point

Grand Canyon Village

Yaki Point

Hermits Rest

**Phantom Ranch** *(see p125)* is the only lodge on the canyon floor, and is accessible by mule, raft, or on foot.

FLAGSTAFF WILLIAMS

Tusayan

**Hermit Road**
*A free shuttle bus runs along this route to the Hermits Rest viewpoint during the summer. It is closed to private vehicles March to November.*

**Kolb Studio**
*Built in 1904 by brothers Emery and Ellsworth Kolb, who photographed the canyon extensively, the Kolb Studio is now a National Historic Site and book store.*

**Point Imperial** is the highest point on the North Rim at 8,803 ft (2,683 m), and offers views of Mt. Hayden and the Painted Desert *(see p55)*.

**LOCATOR MAP**

☐ *Grand Canyon National Park area*

KAIBAB PLATEAU

SHIVITS PLATEAU

COCONINO PLATEAU

Nankoweap Creek

Kwagunt Creek

Vista Encantada

Kwagunt Butte

Atoko Point

Chuar Butte

Cape Solitude

**Colorado River**
*Aided by wind and rain, the Colorado River has shaped the Grand Canyon. The river winds for 277 miles (446 km) through the canyon.*

WALHALLA PLATEAU

Valhalla Overlook

Cape Royal

Colorado River

Comanche Point

Vishnu Temple

GRANITE GORGE

Lipan Point

Desert View

Grandview Point

Moran Point

64

**KEY**

| | |
|---|---|
| ▬ | Major highway |
| — | Park boundary |
| — | Rivers |
| ═ | Highway |
| - - - | Trail route |
| 🚗 | Gas station |
| 🚶 | Ranger station |
| △ | Campground/RV |
| 🎪 | Picnic area |
| ℹ | Visitor information |
| 🌿 | Viewpoint |

0 km          5

0 miles          5

**The Tusayan Ruin** was a pueblo abandoned by the Ancestral Puebloans around 1150. The Tusayan Museum now sits next to the site.

**Desert View Drive**
*This route connects Grand Canyon Village with Desert View, and offers breathtaking views of both the central and eastern canyon.*

# The Geology of the Grand Canyon

G RAND CANYON's multicolored layers of rock provide the best record of the Earth's formation anywhere in the world. Each stratum of rock reveals a different period in the Earth's geological history beginning with the earliest, the Precambrian Era, which covers geological time up to 570 million years ago. Almost two billion years of history have been recorded in the canyon, although the most dramatic changes took place relatively recently, five to six million years ago, when the Colorado River began to carve its path through the canyon walls. The sloping nature of the Kaibab Plateau has led to increased erosion in some parts of the canyon.

**A view of Grand Canyon's plateau and South Rim**

*The canyon's size is awe-inspiring, attracting millions of visitors every year. Pictured here is the North Rim.*

Canyon rim

KAIBAB LIMESTONE
TOROWEAP FORMATION
COCONINO SANDSTONE
HERMIT SHALE

SUPAI GROUP

REDWALL LIMESTONE

TEMPLE BUTTE LIMESTONE

MUAV LIMESTONE

BRIGHT ANGEL SHALE

TAPEATS SANDSTONE

SHINUMO QUARTZITE

HAKATAI SHALE

DIABASE SILL

BASS FORMATION

## RECORD OF LIFE

The fossils found in each layer tell the story of the development of life on Earth. The oldest layer, the Vishnu Schist, was formed in the Proterozoic era, when the first bacteria and algae were just emerging. Later layers were created by billions of small marine creatures whose hard shells eventually built up into thick layers of limestone.

*An asymmetrical canyon, the Grand Canyon's North Rim is more eroded than the South Rim. The entire Kaibab Plateau slopes to the south, so rain falling at the North Rim flows toward the canyon and over the rim, creating deep side canyons and a wide space between the rim and the river.*

*The Surprise Canyon formation, a new strata classified by geologists in 1985, can be seen only in remote parts of the canyon. It was formed 335 million years ago.*

*The Colorado River changed its course about 5 million years ago. It is thought that it was encompassed by another, smaller river that flowed through the Kaibab Plateau. The force of the combined waters carved out the deep Grand Canyon.*

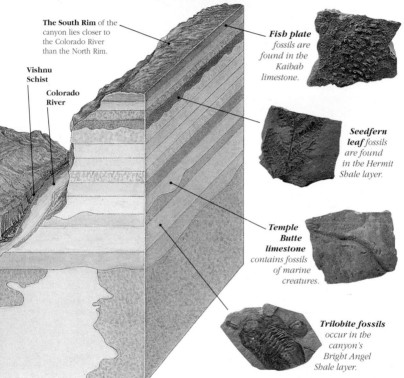

**The South Rim** of the canyon lies closer to the Colorado River than the North Rim.

**Vishnu Schist**

**Colorado River**

*Fish plate* fossils are found in the Kaibab limestone.

*Seedfern leaf* fossils are found in the Hermit Shale layer.

*Temple Butte limestone* contains fossils of marine creatures.

*Trilobite fossils* occur in the canyon's Bright Angel Shale layer.

## HOW THE CANYON WAS FORMED

While the Colorado River accounts for the canyon's depth, its width and formations are the work of even greater forces. Wind rushing through the canyon erodes the limestone and sandstone a few grains at a time. Rain pouring over the canyon rim cuts deep side canyons through the softer rock. Perhaps the greatest canyon-building force is ice. Water from rain and snowmelt works into cracks in the rock. When frozen, it expands, forcing the rock away from the canyon walls. The layers vary in hardness. Soft layers erode quickly into sloped faces. Harder rock resists erosion, leaving sheer vertical faces.

**Crack formed by ice and water erosion**

# Exploring Grand Canyon National Park

**Bell near Hermits Rest**

GRAND CANYON offers awe-inspiring beauty on a vast scale. The magnificent rock formations with towers, cliffs, steep walls, and buttes recede as far as the eye can see, their bands of colored rock varying in shade as light changes through the day. The park's main roads, Hermit Road and Desert View Drive, both accessible from the South Entrance, overlook the canyon. Grand Canyon Village is located on the South Rim and offers a range of facilities. Visitors can also enter the park from the north, although this route (Hwy 67) is closed during winter. Walking trails along the North and South Rims offer staggering views but, to experience the canyon at its most fascinating, the trails that go down toward the canyon floor should be explored.

The Bright Angel Trail on the South Rim, and the North Kaibab Trail on the North Rim, descend to the canyon floor, and are tough hikes involving an overnight stop.

is not only the starting point for most of the mule trips through the canyon, but also the terminus for the Grand Canyon Railway.

### South Rim

Most of the Grand Canyon's 4.3 million annual visitors come to the South Rim, since, unlike the North Rim, it is open year-round and is easily accessible along Highway 180/64 from Flagstaff *(see p64)* or Williams. **Hermit Road** and **Desert View Drive** (Hwy 64) start at Grand Canyon Village and encompass a selection of the choicest views of the gorge. Hermit Road is closed to private vehicles from March to November each year but there are free shuttle buses. Desert View Drive is open all year.

From the village, Hermit Road meanders along the South Rim, extending for 8 miles (13 km). Its first viewpoint is **Trailview Overlook**, which provides an overview of the canyon and the winding course of the Bright Angel Trail. Moving on, **Maricopa Point** offers especially panoramic views of the canyon but not of the Colorado River, which is more apparent from nearby **Hopi Point**. At the end of Hermit Road lies Hermits Rest, where a gift shop, decorated in rustic style, is located in yet another Mary Colter-designed building. The longer Desert View Drive runs in the opposite direction, and covers 26 miles (42 km). It winds for 12 miles (20 km) before reaching **Grandview Point**, where the Spaniards may have had their first glimpse of the canyon in 1540.

Adobe pueblo-style architecture of Hopi House, Grand Canyon Village

### 🏛 Grand Canyon Village
Grand Canyon National Park.
📞 *(928) 638-7888.* ♿ *partial.*

Grand Canyon Village has its roots in the late 19th century. The extensive building of visitor accommodations started after the Santa Fe Railroad opened a branch line here from Williams in 1901, though some hotels had been built in the late 1890s. The Fred Harvey Company constructed a clutch of well-designed, attractive buildings. The most prominent is **El Tovar Hotel** *(see p125).* Opened in 1905, it is named after Spanish explorers who reached the gorge in 1540. The **Hopi House** also opened in 1905 – a rendition of a traditional Hopi dwelling, where locals could sell their craftwork as souvenirs. It was built by Hopi craftsmen and designed

by Mary E. J. Colter. An ex-schoolteacher and trained architect, Colter drew on Southwestern influences, mixing both Native American and Hispanic styles *(see p21).* She is responsible for many of the historic structures that now grace the South Rim, including the 1914 **Lookout Studio** and **Hermits Rest**, and the rustic 1922 **Phantom Ranch** on the canyon floor.

Today, Grand Canyon Village has a wide range of hotels, restaurants, and stores. It is surprisingly easy to get lost here since the buildings are spread out and discreetly placed among wooded areas. The village

The interior of the Hermits Rest gift store with crafts for sale lining the walls

Desert View's stone watchtower, on Desert View Drive

## CALIFORNIA CONDORS

America's largest bird, the California condor, has a wingspan of over 9 ft (2.7 m). Nearly extinct in the 1980s, the last 22 condors were captured for breeding in captivity. In 1996, the first captive-bred birds were released in Northern Arizona. Today, about 50 condors fly the skies over Northern Arizona. They are frequent visitors to the South Rim, though visitors should not approach or attempt to feed them.

**A pair of California condors**

About 10 miles (16 km) farther on lie the pueblo remains of **Tusayan Ruin**, where there is a small museum with exhibits on Ancestral Puebloan life. The road continues on to the stunning overlook of **Desert View**. The watchtower here was Colter's most fanciful creation, its upper floor decorated with early 20th-century Hopi murals.

Just east of Grand Canyon Village is **Yavapai Point** from where it is possible to see Phantom Ranch *(see p125)*. This is the only roofed accommodation available on the canyon floor, across the Colorado River.

### North Rim

Standing at about 8,000 ft (2,400 m), the North Rim is higher, cooler, and greener than the South Rim, with dense forests of ponderosa pine, aspen, and Douglas fir. Visitors are most likely to spot wildlife such as the mule deer, Kaibab squirrel, and wild turkey on the North Rim.

The Rim can be reached via Highway 67, off Highway 89A, ending at **Grand Canyon Lodge** *(see p125 & p134)*, where there are visitor services, a camp-ground, a gas station, restaurant, and a general store. Nearby, there is a National Park information center, which offers maps of the area. The North Rim and all its facilities are closed mid-October to mid-May,

when it is often snowed in. The North Rim is twice as far from the river as the South Rim, and the canyon really stretches out from the over-looks giving a sense of its 10-mile (16-km) width. There are about 30 miles (45 km) of scenic roads along the North Rim, as well as hiking trails to high viewpoints or down to the canyon floor, particularly the **North Kaibab Trail** that links to the South Rim's Bright Angel Trail. The picturesque **Cape Royal Drive** starts north of Grand Canyon Lodge and travels 23 miles (37 km) to Cape Royal on the Walhalla Plateau. From here, several famous buttes and peaks can be seen, including Wotans Throne and Vishnu Temple. There are also several short walking trails around Cape Royal. A 3-mile (5-km) detour leads to **Point Imperial**, the highest point on the canyon rim, while along the way the **Vista Encantada** has delight-ful views and picnic tables overlooking the gorge.

**Mule deer on the canyon's North Rim**

### Bright Angel Trail

This is the most popular of all Grand Canyon hiking trails. The Bright Angel trailhead is at Grand Canyon Village on the South Rim. The trail begins near the **Kolb Studio** at the western end of the village. It then switches dramatically down the side of the canyon for 9 miles (14 km). The trail crosses the river over a suspension bridge, ending a little further on at Phantom Ranch. There are two resthouses and a fully equipped campground along the way. It is not advisable to attempt the whole trip in one day. Many walk from the South Rim to one of the rest stops and then return up to the Rim. Temperatures at the bottom of the canyon can reach 110°F (43°C) or higher during the summer. Day hikers should, therefore, carry a quart (just over a liter) of water per person per hour for summer hiking. Carrying a first-aid kit is also recommended.

**Hikers taking a break on the South Rim's Bright Angel Trail**

Breathtaking view of Grand Canyon at dusk ▷

# Grand Canyon Adventures

THE GRAND CANYON's beauty and grandeur, the diversity of activities it offers, and the availability of top-notch tours and outfitters, have made it one of the most popular outdoor adventure sites in the world. Many of the classic Grand Canyon experiences, such as mule and helicopters tours, Rim-to-Rim hikes and whitewater raft trips, rate as once-in-a-lifetime adventures for many people. But not all Grand Canyon adventures involve white-knuckle thrills. There are activities geared for every interest and physical ability, from birdwatching to ranger-led interpretive walks along the North and South Rims, to a host of educational programs lasting an hour or a week. If there is anything to stymie the would-be adventurer, it is only the sheer number of experiences to choose from.

Hikers studying a map of the Grand Canyon

## HIKING

THE MOST POPULAR day hikes in the park involve a descent into the canyon on well-maintained trails, such as Bright Angel and Hermits Rest *(see pp48–55)*. Once below the Rim, these trails offer ever changing views of the canyon on the way down, sometimes passing by steep overlooks and a few shaded rest areas. Visitors are strongly advised to carry water on these hikes.

For those wanting an easier stroll, there are relatively level trails that follow the edge of the canyon. At the South Rim, the 13-mile (21-km) long Rim Trail can be crowded where it passes through the Grand Canyon Village, but provides wonderful solitude and

stunning vistas just a mile away. At the North Rim, the Transept Trail is an easy 1-mile (1.6-km) hike that winds through thick woods to come out at various points along the canyon's edge.

Many hikers consider a Rim-to-Rim hike (descending from one Rim and hiking up to the other Rim) to be the ultimate canyon hiking experience, but it is also extremely demanding, with more than 10,000 ft (3,048 m) of a vertical descent and ascent over 22 miles (35 km). Bright Angel to North Kaibab, or the reverse, is the most popular Rim-to-Rim route, as it offers the only accessible river crossing. Most Rim-to-Rim hikers spend one or two nights at the Bright Angel campground (advance reservations required).

## CANYON HIKING TIPS

*Over 400 people require medical evacuations from the canyon each year. Most are healthy people under 40 who are dehydrated or exhausted.*
- *Drink plenty of water and/or electrolyte liquids as you hike, even if you don't feel thirsty.*
- *Eat often, even while you are hiking. High-carb and salty foods are good.*
- *Hats, sun protective clothing, and sunscreen are essential.*
- *Do not attempt to hike to the bottom of the canyon and back in a single day.*

## BACKCOUNTRY CAMPING

IN THE GRAND CANYON park, backcountry camping exists primarily to facilitate multi-day hikes into the canyon. In fact, demand far outpaces supply, so visitors should try and reserve camp spaces early if they are contemplating spending a few nights in the canyon. Reservations can be made up to four months in advance. If no camp spaces are available for the time of visit, they could consider signing up for a guided hike with companies that pre-book campsites. **Grand Canyon Hikes** and **Sky Island Treks** are two of the many tour companies in the Grand Canyon that offer three- to seven-day hikes, both for beginners and experienced hikers.

**Camping out in Grand Canyon National Park**

**Mountain bikers in Toroweap Valley, Grand Canyon National Park**

## MOUNTAIN BIKING

A LTHOUGH MOUNTAIN bikes are not allowed on hiking trails within the National Park, there are several scenic roads – both paved and unpaved – in the park on which mountain bikes are permitted. At the North Rim, just outside the park, the Kaibab National Forest offers mountain bikers the 18-mile (29-km) long Rainbow Rim Trail and the Arizona Trail, both of which follow the Rim and offer superb views of the canyon. Both trails have varied sections ranked easy to difficult. **Escape Adventures** offers five-day mountain bike adventures on the North Rim.

## BIRDWATCHING

B IRDWATCHING IS a popular pastime at the Grand Canyon for both serious and casual birders. Hawks and bald eagles can be seen gliding silently above the canyon. Other species, such as canyon wrens, pygmy nuthatch, mountain chickadee, and red crossbill, are quite tame, and can be seen along the tourist trails. Also, many people visit the South Rim for a glimpse of the rare California condors. For those who want a more in-depth experience, birdwatching is a major component of many of the outdoor programs offered by the **Grand Canyon Field Institute**.

## EDUCATIONAL TOURS

T HE GRAND CANYON is a natural classroom for the study of desert and canyon ecology, history, archeology, geology, and natural history. One of the most accessible sources of short educational courses are ranger-led day-programs offered by the National Park. More in-depth, single and multi-day pro-grams are offered by the renowned Grand Canyon Field Institute. Begun in 1993, the institute's programs include wilderness studies, ecology, and photography. The **Museum of Northern Arizona** also offers a variety of educational tours, as do numerous commercial hiking tour operators such as **Discovery Treks**.

## MULE TRIPS

S INCE THEIR inception in 1904, mule rides have been one of the most popular of all Grand Canyon adventures. Although thousands of people undertake these trips each year, they should not be taken lightly – this is a demanding adventure. Run by **Xanterra Parks & Resorts**, the trips fill early and may be booked up to two years in advance. The trip takes two days, descend-ing Bright Angel Trail, with an overnight stay and hearty steak dinner at Phantom Ranch (see p125 & p135). The ride offers ever-changing panoramas of the canyon in both directions. Guides stop frequently to ensure everyone is drinking water, as dehydra-tion is a common and some-times serious problem. Riders must be at least 4.7 ft (1.38 m) tall, weigh less than 200 lbs (91 kg), understand fluent English, and be unafraid of heights. One-day trips that go only half-way into the canyon before returning are also available.

Those wanting a tamer adventure can opt for short trail rides on horseback, which are offered by **Apache Stables** at the South Rim, just outside the park's boundary. For a longer horseback adventure, contact the **Havasupai Tourist Enterprise**, which offers one-day and multi-day adventures into the beautiful Havasu Canyon (see p48).

**Mule rides into Grand Canyon National Park – a popular adventure**

A helicopter conducts an aerial tour of the Grand Canyon, offering breathtaking views

## AIR TOURS

AN AIRPLANE trip over the Grand Canyon offers a unique opportunity to view the vastness of the canyon, and is a particularly good option for those with limited mobility. Tours leave hourly on demand from the Grand Canyon Airport. **Air Grand Canyon** offers tours in small, high-wing aircraft that seat five and provide everyone a window seat. **Grand Canyon Airlines** offer tours in larger twin-engine aircraft that seat 19. Helicopters, which fly at just 500 ft (150 m), compared to 900 ft (275 m) for airplanes, offer an even more intimate look at the canyon. Several operators, such as **Airstar Helicopters**, offer 25–50 minute helicopter tours over the canyon.

The aircraft are not allowed to enter the canyon within the National Park, but full-day trips into the Havasu Canyon (fly in, explore, and fly out) with an optional horseback ride to the Havasu Falls are offered by **Papillon Grand Canyon Helicopters**.

## RIVER TRIPS

PERHAPS NO adventure puts visitors in touch with the essence and natural beauty of the canyon as much as a paddling trip down the Colorado River. The classic river trip, offered by outfits such as **Canyon Explorations**, **OARS**, and **Arizona Raft Adventures** is undertaken in

moderate-sized rubber rafts that seat four to seven people, and are powered by a highly trained guide at the oars. Several rafts usually make the run together, with one or two reserved for provisions. A full-river trip starts at Lees Ferry and covers 280 miles (451 km) over 14–16 days, taking out at Diamond Creek. Stretches of quiet water are interspersed with 49 of America's most impressive whitewater runs. The rafts stop every night to pitch camp and most tour operators pride themselves on providing excellent meals. They also offer hikes into the canyons on the sides, so tourists can view the flora and fauna, and waterfalls in the area. Also available are half-river trips lasting five to nine

days that begin or end at Phantom Ranch and require hiking in or out of the canyon. Some tour companies, such as **Hatch River Expeditions**, offer trips in larger, motorized rafts that seat 15, and can run the canyon in just seven days.

## DORY TRIPS

WHEN JOHN Wesley Powell became the first man to run the canyon, he did so in sturdy open boats, and many believe that this still is the best way to experience the river. Although similar in many ways to rubber rafts, dories are smaller, seating just three to five people. Many people consider the dory experience to be a quieter and more intimate canyon experience.

Dory running on the Specter Rapids, Colorado River

Several tour operators, including **Grand Canyon Dories** and **Grand Canyon Expeditions**, offer 7–14 day dory trips through the canyon.

## KAYAK SUPPORT TRIPS

FOR SKILLED paddlers, nothing beats the experience of running the river under their own power, in whitewater kayaks. The challenge is that park-issued permits to run the river, which are given to single paddlers or groups, have a current waiting list of almost 20 years (the park service is currently reviewing the permit system).

If you do not want to wait that long, the solution may be to sign up for a kayak support trip with tour operators such as **Grand Canyon Discovery** and **Canyon Explorations**. Paddlers sign up for trips on specific dates. The operators provide guides (and kayaks if needed), as well as food and camping gear (which follows along in a support raft). Full- and half-river trips are available, and prices are comparable to rafting trips.

**On the Colorado River in a whitewater kayak**

---

### DIRECTORY

#### BACKCOUNTRY CAMPING

**Grand Canyon Hikes**
7010 Bader Road,
Flagstaff, AZ 86001.
**C** (877) 506-6233,
(928) 779-1614.
**W** www.
grandcanyonhikes.com

**Sky Island Treks**
928, S 7th Ave,
Tucson,
AZ 85701.
**C** (520)622-6966.
**W** www.skyislandtreks.
com

#### MOUNTAIN BIKING

**Escape Adventures**
8221, W Chareston,
#101, Las Vegas,
NV 89117.
**C** (800) 596-2953,
(702) 596-2953.
**W** www.
escapeadventures.com

#### EDUCATIONAL TOURS

**Discovery Treks**
6890, E Sunrise Suite
120-108, Tucson,
AZ 85750.
**C** (888) 256-8731,
(520) 404-1151.
**W** www.
discoverytreks.com

**Grand Canyon Field Institute**
PO Box 399,
Grand Canyon, AZ 86023.
**C** (800) 858-2808.
**W** www.grandcanyon.
org/fieldinstitute

**Museum of Northern Arizona**
3101 N Fort Valley Rd,
Flagstaff, AZ 86001.
**C** 928-774-5211.
**W** www.musnaz.org

#### MULE TRIPS

**Apache Stables**
PO Box 158,
Grand Canyon, AZ 86023.
**C** (928) 638-2891.
**W** www.apachestables.
com

**Havasupai Tourist Enterprise**
Supai, AZ 86435.
**C** (928) 448-2121.

**Xanterra Parks & Resorts**
14001 E Illiff, Ste 600,
Aurora, CO 80014.
**C** (888) 297-2757.
**W** www.
grandcanyonlodges.com

#### AIR TOURS

**Air Grand Canyon**
PO Box 3399,
Grand Canyon,
AZ 86023.
**C** (800) 247-4726,
(928) 638-2686.
**W** www.
airgrandcanyon.com

**Airstar Helicopters**
PO Box 3379,
Grand Canyon,
AZ 86023.
**C** (800) 962-3869,
(928) 638-2622.
**W** www.airstar.com

**Grand Canyon Airlines**
PO Box 3038, National
Park Airport, Grand
Canyon, AZ 86023.
**C** (800) 528-2413,
(928) 638-2359.
**W** www.
grandcanyonairlines.com

**Papillon Grand Canyon Helicopters**
PO Box 455,
Grand Canyon,
AZ 86023.
**C** (800) 528-2418,
(928) 638-2419.
**W** www.papillon.com

#### RIVER TRIPS

**Arizona Raft Adventures**
4050 E Huntington Dr,
Flagstaff,
AZ 86004.
**C** (800) 786-7238,
(928) 526-8200.
**W** www.azraft.com

**Canyon Explorations**
PO Box 310
Flagstaff,
AZ 86002.
**C** (800) 654-0723,
(928) 774-4559.
**W** www.canyonx.com

**Hatch River Expeditions**
PO Box 1200,
Vernal, UT 84078.
**C** (435) 789-3813.
**W** www.hatchriver.com

**OARS**
PO Box 67,
Angels Camp, CA 95222.
**C** (800) 346-6277.
**W** www.oars.com

#### DORY TRIPS

**Grand Canyon Dories**
PO Box 216,
Altaville, CA 95221.
**C** (800) 877-3679.
**W** www.oars.com

**Grand Canyon Expeditions**
PO Box 0,
Kanab, UT 84741.
**C** (800) 544-2691.
**W** www.gcex.com

#### KAYAK SUPPORT TRIPS

**Canyon Explorations**
PO Box 310,
Flagstaff, AZ 86002.
**C** (800) 654-0723,
(928) 774-4559.
**W** www.canyonx.com

**Grand Canyon Discovery**
4050, E Huntington Dr,
Flagstaff, AZ 86004.
**C** (800) 786-7238.
**W** www.
grandcanyondiscovery.com

# Lake Powell & Glen Canyon National Recreation Area ❷

THE BUILDING OF Glen Canyon Dam in 1963 created the 185-mile (298-km) long Lake Powell. Originally intended as a reservoir to provide drinking and irrigation water, it got a boost in 1972 with the opening of the Glen Canyon National Recreation Area (NRA). Covering more than one million acres of dramatic desert and canyon country, mostly along the Utah side of Lake Powell, the area is a popular hiking and 4WD destination. Initially built for dam workers, the town of Page is now the starting point for exploring Lake Powell and the NRA. Along the lake shore, the Wahweap and Bullfrog marinas hum with activity and houseboating and watersports are popular. In recent years prolonged drought has lowered lake levels.

**Rainbow Bridge National Monument**
*Rising 290 ft (88 m) above Lake Powell, Rainbow Bridge is the largest natural bridge in North America, only accessible by boat from Wahweap or Bullfrog marinas.*

**View of Lake Powell**
*The blue waters of the man-made Lake Powell are encircled by colorful sandstone coves – once Glen Canyon's side canyons – and dramatic buttes and mesas.*

**Glen Canyon Dam** was completed in 1963 and rises 710 ft (213 m) above the bedrock of the Colorado River.

WATERPOCKET FOLD

Escalante River

FIFTYMILE MOUNTAINS

Dangling Rope Marina

Lake Powell

WEST CANYON

NAVAJO CANYON

Wahweap

Page

89

TO GRAND CANYON

**Antelope Canyon**
*Bands of sandstone curve sinuously together, sometimes just a few feet apart, in this famously deep "slot" canyon.*

**Lees Ferry** was a Mormon settlement in the 19th century. Today, this outpost offers tourist facilities, including a ranger station and campground.

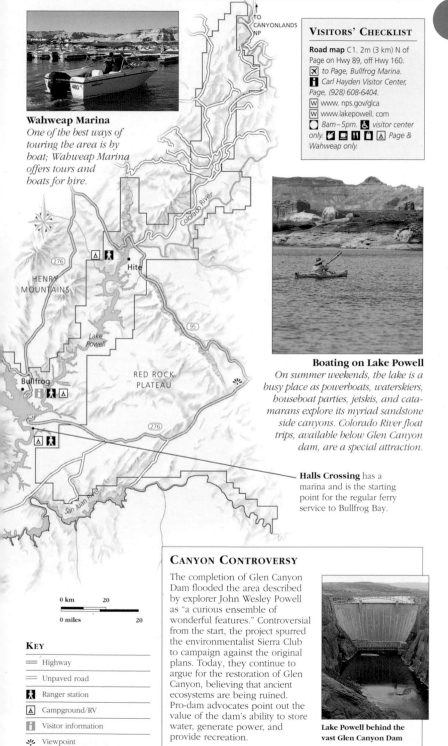

**Wahweap Marina**
*One of the best ways of touring the area is by boat; Wahweap Marina offers tours and boats for hire.*

**Boating on Lake Powell**
*On summer weekends, the lake is a busy place as powerboats, waterskiers, houseboat parties, jetskis, and catamarans explore its myriad sandstone side canyons. Colorado River float trips, available below Glen Canyon dam, are a special attraction.*

**Halls Crossing** has a marina and is the starting point for the regular ferry service to Bullfrog Bay.

## CANYON CONTROVERSY

The completion of Glen Canyon Dam flooded the area described by explorer John Wesley Powell as "a curious ensemble of wonderful features." Controversial from the start, the project spurred the environmentalist Sierra Club to campaign against the original plans. Today, they continue to argue for the restoration of Glen Canyon, believing that ancient ecosystems are being ruined. Pro-dam advocates point out the value of the dam's ability to store water, generate power, and provide recreation.

**Lake Powell behind the vast Glen Canyon Dam**

### KEY

═══ Highway

━━━ Unpaved road

🏃 Ranger station

△ Campground/RV

ℹ Visitor information

☆ Viewpoint

0 km — 20
0 miles — 20

# Flagstaff ❸

**Colorful Lowell Observatory sign**

Nestling among the pine forests of Northern Arizona's San Francisco Peaks, Flagstaff is one of the region's most attractive towns. It is a lively, easy-going place with a good selection of bars and restaurants among the maze of old red-brick buildings that make up its compact downtown. Flagstaff's first Anglo settlers were sheep ranchers who arrived in 1876. The railroad came in 1882, and the town developed as a lumber center.

Flagstaff is the home of Northern Arizona University, which has two appealing art galleries, and is a good base for visiting Grand Canyon's South Rim, just under two hours' drive away. The surrounding mountains attract hikers in summer and skiers in winter.

**The town of Flagstaff with the San Francisco Peaks as a backdrop**

## Exploring Flagstaff

Flagstaff's center is narrow and slender, channeling north toward the Museum of Northern Arizona and south to the university. At its heart is a pocket-sized historic district, an attractive ensemble of red-brick buildings, which houses the best restaurants and bars. Lowell Observatory is located on Mars Hill, a short distance from downtown, and the popular Arizona Snowbowl ski resort is an enjoyable ten-minute drive to the north of the town.

### 🏛 Lowell Observatory
1400 West Mars Hill Rd.
📞 *(928) 774-3358.* ⏲ *Mar–Oct: 9am–5pm; Nov–Feb: noon–5pm. Call for details.* 🅿 *public hols.* 🎫 ♿ 🎦
🌐 *www.lowell.edu*
Tucked away on a hill about a mile northwest of the town center, the Lowell Observatory was founded in 1894 and named for its benefactor, Percival Lowell, a member of one of Boston's wealthiest families. He financed the observatory to look for life on Mars and chose the town because of its high altitude and clear mountain air. The observatory went on to establish an international reputation with its documented evidence of an expanding universe, data

**The 1930 Pluto dome, Flagstaff Lowell Observatory**

that was disclosed to the public in 1912. One of the observatory's famous astronomers, Clyde Tombaugh, discovered the planet Pluto on February 18, 1930.

Visitors can inspect the main rotunda, with its assorted astronomical paraphernalia, and view the original photographic plates made by Tombaugh. A guided tour includes a video presentation on the observatory's history. Evening astronomy sessions can be arranged in advance.

### 🏚 Historic Downtown
Just ten minutes' walk from end to end, Flagstaff's historic downtown dates mainly from the 1890s. Many buildings sport decorative stone and stucco friezes, and are now occupied by cafés, bars, and stores. Architecturally, several buildings stand out, particularly the restored Babbitt Building and the 1926 train station that today houses the visitor center. Perhaps the most attractive building is the Weatherford Hotel, which was opened on January 1, 1900. It was named after its owner, Texan entrepreneur John W. Weatherford, and was much admired for its grand two-story wraparound veranda and its sunroom.

### 🏛 Northern Arizona University
624 S Knoles Dr. 📞 *(928) 523-9011.* ⏲ *Times vary, so call in advance.* 🌐 *www.nau.edu*
Flagstaff's lively café society owes much to the 16,000 students of Northern Arizona University. The main entrance point to the campus is located on Knoles Drive. Green lawns, stately trees, and several historic buildings make for a pleasant visit. Of particular note are two campus art galleries: the Beasley Gallery in the Fine Art Building, which features temporary exhibitions and student work, and the Old Main Art Museum and Gallery housed in Old Main Building – the university's oldest. This features the permanent Weiss Collection, which includes works by the famous Mexican artist Diego Rivera.

**Arts and Crafts swinging settee at Riordan Mansion**

## 🏛 Riordan Mansion State Historic Park

409 Riordan Rd. 📞 (928) 779-4395.
🕐 May–Oct: 8:30am–5pm;
Nov–Apr: 10:30am–5pm. ⬤ Dec 25.
📷 👤 ⓦ www.azstateparks.com
In the mid-1880s, Michael and Timothy Riordan established a lumber company that quickly made them a fortune. The brothers then built a house of grandiose proportions, a 40-room log mansion with two wings, one for each of them. Completed in 1904 and now preserved as a State Historic Park, the house has a rustic, timber-clad exterior, and Arts and Crafts furniture inside.

## 🏛 Pioneer Museum

2340 Fort Valley Rd. 📞 (928) 774-6272. 🕐 9am–5pm Mon–Sat.
⬤ Sun, public hols. 📷
Flagstaff's Pioneer Museum occupies an elegant stone building that was originally built as a hospital in 1908. The museum opened in 1960 and incorporates the Ben Doney homestead cabin. On display in the grounds are a steam locomotive of 1929 and a Santa Fe Railroad caboose. Inside, a particular highlight is a selection of Grand Canyon photographs taken in the early 1900s by photographers Ellsworth and Emery Kolb.

## Arizona Snowbowl

Snowbowl Rd, off Hwy 180.
📞 (928) 779-1951. 📷 Flagstaff Snow Report: (928) 779-4577.
🕐 Dec–mid-Apr.
ⓦ www.arizonasnowbowl.com
Downhill skiing can be enjoyed at Arizona Snowbowl just 7 miles (11 km) north of town. The mountains here are the San Francisco Peaks, which receive an average of 260 in (660 cm) of snow annually,

**VISITORS' CHECKLIST**

**Road map:** C3. 🏠 58,000.
✈ Pulliam Airport, 4 miles (6 km) south of town. 🚆 Amtrak Flagstaff Station, 1 E Rte 66. 🚌 Flagstaff bus station, 399 S Malpais Lane.
🛈 Flagstaff Visitor Center, at Amtrak depot, 1 E Rte 66, Flagstaff, (928) 774-9541. 🕐 Sep–May: 8am–5pm; June–Aug: 7am–7pm. ⬤ Thanksgiving, Dec 25. 🎭 Flagstaff Festival of the Arts (early July to mid-August).

enough to supply the various ski runs that pattern the lower slopes of the 12,356-ft (3,707-m) high Agassiz Peak. Facilities include four chairlifts, and a ski school for beginners. In summer, there is a hiking trail up to the peak, while for those less inclined to walk, the Arizona Scenic Skyride is a cable car trip that offers spectacular views of the scenery.

## 🏛 Museum of Northern Arizona

(see p66)

**FLAGSTAFF**

Historic Downtown District ②
Lowell Observatory ①
Northern Arizona University ③
Riordan Mansion State Historic Park ④

Arizona Snowbowl
Museum of Northern Arizona
Pioneer Museum

**KEY**

🚆 Train station
🚌 Bus station
🅿 Parking
🛈 Visitor information

0 meters 300
0 yards 300

# Flagstaff: Museum of Northern Arizona

THE MUSEUM OF NORTHERN ARIZONA holds one of the Southwest's most comprehensive collections of archeological artifacts, as well as fine art and natural science exhibits. The collections are arranged in galleries around a central courtyard. The Archeology Gallery gives an introduction to the historic cultures. The award-winning anthropology exhibition in the Ethnology Gallery documents 12,000 years of tribal cultures on the Colorado Plateau, while the Babbitt Gallery showcases traditional and modern pottery of the Hopi people. The Museum Shop sells contemporary Native arts and crafts.

**VISITORS' CHECKLIST**

3101 N Fort Valley Rd. ☎ (928) 774-5213. ◻ 9am–5pm. ● public hols. ▨ & ▯
ⓦ www.musnaz.org

**The historic courtyard** has exhibits that focus on the variety of plants and animals found on the Colorado Plateau through the ages.

★ **Ethnology Gallery**
*This well-organized gallery houses important examples of Hopi silverwork, Zuni pottery, and* kachina *dolls* (see p19) *dating from 1880.*

**The Kiva Gallery** replicates the inside of a *kiva* (see pp36–7).

**Babbitt Gallery**

**KEY**

- ◻ Archeology Gallery
- ◻ Ethnology Gallery
- ◻ Babbitt Gallery
- ◻ Geology Gallery
- ◻ Historic courtyard
- ◻ Temporary exhibition space
- ◻ Non-exhibition space

**Entrance**

**Archeology Gallery**

**STAR SIGHT**

★ **Ethnology Gallery**

**Geology Gallery**
*A lifesize skeletal model of a Dilophosaurus is ringed by dioramas of ancient Arizona desert scenes.*

**Museum Façade**
*Built in 1935, the museum has a stone façade and is listed on the National Register of Historic Places.*

# Wupatki National Monument ❹

**Road map** C3. Forest Service Rd 545, Sunset Crater/Wupatki Loop Rd. ☎ *(928) 679-2365.* 🚌 *Flagstaff.* ⊞ *Flagstaff.* ⏱ *8am–6pm summer; 9am–5pm winter; 8am–5pm spring, fall.* ● *Dec 25.* 📷 ♿ *partial.* ☑ W *www.nps.gov/wupa*

COVERING MORE than 35,000 acres (14,000 ha) of sun-scorched wilderness to the north of Flagstaff, the Wupatki National Monument incorporates about 2,700 historic sites once inhabited by the ancestors of the Hopi people. The area was first settled after the eruption of Sunset Crater in 1064. The Sinagua people and their Ancestral Puebloan cousins *(see pp36–7)* realized that the volcanic ash had made the soil more fertile and consequently favourable for farming. The power of the volcanic eruption may also have have appealed to their spirituality. They left the region in the early 13th century, but no one really knows why.

The largest site here is the Wupatki Pueblo, built in the 12th century and once a four-story pueblo complex of 100 rooms, housing more than 100 Sinagua. The structures rise from their rocky outcrop overlooking the desert. A trail from the visitor center explores the remains of the complex, whose most unusual feature is its ballcourt. Here the Sinagua may have played at dropping a ball through a stone ring without using their hands or feet.

# Sunset Crater Volcano National Monument ❺

**Road map** C3. Hwy 545 off Hwy 89, Sunset Crater/ Wupatki Loop Rd. ☎ *(928) 556-7042.* 🚌 *Flagstaff.* ⊞ *Flagstaff.* ⏱ *Mar–May & Sep–Nov: 8am–5pm; June–Aug: 8am–6pm; Dec–Feb: 9am–5pm.* ● *Dec 25.* 📷 ♿ ☑ W *www.nps.gov/sucr*

A MIGHTY volcanic eruption in 1064 formed the 400-ft (120-m) deep Sunset Crater, leaving a cinder cone that is 1,000-ft (300-m) high. The cone is black at the base and tinged **Petroglyph from** with reds and oranges **Walnut Canyon** farther up. The one-mile (1.6-km) Lava Trail offers an easy stroll around the ashy landscape with its lava tubes, bubbles, and vents. Sunset Crater is the youngest volcano on the Colorado Plateau.

# Walnut Canyon National Monument ❻

**Road map** C3. Hwy 40 exit 204. ☎ *(928) 526-3367.* 🚌 *Flagstaff.* ⊞ *Flagstaff.* ⏱ *Mar–May, Sep–Nov: 8am–5pm; Jun–Aug: 8am–6pm; Dec–Feb: 9am–5pm.* ● *Dec 25.* 📷 ♿ *partial.* 🎥 W *www.nps.gov/waca*

LOCATED ABOUT ten miles (16 km) east of Flagstaff, off Interstate Highway 40,

the Walnut Canyon National Monument houses an intriguing collection of single-story cliff dwellings. These were inhabited by the Sinagua people in the 12th and 13th centuries. The Sinagua were attracted to the canyon because of its fertile soil, and the abundance of water from the nearby Walnut Creek.

Today, visitors to Walnut Canyon can tour the 25 cliff dwellings huddled underneath the natural overhangs of its eroded sandstone and limestone walls. Sinagua artifacts are on display in the Walnut Canyon Visitor Center, which also houses a small museum.

# Petrified Forest National Park ❼

**Road map** D3. Off Hwy I-40. ☎ *(928) 524-6228.* ⏱ *8am–5pm.* ● *Dec 25.* 📷 ♿ *partial.* W *www.nps.gov/pefo*

THE PETRIFIED Forest National Park is one of Arizona's most unusual attractions. Millions of years ago rivers swept trees downstream into a vast swamp in the area. Groundwater transported silica dioxide, and eventually turned the timber into the quartz stone logs seen today, with colored crystals preserving the trees' shape and structure.

Running the length of the forest is the famous Painted Desert, an area of colored bands of sand and rock that change from blues to reds as the shifting light catches the different mineral deposits. The Painted Desert Visitor Center offers an orientation film.

From here, a 28-mile (45-km) scenic road travels the length of the park. There are nine overlooks, including Kachina Point, where the Painted Desert Wilderness trailhead is located. Near the south end of the road is the **Rainbow Forest Museum**.

🏛 **Rainbow Forest Museum** Off Hwy 180 (S entrance). ☎ *(928) 524-6822.* ⏱ *8am–5pm (call for extended hours schedule).* ● *Dec 25.* 📷

**Ruins of a 12th-century pueblo building at Wupatki National Monument**

# Sedona ❽

**Sign of Sedona city**

Founded by Theodore Schnelby in 1902, and named after his wife, Sedona was a quiet town until 1981. That year, author and renowned psychic, Page Bryant, claimed to have located seven "vortexes" emanating powerful spiritual energy in and around this beautiful town, and declared it the "heart-chakra of the planet." Since then, New Agers have developed Sedona as a spiritual, artistic, and outdoor-oriented resort town. Today, artists of all kinds sell their works in a growing number of galleries, such as those in Tlaquepaque, a superbly rendered village of artists, craftspeople, and imaginative shops.

**VISITORS' CHECKLIST**

**Road map** B3. 🏠 16,000.
✈ Pulliam Airport, Flagstaff (no commercial flights into Sedona Airport). 🚹 331 Forest Road, (800) 288-7336.
📷 Sedona Jazz on the Rocks (late Sep). Ⓦ www.visitsedona.com
**Spas** Mii Amo at Enchantment Resort, (800) 826-4180; Los Abrigados Resort & Spa, (800) 418-6499.
**Art Shopping** Tlaquepaque Art Village, (928) 282-4838.

## CATHEDRAL ROCK
One of Sedona's seven "energy vortexes," Cathedral Rock is revered in Native American mythology as the birthplace of the "First Man" and "First Woman." It is a popular place for sunrise and sunset hikes, and the view of Cathedral Rock overlooking Oak Creek is one of the most photographed scenes in Arizona.

**Crystal Therapy**
*Sedona's New Age centers offer a dazzling array of alternative therapies.*

**Havasupai Storyteller**
*Native American themes and traditions are often components of many of the programs offered in and around Sedona.*

**Tlaquepaque Art Village**
*Sedona has attracted many artists and craftspeople, whose creations are on display in fine shops and galleries.*

**Spa Resorts**
*Sedona's natural desert beauty and reputed healing energies have made it a premier center for spas and resorts.*

# Oak Creek Canyon ❾

**Road map** B3. 🛈 *(800) 228-7336.*

JUST SOUTH OF Flagstaff, Highway 89A weaves a charming route through Oak Creek Canyon on its way to Sedona. In the canyon, dense woods shadow the road, and the steep cliffs are colored in bands of red and yellow sandstone, pale limestone, and black basalt. The canyon is a popular summer vacation area with many day-hiking trails, such as the East Pocket Trail, a steep, wooded climb to the canyon rim. One of the prettiest and easiest hikes in Oak Creek is along the 3-mile (5-km) West Fork Trail, which follows a stream past abandoned apple orchards and into a narrow red rock canyon. At nearby Slide Rock State Park, swimmers enjoy sliding over the rocks that form a natural water chute.

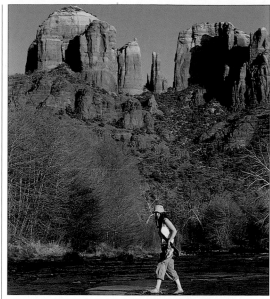

Picturesque Oak Creek Canyon – a popular summer destination

# Williams ❿

**Road map** B3. 🏃 *2,700.*
🚉 🛈 *200 W Railroad Ave, (928) 635-4061.* Ⓦ *www. williamschamber.com*

THIS DISTINCTIVE little town was named in 1851 for Bill Williams (1787–1849), a legendary mountain man and trapper who lived for a time with the Osage Indians in Missouri. The town grew around the railroad that came in the 1880s, and when this was followed by a spur track to Grand Canyon's South Rim in 1901, Williams became established as a tourist center. By the late 1920s, it was also a popular rest stop on Route 66 *(see pp28–9).*

The town retains its frontier atmosphere, complete with Stetson-wearing locals. Most hotels and diners are located on a loop that follows Route 66 on one side, and Interstate Highway 40 on the other. Diners evoke the 1950s, and are filled with Route 66 memorabilia, including original soda fountains and posters.

# Tuzigoot National Monument ⓫

**Road map** B3. *Follow signs from Hwy 89A.* ☎ *(928) 634-5564.* ⏲ *end May–early Sep: 8am–6pm; early Sep–end May: 8am–5pm.* ⬤ *Dec 25.* ♿ Ⓦ *www.nps.gov/tuzi*

PERCHED ON A solitary and slender limestone ridge, the ruins of Tuzigoot National Monument offer fine views of the Verde River Valley. The pueblo was built by the Sinagua people between the 12th and 15th centuries and, at its peak, had a population of around 300. It was abandoned in the early 15th century, when the Sinagua are believed to have migrated north.

Tuzigoot was partly rebuilt by a local and federally funded program during the Depression in the 1930s. This emphasized one of the most unusual features of pueblo building, the lack of doorways. The normal pueblo room was entered by ladder through a hatchway in the roof. Sinaguan artifacts and art are on display at the visitor center here.

# Jerome ⓬

**Road map** B3. 🏃 *500.*
🛈 *Box K, Jerome, www.azjerome.com*

APPROACHED FROM the east along Highway 89A, Jerome is easy to spot, with its old brick buildings high above the valley. Silver mining began here in the 1870s, but the town's big break came in 1912 when prospectors struck substantial copper. World War I sent the price of copper sky-high, and Jerome boomed. In the Wall Street Crash of 1929, however, copper prices tumbled, and the boom times were over. Jerome was a ghost town by the early 1960s, but its fortunes have now been revived by an influx of artists and artisans.

Façade of an early 20th-century store on Jerome's historic Main Street

# Heart of Arizona Tour ⓭

THE VERDE RIVER passes through the wooded hills
and fertile meadows of Central Arizona, before
opening into a wide, green valley between Flagstaff
and Phoenix. The heart of Arizona is full of charming towns such as Sedona, hidden away among
stunning scenery, and the former mining town of
Jerome. Over the hills lies Prescott, once state capital and now a busy, likable little town with a center full of dignified Victorian buildings. The area's
ancient history can be seen in its two beautiful
pueblo ruins, Montezuma Castle and Tuzigoot.

## TIPS FOR DRIVERS

*Recommended route:* From
Sedona, take Hwy 89A to
Tuzigoot, Jerome, and Prescott.
Hwy 69 runs east from Prescott to
Interstate Hwy 17, which
connects to Camp Verde, Fort
Verde, and Montezuma Castle.
*Tour length:* 85 miles (137 km).
*When to go:* Spring and fall are
delightful; summer is very hot.

**Sedona** ①
Set among dramatic
red rock hills, Sedona
*(see p68)* is a popular
resort, known for its
New Age stores and
galleries, as well as for
its friendly ambience.

## KEY

━━ Tour route

═══ Other roads

**Tuzigoot National Monument** ②
Stunning views of Verde River
Valley are seen at this ruined
pueblo *(see p69)*, occupied
until 1425.

FLAGSTAFF

Cottonwood

Verde River

179

89A

260

Prescott Valley

④

③

⑤

⑥

**Jerome** ③
A relic of the
mining boom,
Jerome *(see p69)* is
known for its 1900s brick
buildings that cling to the
slopes of Cleopatra Hill.

69

17

PHOENIX

0 km    10

0 miles    10

**Prescott** ④
This cool hilltop town is set
among the rugged peaks and
lush woods of Prescott National
Forest, making it a popular center
for many outdoor activities.

**Montezuma Castle
National Monument** ⑥
The Ancestral Puebloan
ruins here date from the
1100s and occupy one of
the loveliest sites in
the Southwest.

**Camp Verde** ⑤
A highlight of this little town is
Fort Verde. Built by the US Army
in 1865, the fort is manned by
costumed guides.

## Montezuma Castle National Monument ⑭

**Road map** B3. Hwy I-17 exit 289.
▮ (928) 567-3322. ◯ early Sep–end May: 8am–5pm; end May–early Sep: 8am–6pm. ▨ �W www.nps.gov/moca

DATING FROM the 1100s, the pueblo remains that make up Montezuma Castle occupy an idyllic location, built into the limestone cliffs high above Beaver Creek, a couple of miles to the east of Interstate Highway 17. Once home to the Sinagua people, this cliff dwelling originally contained 20 rooms on five floors. Montezuma Castle was declared a National Monument in 1906 to preserve its excellent condition. The visitor center has a display on Sinaguan life, and is found at the start of an easy trail along Beaver Creek. The National Monument also incorporates Montezuma Well, situated about 11 miles (18 km) to the northeast. This natural sinkhole, 50 ft (15 m) deep and 470 ft (140 m) in diameter, had religious significance for Native Americans, who believed it was the site of the Creation. Over 1,000 gallons (3,790 liters) of water flow through the sinkhole every minute, an inexhaustible supply that has long been used for irrigation. A narrow trail leads around the rim before twisting its way down to the water's edge.

Pueblo remains of Montezuma Castle, built into limestone cliffs

Costumed guides at Fort Verde State Historic Park

## Camp Verde ⑮

**Road map** B3. ▨ 6,000. ▮ 385 S Main St, (928) 567-9294. ▨ �W www.campverde.org

FARMERS FOUNDED the small settlement of Camp Verde in the heart of the Verde River Valley in the 1860s. It was a risky enterprise as the Apache lived nearby, but the US Army quickly moved in to protect the settlers, building **Fort Verde** in 1865. Today, Camp Verde remains at the center of a large and prosperous farming and ranching community. It was from Fort Verde that the army orchestrated a series of brutal campaigns against the Apache, which ended with the Battle of the Big Dry Wash in 1882. Once the Apache had been sent to reservations, Fort Verde was no longer needed and it was decommissioned in 1891. Four of its original buildings have survived. The former army administration building contains a collection of exhibits on army life. The interiors of the other three houses, on Officers' Row, have been restored. On weekends, from spring to fall, volunteers dressed in period costume act as guides and re-enact scenes from the fort's daily life.

🏛 **Fort Verde at Camp Verde State Historic Park**
Off Hwy I-17. ▮ (928) 567-3275.
◯ 8am–5pm. ● Dec 25. ▨

## Prescott ⑯

**Road map** B3. ▨ 34,000. ✕ ▯
▮ 117 W Goodwin St, (928) 445-2000. �W www.prescott.org

SURROUNDED BY high-country and lakes, this attractive Victorian town gives little evidence of its early days as a hard-drinking frontier area. Perhaps the three years spent as the early capital of the Arizona Territories gave it some respectability. Palace Saloon is the only structure left from "Whiskey Row," where over 20 saloons once stood. The Governor's Mansion – really just a large log cabin – is part of the **Sharlot Hall Museum**. This exceptional museum is named for Sharlot Hall, a pioneer, writer, and early activist who served as Arizona's first salaried historian. Her paintings and photographs form the core of a collection that fills nine buildings.

Fans of Native history should visit **Smoki Museum**. Located in a replica of a Hopi pueblo, the museum contains over 2,000 Native artifacts from prehistoric to modern. The museum's basket collection is said to be one of the best in the United States. Also of note is the **Phippen Art Museum**, which has an impressive collection of historic and contemporary Western art.

🏛 **Sharlot Hall Museum**
415 W Gurly St. ▮ (928) 445-3122.
◯ May–Oct: 10am–5pm Mon–Sat, 10am–2pm Sun; Nov–Apr: 10am–4pm Mon–Sat. �W www.sharlot.org
🏛 **Smoki Museum**
147 N Arizona St. ▮ (928) 445-1230.
◯ 10am–4pm Mon–Sat, 1pm–4pm Sun. �W www.smokimuseum.org
🏛 **Phippen Art Museum**
4701 Hwy 89 N. ▮ (928) 778-1385.
◯ 10am–4pm Tue–Sat, 1pm–4pm Sun. ● early Jan, Thanksgiving, Dec 25; Mon. �W www. phippenartmuseum.org

# Hoover Dam ⑰

**Road map** A2. **ℹ** *Hoover Dam
Visitor Center, Hoover Dam, Boulder
City, (702) 597-5970, (866) 291-
8687.* ☐ *9am–4:45pm.*
● *Thanksgiving, Dec 25.* 📷 ♿

NAMED AFTER Herbert
Hoover, the 31st presi-
dent, the historic Hoover Dam
is situated at Arizona's border
with Nevada. Built between
1931 and 1935 across the
Colorado River's Black Canyon,
the dam is 30 miles (48 km)
east of the city of Las Vegas.
Hailed as an engineering victory, the dam gave this desert
region a reliable water supply
and provided inexpensive
electricity. Today, it supplies
water and electricity to the
three states of Nevada, Arizona,
and California, and has created
Lake Mead – a popular tourist
center. Visitors to the dam can
take the Discovery Tour, which
includes a trip to the observation deck and elevator ride
deep inside the dam to the
generator viewing area.
   Located eight miles (13
km) west of Hoover Dam is
**Boulder City**, which was
built as a model community
to house dam construction
workers. With its neat yards
and suburban streets, it is one
of Nevada's most attractive
and well-ordered towns. Its
Christian founders banned

Lake Mead, a popular tourist destination for watersports

casinos, and there are none
here today. Several of its
original 1930s buildings
remain, including the restored
1933 Boulder Dam Hotel,
which houses the **Hoover
Dam Museum**.
   The museum tells the
history and development of
Boulder City, Hoover Dam,
Lake Mead, and the Lower
Colorado River region through
3-D interactive displays and
exhibits. Several artifacts and
photographs, which highlight
the lives of the workers who
built the dam, provide a
sense of the complexity and
the immense scale of the
Hoover Dam project.

**🏛 Hoover Dam Museum**
1305 Arizona St, Boulder City.
**☏** *(702) 294-1988.* ☐ *10am–5pm
Mon–Sat; noon–5pm Sun.* 📷 ♿
**W** www.bcmha.org

# Lake Mead National Recreation Area ⑱

**Road map** A2. 🚌 *Las Vegas.*
**ℹ** *Alan Bible Visitor Center,
(702) 293-8990.* ☐ *8:30am–
4:30pm.* ● *Jan 1, Thanksgiving,
Dec 25.* 📷 ♿ *limited.* 🅰
**W** www.nps.gov/lame

AFTER THE completion of the
Hoover Dam, the waters
of the Colorado River filled
the deep canyons that once
towered above the river to
create a huge reservoir. This
lake, with its 700 miles
(1,130 km) of shoreline, is the
centerpiece of Lake Mead
National Recreation Area, a
1.5-million-acre (600,000-ha)
tract of land. The focus is on
watersports, especially sailing,
waterskiing, and fishing.
Striped bass and rainbow
trout are popular catches.
There are also several campgrounds and marinas.

# Kingman ⑲

**Road map** A3. 🏘 *35,000.* ✈
🚌 🚆 **ℹ** *120 W Andy Devine Ave,
(928) 753-6106.* **W** *www.
kingmantourism.org*

LOCATED IN the middle of the
desert, Kingman was
founded by the Santa Fe
Railroad as a construction
camp in 1882. In the 1920s,
the town became an impor-
tant stop on Route 66
*(see pp28–9)*, and during
the 1930s depression it was
crowded with migrants
fleeing the Midwest. Today,
Kingman's claim to fame is
being situated on the longest

---

### THE CONSTRUCTION OF THE HOOVER DAM

**Hoover
Dam sign**

More than 1,400 miles (2,250 km) in length, the
Colorado River flows through seven states from
the Rocky Mountains to the Gulf of California.
A treacherous, unpredictable river, it used to be
a raging torrent in spring and a trickle in the
heat of summer. As a source of water it was
therefore unreliable and, in 1928, the seven
states it served signed
the Boulder Canyon
Project Act to define how much
water each state could siphon
off. The agreement paved the
way for the Hoover Dam, and its
construction began in 1931. It
was a mammoth task, and more
than 5,000 men toiled day and
night to build what was, at 726
ft (218 m), the world's tallest
dam. The dam contains 17
hydroelectric generating units.

**View of the Hoover Dam**

remaining stretch of Route 66. Renewed interest in the road has resulted in the renovation of many of Kingman's Route 66 diners, motels, and tourist stops. The visitor center, housed in the "Powerhouse," which was built in 1907, features a replica Route 66 diner and the Route 66 Museum, which traces the road's journey from its origins.

**Chloride**, a former mining town, is an enjoyable day trip from Kingman. A boomtown during the late 19th century, it still has many of its original structures, including a raised wooden sidewalk, and some shops and galleries.

Oatman – a boomtown of the early 20th century

## Oatman ⑳

Road map A3. 🏃 100. ℹ️ PO Box 423, Oatman, (928) 768-6222.

PROSPECTORS STRUCK gold in 1904 in the Black Mountains and Oatman became their main supply center. Today, it is popular with visitors wanting a taste of its boomtown past, such as the 1920s hotel, where Carole Lombard and Clark Gable honeymooned in 1939.

## Lake Havasu City ㉑

Road map A3. 🏃 45,000. ✈️ 🚌 ℹ️ 314 London Bridge Rd, (928) 453-3444. ⓦ www.golakehavasu.com

CALIFORNIA businessman Robert McCulloch founded Lake Havasu City in 1964. The resort city he built on the Colorado River was popular with the land-locked citizens of Arizona. His real brainwave, however, came four years later when he bought the historic London Bridge and transported it all the way from England to Lake Havasu.

Some mocked McCulloch, suggesting that he had thought he was buying London's Gothic Tower Bridge, not this much more ordinary one. There was more hilarity when it appeared that there was nothing in Havasu City for the bridge to span. Undaunted, McCulloch simply created the waterway he needed. The bridge, and its adjoining mock-Tudor village complex, have since become one of Arizona's most popular tourist attractions. They are the center point for a resort that specializes in watersports of every kind, from powerboating and houseboating to jetskiing and kayaking. Golf, hiking, and 4WD adventures are also very popular.

## Quartzsite ㉒

Road map A4. 🏃 3,300. 🚌 ℹ️ Quartzsite Chamber of Commerce, 100 E Main, (928) 927-5600. ⓦ www.quartzsitechamber.com

THIS QUIET VILLAGE, located in the low desert, 10 miles (16 km) east of the Colorado River, has long been a favorite collecting site for rockhounds *(see pp26–7)*. In the 1970s, the winter population began to swell as escapees from the northern cold arrived in droves to park their RVs for a modest sum on government land. Many were rockhounds, and they started Quartzsite's first gem and mineral show. Today, over a million people visit the town every winter, and eight major gem and mineral shows take place in January and February. Everything from antiques and collectibles to solar panels to eyeglasses can be purchased in what must be the most curious and diverse flea market in America.

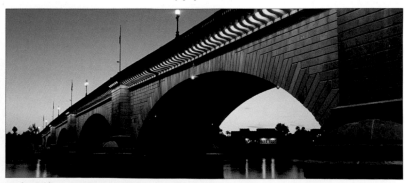

London Bridge spanning a man-made waterway in Lake Havasu City

# PHOENIX &
# SOUTHERN ARIZONA

OUNTAIN RANGES and sun-bleached pla-teaus ripple the wide landscapes of Southern Arizona, a spectacular region dominated by pristine tracts of desert, parts of which are protected within the Saguaro National Park and the Organ Pipe Cactus National Monument. This land was first farmed around 400 BC by the Hohokam people *(see p35)*, who care-fully used the meager water supplies to irrigate their crops. When the Spanish arrived in the 16th century they built forts and established settlements across the region. This Hispanic heritage is recalled by the

beautiful mission churches of San Xavier del Bac and Tuma-cacori, and in the popular historic city of Tucson that grew up around the 1776 Spanish fort. When silver was discovered nearby in the 1870s, the scene was set for a decade of rowdy frontier life. Today, towns such as Tombstone, famous for the "Gunfight at the OK Corral," re-create this Wild West era. The influx of miners also spurred the growth of Phoenix, a farming town established on the banks of the Salt River in the 1860s. Phoenix is now the largest city in the Southwest, known for its warm winter climate and recreational facilities.

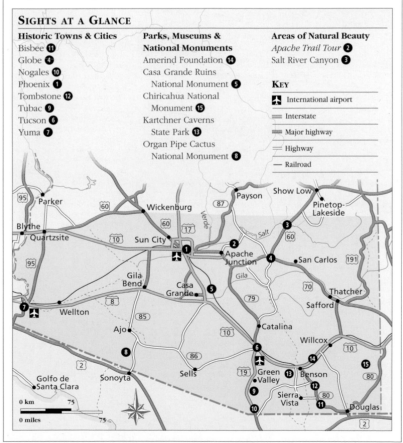

## SIGHTS AT A GLANCE

**Historic Towns & Cities**
Bisbee ⑪
Globe ④
Nogales ⑩
Phoenix ①
Tombstone ⑫
Tubac ⑨
Tucson ⑥
Yuma ⑦

**Parks, Museums & National Monuments**
Amerind Foundation ⑭
Casa Grande Ruins
  National Monument ⑤
Chiricahua National
  Monument ⑮
Kartchner Caverns
  State Park ⑬
Organ Pipe Cactus
  National Monument ⑧

**Areas of Natural Beauty**
*Apache Trail Tour* ②
Salt River Canyon ③

**KEY**

✈ International airport

═ Interstate

═ Major highway

━ Highway

— Railroad

⊲ **Visitors riding the range at the Lazy K Bar Guest Ranch near Tucson**

# Phoenix ❶

PHOENIX IS A HUGE metropolis, stretching across the Salt River Valley. Farmers and ranchers settled here in the 1860s. By 1912, the city had developed into the political and economic focus of Arizona and was the state capital. As it grew, it absorbed surrounding towns, although each district still maintains its identity. Downtown Phoenix is now being reinvigorated and is home to many historic attractions. These include restored Victorian houses in Heritage Square, the Phoenix Art Museum, and the Heard Museum (see pp78–9) with its excellent collection of Native American artifacts.

**Cash register at the Museum of History**

**The 1900 façade of the Arizona State Capitol Building**

## Exploring Downtown Phoenix

Downtown Phoenix, where the city began in the 19th century, is centered on Washington and Jefferson Streets, which run east to west between 7th Street and 19th Avenue. Central Avenue is the main north–south axis: to its east, parallel roads are labeled as "Streets," while roads to the west are "Avenues." City sights are mostly too far apart to see on foot, and driving is the best option. A DASH bus runs from downtown to the State Capitol regularly on weekdays.

### 🏛 Arizona State Capitol Museum

1700 West Washington St.
℡ (602) 542-4675.
🕐 8am–5pm Mon–Fri.
⬤ public hols. 🚻 ♿
ⓦ www.lib.az.us/museum
Completed in 1900, the Arizona State Capitol housed the state legislature until they moved into new premises in 1960. The handsome building is topped by a copper dome.

The interior is now a museum; guided tours include both original legislative chambers, which have been carefully restored, and a series of sepia photographs that document the history of Phoenix.

### 🏛 Arizona Mining & Mineral Museum

1502 W Washington St. ℡ (602) 255-3777. 🕐 8am–5pm Mon–Fri; 11am–4pm Sat. ⬤ public hols. 🚻 ♿ 🚹
ⓦ www.admmr.state.az.us
The search for precious stones and metals brought waves of prospectors to the Southwest in the years following the Civil War (1861–65). The riches they unearthed in Arizona's sun-seared hills were fabulous. A mountain of silver was discovered in the Dragoon Mountains near Tucson, while quantities of gold, silver, copper, and turquoise were found farther north in the Cerbat Mountains outside Kingman (see p72). As word of the fortunes to be made in the

**Azurite and malachite rock**

area spread, thousands of prospectors converged on the Superstition Mountains (see p84) to the east of Phoenix. However, many ended up destitute, never discovering the large deposits of gold rumored to be hidden in the hills.

This museum traces the history of Arizona mining through photographs and displays of historic tools. There are also glittering examples of the various rocks the miners quarried, the most striking of which are the copper-bearing ores such as malachite and azurite, in vivid greens and blues.

### 🏛 Heritage Square

115 N 6th St. ♿ partial. **Rosson House** ℡ (602) 262-5071.
ⓦ www.rossonhousemuseum.org
Phoenix is a thoroughly modern city, which grew rapidly after World War II. Many of its older buildings did not survive this expansion. However, a few late 19th- and early 20th-century buildings remain, and the most interesting of these are found on Heritage Square. **Rosson House** is a handsome wooden mansion on Monroe Street dating from 1895. It has a wraparound veranda and distinctive hexagonal turret. Visitors may tour the house, which is furnished in period style. Next door is the Burgess Carriage House, constructed in an expansive colonial style rare in the Southwest. The 1900 Silva House features exhibits detailing Arizona's history. The tree-lined square with its cafés is pleasant for a stroll.

### KEY

| | |
|---|---|
|  | Visitor information |
| 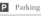 | Parking |

## 🏛 Arizona Science Center

600 E Washington St. 📞 *(602) 716-2000.* 🕐 *10am–5pm.* ⬤ *Thanksgiving, Dec 25.* 🎫 ♿ 🅆 *www.azscience.org*

This ultra-modern facility has over 300 interactive science exhibits, covering everything from physics and energy to the human body, spread over three levels. The popular "All About You" gallery on Level One focuses on human biology. Here, visitors can take a virtual reality trip through the body. Level Three has "The World Around You," where visitors explore a 90-ft (27-m) long rock wall, and test the surface temperature of different substances. The center also has a large-screen cinema on Level One. It is popular with children, but there is something here for everyone.

artifacts, including 19th-century land surveying equipment, a steam-powered bicycle, Phoenix's first printing press, and reconstructions of a general store and the first jail.

## 🏛 Phoenix Art Museum

1625 Central Ave. 📞 *(602) 257-1222.* 🕐 *10am–5pm Tue, Wed, Fri, Sat & Sun; 10am–9pm Thu.* ⬤ *public hols.* 🎫 ♿ 🖥 🅿 🅆 *www.phxart.org*

Housed in an austere modern building, the highly aclaimed Phoenix Art Museum has an enviable reputation for the quality of its temporary exhibitions. These usually share the lower of the museum's two floors with a permanent collection of contemporary European and US art. The second floor features 18th- and 19th-century American artists, with a focus on painters connected to the Southwest. The exhibit here includes first-rate work from the Taos art colony of the 1900s and Georgia O'Keeffe (1887–1986), the most distinguished member of the group. Among other featured artists are Gilbert Stewart (1755–1828), whose celebrated *Portrait of George Washington* (1796) is seen on every dollar bill.

## 🏛 Phoenix Museum of History

105 N 5th St. 📞 *(602) 253-2734.* 🕐 *10am–5pm Tue–Sat.* ⬤ *public hols.* 🎫 ♿ 🅆 *www.pmoh.org*

This inventive museum concentrates on the early years of the city's history. There is a fascinating range of unusual

### SIGHTS AT A GLANCE

*Heard Museum*

0 meters    500
0 yards     500

**Outside view of the Phoenix Museum of History**

# Phoenix: Heard Museum

THE HEARD MUSEUM was founded in 1929 by Dwight Heard, a wealthy rancher and businessman who, with his wife, Maie, assembled an extraordinary collection of Southwest Native American art in the 1920s. Several benefactors later added to the collection; they included Senator Barry Goldwater of Arizona and the Fred Harvey Company, who donated their *kachina* dolls. The museum exhibits more than 30,000 works, but its star attraction is their display of more than 500 dolls. Additionally, the museum showcases baskets, pottery, textiles, and fine art, as well as sumptuous silverwork by the Navajo, Zuni, and Hopi peoples.

**Heard Museum's Spanish Colonial Revival style, retained in the 1999 expansion**

**Main entrance**

**Central courtyard leading to main entrance**

**Red Totem** *(1980)*
*George Morrison's sculpture reflects the fusion of traditional and contemporary styles in the Native American Fine Art Movement.*

**Flagsong** *(1983)*
*This sculpture by Native American artist Doug Hyde is located in one of the Heard's tranquil courtyards.*

**The Samuel and Betty Kitchell Gallery** explores the traditions of Native art.

**Red-Tailed Hawk**
*Painted in 1986 by Dan Naningha, this is an impressionistic view of a Hopi kachina in hawk form. It is displayed as part of the Heard's fine art collection.*

**VISITORS' CHECKLIST**

2301 N Central Ave, Phoenix, AZ 85004. 🚌 *Phoenix Greyhound Station.* 📞 *(602) 252-8840.* 📠 *(602) 252-8848.* 🕐 *9:30am–5pm.* ⬤ *public hols.* ♿ 🎥 🎫 🍴 🎁 W www.heard.org

**Navajo Child's Blanket**
*Woven in the 1870s, this richly colored, traditional blanket is one of the highlights of the Sandra Day O'Connor Gallery. The museum's history is documented at the gallery, which also showcases the Heard family's early collection of Native American artifacts.*

**KEY**

- Samuel and Betty Kitchell Gallery
- Crossroads Gallery
- Sandra Day O'Connor Gallery
- Ullman Learning Center
- Freeman Gallery
- Home: Native Peoples in the Southwest Gallery
- Lincoln Hall
- Pritzlaff Courtyard
- Non-exhibition space

**Ullman Learning Center** features interactive exhibits related to Native American life in Arizona.

**Every Picture Tells a Story**
*An interactive hands-on display shows how artists interpret their environments through art.*

**The South Courtyard** offers additional space for the museum's fine sculptures.

**★ Home: Native Peoples in the Southwest**
*This award-winning collection of over 2,000 Native artifacts spans 14 centuries, and includes jewelry, basketry, textiles, pottery and one of the West's best collections of kachinas.*

**STAR COLLECTION**

**★ Home: Native Peoples in the Southwest**

# Exploring Metropolitan Phoenix

PHOENIX IS ONE of North America's largest cities. In addition to its city population of more than one million, Phoenix has a burgeoning number of residents in its metropolitan area, totaling more than three million. The city fills the Salt River Valley, occupying more than 2,000 sq miles (5,200 sq km) of the Sonoran Desert. It is famous for winter temperatures of 60–70°F (16–21°C) and around 300 days of sunshine a year. This makes Phoenix a popular destination with both tourists and "snowbirds," visitors who spend their winters here.

Metropolitan Phoenix includes the former town of Scottsdale, 12 miles (19 km) northeast of downtown. With air-conditioned malls, designer stores, hotels, and restaurants, it is a good base for visiting Taliesin West and Papago Park, and is famous for its world-class golf courses *(see pp154–5)*. Tempe, 6 miles (10 km) east of downtown, is home to Arizona State University and the Pueblo Grande Museum, while Mesa has the Arizona Temple, a large Mormon church built in 1927.

between 2nd Street and Indian School Road, the streets are lined with low, brightly painted adobe buildings, which house many of the city's most fashionable restaurants as well as bars, antiques stores, and art galleries. In addition to the Renaissance-style Borgata shopping mall, there is the El Pedregal Festival Marketplace, and Scottsdale Downtown with its arts shopping district around Main Street, Marshall Way, Old Town, and Fifth Avenue. Scottsdale is also the location for Phoenix's most popular shopping mall, **Fashion Square,** which has an array of designer stores and excellent restaurants *(see p144).*

## SIGHTS AT A GLANCE

Camelback Mountain ④

Challenger Space Center ⑧

Cosanti Foundation ③

Mystery Castle ⑦

Papago Park ⑥

Pioneer Living History Village ⑨

Pueblo Grande Museum &
    Archeological Park ⑤

Scottsdale ①

Taliesin West ②

### KEY

| | |
|---|---|
| ▨ | Downtown Phoenix |
| ▢ | Metropolitan Phoenix |
| ✈ | International airport |
| ▬ | Interstate |
| ▬ | Major highway |
| ═ | Highway |
| — | Railroad |

Scottsdale's elegant shopping mall, Fashion Square

🏛 **Taliesin West**

Cactus Rd at Frank Lloyd Wright Blvd, Scottsdale. ☎ *(480) 860-8810.* ◯ *9am–4pm.* ⬤ *Thanksgiving, Dec 25, Jan 1.* ✎ & ☑ W www.franklloydwright.org

Generally regarded as the greatest American architect of all time, Frank Lloyd Wright (1869–1959) established the 600-acre (240-ha) Taliesin West complex as a winter school for his students in 1937. Wright had come to prominence in Chicago during the 1890s with a series of strikingly original houses that featured an elegant open-plan style. Although noted for his use of local materials such as desert rocks and earth, he also pioneered the use of pre-cast concrete. Today, Taliesin West is home to the

## Scottsdale

Founded in the late 19th century, Scottsdale was named after its developer, army chaplain Winfield Scott (1837–1910), whose religious scruples helped keep the early settlement free from saloons and gambling. Scottsdale's quiet, tree-lined streets and desert

setting attracted the architect Frank Lloyd Wright *(see p21)*, who established Taliesin West here in 1937. The area still attracts artists and designers, but it is best known for its many golf courses – there are 175 in and around Scottsdale. At the center of the district, to either side of Scottsdale Road

**Innovative design of the Cosanti Foundation gift shop**

Wright School of Architecture, where students live and work for up to five years. The students also work as guides to the complex. There are a variety of tours, from one to three hours. One-hour tours begin every half hour from 10am to 4pm.

Taleisin West is approached along a winding desert road. The muted tones of the low-lying buildings reflect Wright's enthusiasm for the desert setting. He was careful to enhance, rather than dominate, the landscape.

### 🏛 Cosanti Foundation

6433 Doubletree Ranch Rd, Paradise Valley. ☎ *(480) 948-6145.* ⏰ *9am–5pm Mon–Sat; 11am–5pm Sun.* ● *public hols.* 💰 *donation requested.* ♿

In 1947, Italian architect Paolo Soleri (b. 1919) came to study at Taliesin West. He set up the Cosanti Foundation in Scottsdale nine years later to further his investigations into what he termed "arcology": a combination of architecture and ecology to create new urban habitats *(see p21).*

Today, the Cosanti site consists of simple, low structures housing studios, a gallery, and workshops. This is where Soleri and his workers make and sell their trademark windbells. Guided visits can be arranged with advance notice.

Visitors can also take a tour of Soleri's main project, Arcosanti, which lies 60 miles (100 km) north of Phoenix on Interstate Highway 17. The project began in 1970 and, once completed, it will house 6,000 people in homes that will combine work and leisure space. Currently, 60 residents live there, using energy generated by solar greenhouses.

### 🏔 Camelback Mountain

Named for its humped shape, this mountain rises high above its suburban surroundings just 7 miles (11 km) northeast of downtown Phoenix. One of the city's most distinctive landmarks, the mountain is a granite and sandstone outcrop formed by prehistoric volcanic forces. It is best approached from the north via the marked turn off McDonald Drive near the junction of Tatum Boulevard. From the parking lot, a well-marked path leads to the summit, a steep climb that covers 1,300 ft (390 m) in the space of a mile.

Camelback Mountain is adjacent to the Echo Canyon Recreation Area, a lovely wooded enclave with a choice of shaded picnic sites.

### 🏛 Pueblo Grande Museum & Archeological Park

4619 E Washington St. ☎ *(602) 495-0901.* ⏰ *9am–4:45pm Mon–Sat; 1pm–4:45pm Sun.* ● *public hols.* 📷 ♿ 🖥 *www.ci.phoenix.az.us/parks/pueblo.html*

Located 5 miles (8 km) east of downtown Phoenix, the Pueblo Grande Museum displays a Hohokam ruin and many artifacts, including cooking utensils and pottery. Many of these pieces come from the adjacent Archeological Park, the site of a Hohokam settlement from the 8th to the 14th centuries. The site was originally excavated in 1887, and today has a path through the ruins. Informative signs point out the many irrigation canals once used by the Hohokam to water their crops.

**Taliesin West façade, designed by Frank Lloyd Wright to blend with desert landscape**

**Cacti in the Desert Botanical Garden at Papago Park**

### 🌵 Papago Park

Galvin Parkway & Van Buren St. ( (602) 256-3220. W www.phoenix. gov/parks/papago.html

Papago Park is situated 6 miles (10 km) east of downtown Phoenix, and is a popular place to unwind, with a number of hiking and cycling trails, picnic areas, and fishing ponds. Many of Phoenix's top attractions are located within the rambling boundaries of Papago Park. The most famous of these is the award-winning **Desert Botanical Garden**. Covering over 145 acres (59 ha), the park displays more than 20,000 cacti and protected desert flora from around the world. The most popular part of the garden is the paved Desert Discovery Trail, which winds past half the known species of cacti in the world. Some of the rarer and more fragile specimens can be found in the nearby Cactus House and Succulent House. Of particular interest are the Center for Desert Living, and Desert House, both of which demonstrate low-impact, environmentally sensitive ways for humans to co-exist in harmony with the desert. The garden is prettiest in spring, when many species flower. Guided tours explain the extraordinary life cycles of the desert plants seen here. The rolling hills and lakes of

**Trail's End sign at Phoenix Zoo**

**Phoenix Zoo** also occupy a large area of the Papago Park. A series of natural habitats, including the Arizona-Sonora Desert and a tropical rainforest, have been reproduced at the zoo. It is home to more than 1,300 animals from around the world; the animals' movements are controlled by banks and canals rather than fences. The Arizona Trail area of the zoo gives visitors a chance to encounter rarely seen animals that are native to Arizona's deserts and mountains. A Safari Train provides a narrated tour of the zoo.

Also in Papago Park is the **Hall of Flame Museum**, which houses an exceptional collection of fire engines and firefighting equipment, dating from 1725. The museum traces the history of organized firefighting, displaying over 130 wheeled pieces and thousands of smaller items. Arranged chronologically, the first gallery features hand- and horse-drawn fire equipment from the 18th and 19th centuries. The second gallery contains over 25 motorized fire engines from the early 20th century, while those dating from 1930 to the present are showcased in the third and fourth galleries.

Also part of the museum is the National Firefighting Hall of Heroes, which honors firefighters who have died in the line of duty, or been decorated for heroic service. In August 2003, the museum opened a 2,000 sq ft (186 sq m) gallery on the subject of wildland firefighting.

### 🌵 Desert Botanical Garden

1201 N Galvin Parkway. ( (480) 941-1225. ◯ May–Sep: 7am–8pm; Oct–April: 8am–8pm. ● major public hols. 🏛 & 📷 W www.dbg.org

### 🐾 Phoenix Zoo

455 N Galvin Parkway. ( (602) 273-1341. ◯ Sep–May: 9am–5pm; Jun–Aug: 7am–8pm. ● Dec 25. 🏛 & W www.phoenixzoo.org

### 🏛 Hall of Flame Museum

6101 N Van Buren St, Phoenix. ( (602) 275-3473. ◯ 9am–5pm Mon–Sat; noon–4pm Sun. ● Jan 1, Thanksgiving, Dec 25. 🏛 W www.hallofflame.org

### ♠ Mystery Castle

800 E Mineral Rd. ( (602) 268-1581. ◯ Oct–Jun: 11am–4pm Thu–Sun. 🏛 📷

Mystery Castle is possibly Phoenix's most eccentric attraction. In 1927, a certain Boyce Luther Gulley came to the city hoping that the warm climate would improve his ailing health. His young daughter, Mary Lou Gulley, loved building sandcastles on the beach and, since Phoenix was so far away from the ocean, Gulley set about creating a real-life fairy-tale sandcastle for her.

He started work in 1930 and continued for 15 years, until his death in 1945. Discarded bricks, desert rock, railroad refuse, and an assortment of scrapyard junk, including old car parts, have been used to build the structure. The 18-room interior has 13 fireplaces, and can be seen on a guided tour, which explores the quirky building and its eclectic collection of antiques and furniture from around the world.

**Exterior of Phoenix's unusual Mystery Castle**

Entrance to the Challenger Space Center

## ⛫ Challenger Space Center

21170 N 83rd Ave, Peoria.
📞 (623) 322-2001. ⏱ 9am–4pm
Mon–Fri; 10am–4pm Sat.
⬤ major hols. **Public programs**
10am, 11am, 1pm, 3pm Sat. 🏫
🌐 www.azchallenger.org/index.htm

Named in honor of the *Challenger* shuttle crew that lost their lives in the 1986 disaster, the center's mission is "to inspire, excite, and educate people of all ages about the mysteries and wonders of space, science, and the universe in which we live." Their main objective is to provide educational programs for school children. The same two-hour programs are run on Saturdays for the public, and are geared for both adults and children. Utilizing the center's multimillion dollar simulated space station and mission control center, the programs integrate teamwork, math, science, and leadership skills into exciting programs that replicate voyages to Mars or to a comet hurtling through space. There are also daily tours of the facility that include an introduction to the center's ongoing programs, and a wide variety of displays and exhibits. One of the highlights of the tour is a stroll along a floating balcony to view "A Tour of the Universe" – a breathtaking six-story tall, 27,000 sq ft (2,508 sq m) mural by official NASA space artist, Robert McCall. The mural, which depicts

man's quest in space, wraps 360 degrees around the inside of the center's vast rotunda. The center also hosts star gazing and other fun, educational family programs throughout the year.

## ⛫ Pioneer Living History Village

3901 W Pioneer Rd.
📞 (623) 465-1052. ⏱ Oct–May:
9am–5pm Wed–Sun; Jun–Sep:
8am–3pm Wed–Sun.
🌐 www.pioneer-arizona.com

Unlike some of Arizona's Hollywood-inspired Wild West towns, Arizona Pioneer Historical Village puts historical accuracy and education at the forefront of the experience. That doesn't stop them from staging a gunfight in

the street, but at least it is a historically accurate gunfight. The village, with the help of several costumed re-enactors, re-creates a frontier town from Arizona's territorial heyday circa 1860 to 1912. There are 29 buildings, 24 of which are originals moved to this site from other parts of Arizona. The remaining buildings, for instance the blacksmith's shop, are replicas of buildings that once stood in the territory – in this case a duplicate of the shop that stood in Globe in the 1870s. Also of note are the bank, sheriff's office, a ranch complex, and even an opera house that once hosted the legendary actress, Lillie Langtry.

Educational tour for school children at Challenger Space Center

# Apache Trail Tour ❷

THE TOWERING ROCKY spires and canyons of the Superstition Mountains are the setting for this loop-trail that weaves together desert beauty and Western legends. Starting at Apache Junction, the route climbs to the Tonto National Monument and the Lost Dutchman State Park. The road turns to gravel as it rises past three cool, man-made lakes, and continues to Globe. Descending, the road offers stunning views as it winds through red rock canyons to the town of Superior, and the lovely gardens and shady trails of Boyce Thompson Arboretum.

### TIPS FOR DRIVERS

**Tour length:** 120 miles (193 km).
**Tour route:** Drive this route clockwise starting north on Route 88, from Lost Dutchman State Park to Roosevelt Dam.
**When to go:** Spring and fall are the most pleasant. Summer can be very hot, and winter can be cold with occasional snow.

**Tonto National Monument ③**
These cliff dwellings were occupied by the Salado Indians from the 13th to the 15th centuries. The museum here contains fine examples of their pottery and textiles.

```
0 km          5
0 miles       5
```

Roosevelt Lake

Goldfield
Tortilla Flat
Apache Junction
Florence Junction

**Lost Dutchman State Park ②**
Named after the mystery mine, the park offers hiking trails through a high Sonoran Desert landscape, and great views of the surrounding mountains.

## LOST DUTCHMAN MINE MYSTERY

In the 1870s, Prussian immigrant Jacob Waltz left his home in Phoenix, returning with high-grade gold ore. Drinking and spending lavishly, he often spoke of a rich mine in the Superstition Mountains. Years later, on his deathbed, he purportedly told his caregiver the location of the mine. She and countless others have since tried to find the "Lost Dutchman Mine" without success. It remains one of the most captivating mysteries of the Wild West.

**Weaver's Needle peak, fabled location of the mystery mine**

**Superstition Mountains ①**
Rising over 6,000 ft (1,829 m), this wild and rocky mountain range is 40 miles (64 km) from Phoenix. Prospectors have long sought wealth here.

**Roosevelt Dam** ④
Completed in 1911, it
supplies water to Phoenix.
The lake here is a favorite
with boaters and fishermen.

**Superior** ⑤
Settled in 1870, the
town boasts the
world's smallest mus-
eum, which houses
the largest Apache
Tear gemstone on

**Boyce Thompson
Arboretum** ⑥
Dedicated to propagating
desert species, the arboretum
is very beautiful when the
spring flowers bloom.

## KEY

| | |
|---|---|
| ▬▬ | Tour route |
| ⇉ | Other roads |
| **i** | Visitor information |

# Salt River Canyon ❸

**Road map** C4. **i** *White Mountain
Apache Reservation Tourism Office,
Fort Apache, (928) 338-1230.*

THE APACHES used this deep,
wild canyon as a refuge
from US troops in the 1800s.
Today, the Salt River marks the
border between the San Carlos
Apache Reservation and the
White Mountain Apache
Reservation. The 9-mile
(15-km) rim-to-rim drive on
Highway 60 is truly awe-
inspiring as the road drops
almost 2,000 ft (610 m) in a
series of hairpin turns to cross
the river on a narrow bridge.
Occasionally a driver forgets to
pay attention, or loses control
on the descent, and the resulting twisted wreckage sometimes stays for weeks at the
bottom of the gorge as a visual
warning to others. Numerous
pullouts exist along the road
for those who want to stop
and admire the view. At the
bottom, near the bridge, there
is a parking area with interpretive signage. Several companies *(see p150)* offer single and
multi-day whitewater rafting
tours, which provide tremendous views of the 32,000 acre
(12,950 ha) wilderness that
surrounds the river.

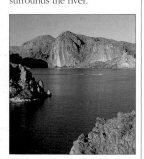

**The beautiful and dramatic
wilderness of Salt River Canyon**

# Globe ❹

**Road map** C4. 🏘 6,000. 🚌
**i** *Globe Chamber of Commerce,
1360 N Broad St, (928) 425 4495.* Ⓐ

THE MINING town of Globe
lies about 100 miles
(160 km) east of Phoenix in
the wooded Dripping Spring
and Pinal Mountains. In 1875,

prospectors struck silver here,
in what was then part of an
Apache reservation. The silver-
bearing hills were annexed
from the reservation, and
Globe was founded as a
mining town. It was named
for a massive nugget of silver,
shaped like a globe, which
was unearthed in the hills
nearby. The silver was quickly
exhausted, but copper mining
thrived until 1931, and continues today. Globe has an attractive historic district, and its
history is outlined in the **Gila
County Historical Museum**.
On the south side of town are
the Besh-Ba-Gowah Ruins,
home of the Salado people in
the 13th and 14th centuries.

🏛 **Gila County
Historical Museum**
1330 N Broad St. **C** *(928) 425-
7385.* ☐ *10am–4pm Mon–Fri;
11am–3pm Sat; Sun by appointment.*
⬤ *Jan 1, Dec 25.*

# Casa Grande
Ruins National
Monument ❺

**Road map** C4. **C** *(520) 723-3172.*
☐ *8am–5pm.* ⬤ *Dec 25.* 🈺
♿ **w** *www.nps.gov/cagr*

FROM AROUND 200 BC until
the middle of the 15th
century, the Hohokam people
farmed the Gila River Valley to
the southeast of Phoenix.
Among the few Hohokam
sites that remain, the fortress-
like structure that makes up
the Casa Grande National
Monument is one of the most
distinctive. Built in the early
decades of the 14th century,
and named the "Big House"
by a passing Jesuit missionary
in 1694, this sturdy four-story
structure has walls up to 4-ft
(1.2-m) thick. The interior is
out of bounds, but visitors can
stroll around the exterior. The
visitor center has a small
museum with some interesting
exhibits on Hohokam history
and culture. Casa Grande is
located 15 miles (24 km) east
of Interstate Highway 10 (I-10)
on the outskirts of Coolidge. It
should not be confused with
the town of Casa Grande,
found to the west of I-10.

# Tucson ⑥

**D**ESPITE BEING ARIZONA's second largest city, Tucson has a friendly, welcoming atmosphere and a variety of interesting attractions to entertain the increasing number of visitors it receives each year. The city is located on the northern boundary of the Sonoran Desert in Southern Arizona, in a basin surrounded by five mountain ranges. When the Spanish colonizers arrived in the early 18th century they were determined to seize land from the local Tohono O'odham and Pima Native tribes, who put up strong resistance. This led the Spanish to move their regional fortress, or presidio, from Tubac to Tucson in the 1770s. The city was officially founded by Irish explorer Hugh O'Connor in 1775. Tucson's pride in its history is reflected in the careful preservation of 19th-century downtown buildings in the Barrio Historic District.

**Exhibit at Arizona University**

Contemporary glass skyscrapers in downtown Tuscon

## Exploring Tucson

Tucson's major art galleries and museums are clustered around two central areas: the University of Arizona (UA) campus, lying between Speedway Blvd, E Sixth Street, Park, and Campbell Avenues, and the downtown area, which includes the Barrio and El Presidio historic districts. The latter contains many of the city's oldest buildings, and is best explored on foot, as is the Barrio Historic District, south of Cushing Street.

## 🏛 Tucson Museum of Art & Historic Block

140 N Main Ave. ☎ (520) 624-2333.
🕐 10am–4pm Tue–Sat; noon–4pm Sun. ● Mon; public hols. 🎫 (free on 1st Sun of month). ⛶ 🗗
🖳 www. tucsonarts.com
The Tucson Museum of Art opened in 1975 and is located on the Historic Block, which also contains five of the

presidio's oldest dwellings – most of which are at least a 100 years old. These historic buildings form part of the art museum and house different parts of its extensive collection. The museum's sculpture gardens and courtyards also form part of the Historic Block complex.

The art museum itself displays contemporary and 20th-century European and American works. In the adobe Stevens House (1866), the museum has its collection of pre-Columbian tribal artifacts, some of which are 2,000 years old. There is the Spanish Colonial collection with some stunning pieces of religious art. The 1850s Casa Cordova houses *El Nacimiento*, a

Nativity scene with more than 300 earthenware figurines, on display from December to March. The **J. Knox Corbett House**, built in 1907, has Arts and Crafts Movement pieces such as a Morris chair.

Both guided and self-guided walking tours of this district are available from the Tucson Museum of Art.

## 🏛 Pima County Courthouse

115 N Church Ave.
The courthouse's pretty tiled dome is a downtown landmark. It was built in 1927, replacing its predecessor, a one-story adobe building dating from 1869. The position of the original presidio wall is marked out in the courtyard, and a section of the wall, 3-ft (1-m) thick and 12-ft (4-m) high, can still be seen inside the building.

## 🏚 El Presidio Historic District

The El Presidio Historic District occupies the area where the original Spanish presidio, San Agustin del Tucson, was built in 1775. More than 70 of the houses here were constructed during the Territorial period, before Arizona became a state in 1912. Today, these historic buildings are largely occupied by shops, restaurants, and offices. However, archeological excavations in the area have found artifacts from much earlier residents, the Hohokam Indians.

## ⛪ St. Augustine Cathedral

192 S Stone Ave. ☎ (520) 623-6351.
🕐 Services only; call for times.
St. Augustine Cathedral was begun in 1896 and modeled after the Spanish Colonial style of the Cathedral of Querétaro in central Mexico. This gleaming white building features an imposing sandstone façade with intricate carvings of the yucca, the saguaro, and the horned

Stained-glass window in the cathedral

toad – three symbols of the Sonoran Desert – while a bronze statue of St. Augustine, the city's patron saint, stands above the main door.

One of many 19th-century adobe houses in the Barrio Historic District

**🏛 Barrio Historic District**

This area was Tucson's business district in the late 19th century. Today, its streets are quiet and lined with original adobe houses painted in bright colors. On nearby Main Street is the "wishing shrine" of **El Tiradito**, which marks the spot where a young man was killed as a result of a lovers' triangle. Local people lit candles here for his soul, and still believe that if their candles burn for a whole night, their wishes will come true.

**🏛 University of Arizona**

ℹ️ Visitors' Center, 845 E University Blvd, Suite 145. ☎ *(520) 884-7516.*
Several museums are located on or near the UA campus, about a mile (1.6 km) east of downtown. The **Arizona Historical Society Museum** traces Arizona's history from the arrival of the Spanish in 1539 to modern times. The **University of Arizona Museum of Art** focuses on European and American fine art from the Renaissance to the 20th century. Opposite the

museum is the **Center for Creative Photography**, which contains the work of many of the 20th century's greatest American photographers. Visitors can view the archives by advance reservation. The **Flandrau Science Center** features a range of child-friendly interactive exhibits.

One of the most renowned collections of artifacts, covering 2,000 years of Native history, is displayed by the **Arizona State Museum**, which was founded in 1893.

**DOWNTOWN TUCSON**

Barrio Historic District ⑤
El Presidio Historic
    District ③
Pima County Courthouse ②
St. Augustine Cathedral ④
Tucson Museum of Art
    & Historic Block ①

University of
Arizona →

**KEY**

🚉 Train station
ℹ️ Visitor information
P Parking

0 meters          100
0 yards            100

# Exploring Around Tucson

B EYOND DOWNTOWN, metropolitan Tucson extends north to the Santa Catalina Mountains, the foothills of which are the start of a scenic drive to the top of Mount Lemmon. To the west are the Tucson Mountains, which frame Saguaro National Park West. This park has a sister park to the east of the city. To the south lies the beautiful mission church of San Xavier del Bac, which stands out from the flat, desert landscape of the Tohono O'odham Indian Reservation.

## SIGHTS AT A GLANCE

Arizona-Sonora Desert
  Museum ②
Mount Lemmon ⑦
Old Tucson Studios ③
Pima Air & Space Museum ⑤
Sabino Canyon Tours ⑥
Saguaro National Park
  (East & West) ①
San Xavier del Bac Mission
  See pp92–3 ④

## KEY

| | |
|---|---|
| ▨ | Downtown Tucson |
| ▧ | Greater Tucson |
| ✈ | International airport |
| ══ | Interstate |
| ▬ | Major highway |
| ══ | Highway |
| ── | Railroad |

**Vistas of tall saguaro cacti in Saguaro National Park**

## 🏛 Arizona-Sonora Desert Museum

2021 N Kinney Rd. 【 (520) 883-2702. 🕐 Mar–Sep: 7:30am–5pm; Oct–Feb: 8:30am–5pm. 🈂 🛗 Ⓦ www.desertmuseum.org

This fascinating natural history park covers more than 21 desert acres (8.5 ha), and includes a botanical garden, zoo, and natural history museum. At the museum, displays describe the history, geology, and flora and fauna of the Sonoran Desert region. Outside, a 2-mile (3-km) walkway passes more than 1,200 varieties of plants, which provide the setting for a range of creatures, including hummingbirds, wildcats, and Mexican wolves.

**One of many flowering cacti at the Arizona-Sonora Desert Museum**

## 🎬 Old Tucson Studios

201 S Kinney Rd. 【 (520) 883-0100. 🕐 10am–3pm Sun–Fri, 10am–4pm Sat. ● Thanksgiving, Dec 24, 25. 🈂 🛗 Ⓦ www.oldtucson.com

Modeled on a Western town of the 1860s, the park was built as a set for a Western movie in 1939. Since then, Old Tucson Studios has formed the backdrop for some of Hollywood's most famous Westerns, such as *Gunfight at the OK Corral* (1957) and *Rio Bravo* (1958).

## 🌵 Saguaro National Park

3693 S Old Spanish Trail. 【 (520) 733-5153. 🕐 9am–5pm daily. ● Dec 25. 🈂 Loop Dr only. 🛗 Ⓦ www.nps.gov/sagu

The saguaro (pronounced sa-wah-ro) cactus is unique to the Sonoran Desert. The largest cactus species in the US, it has a life span of up to 200 years. Those that survive into old age may reach heights of up to 50 ft (16 m) and weigh more than 8 tons (7 kg).

Set up in 1994, the park comprises two tracts of land on the eastern and western

flanks of Tucson, that together cover more than 91,000 acres (36,800 ha). The 9-mile (14.5-km) Bajada Loop Drive runs deep into the park on a dirt road, past hiking trails and picnic areas. One of these trails leads to Hohokam petroglyphs carved into volcanic rock. The eastern park has the oldest saguaros, which can be seen along the 8-mile (13-km) Cactus Forest Drive. There are also more than 100 miles (160 km) of hiking trails here. The park offers guided walks during the summer season.

The popular 1970s TV series *Little House on the Prairie* was also filmed here. More recently, movies such as *The Three Amigos* (1986) and *Tombstone* (1993) were partly shot here.

Main Street's 1860s frontier atmosphere provides an authentic setting for performers in period costume, who entertain visitors with stunt shows, mock gunfights, and stagecoach rides. Visitors can also take part in such activities as panning for gold.

## BIRDWATCHING IN THE CANYONS OF SOUTHERN ARIZONA

The landscape of Southern Arizona may seem dry, but this high desert environment gets about 11 in (280 mm) of rain annually. This enables vegetation to flourish which, in turn, attracts a variety of birds. In fact, the area is one of the top five birdwatching locations in the US. Just off I-19, near Green Valley, Madera Canyon plays host to some 400 bird species. Along with the more common varieties of hummingbirds, flycatchers, and warblers, many rare species, such as the brown-crested flycatcher and the black-and-white warbler, are often sighted here. Farther afield, Ramsey Canyon in the Huachuca Mountains is the country's hummingbird capital with 14 varieties of these tiny, delicate creatures.

**Broad-billed hummingbird**

**Gunfight staged outside the mission at Old Tucson Studios**

### 🛕 San Xavier del Bac Mission
*See pp92–3.*

### 🏛 Titan Missile Museum
1580 W Duval Mine Rd, Sahuarita. **(** (520) 625-7736. ⊙ *9am–5pm. Thanksgiving, Dec 25.* 🅿 ☑ *9am–4pm.* ♿ ⓦ *www.pimaair.org*

This remote site, 25 miles (40 km) south of Tucson, is a great place to get in touch with the potential horror of the Cold War years. Built in 1963, this is one of 18 Titan II silos constructed around the Tucson area (out of 54 in the United States). This station and its single, multiple-warhead nuclear missile – the largest ever built in the US – stood ready to launch within minutes for over 20 years. Today, it is one of only two remaining Titan II missiles

and launch sites left, as all the others were decommissioned by 1987. The museum tour includes a walk through the buildings and a peek down into the silo, followed by a visit to the below-ground missile launch facility and a look at the missile from within the silo.

### 🏛 Pima Air & Space Museum
6000 E Valencia Rd. **(** (520) 574-0462. ⊙ *9am–5pm.* ● *Thanksgiving, Dec 25.* 🅿 ♿ ⓦ *www.pimaair.org*

Located nine miles (14 km) southeast of downtown Tucson, the Pima Air and Space Museum contains one of the largest collections of aircraft in the world. Visitors are met with the astonishing sight of more than 250 vintage aircraft arranged in ranks across the desert.

Three presidential jets are displayed – Eisenhower's, Kennedy's, and Johnson's – as well as a replica of the Wright brothers' famous 1903 aircraft. The adjacent

Davis-Monthan Air Force Base displays more than 2,000 planes, including B-29s and supersonic bombers.

### 🏛 Colossal Cave
Colossal Cave Mountain Park, PO Box 70, 16721 E Old Spanish Trail, Vail. **(** (520) 647-7275. ⊙ *mid-Mar–mid-Sep: 8am–6pm Mon–Sat, 8am–7pm Sun; mid-Sep–mid-Mar: 9am–5pm Mon–Sat, 9am–6pm Sun.* 🅿 ☑ ⓦ *www.colossalcave.com*

The first European to discover Colossal Cave was Solomon Lick in 1879, but he was a relative latecomer. The cave was used by the Solobai people as early as 1450, and later by the Hohokam. Although opened for tours in 1923, it has never been fully explored – it took over two years to map the first two miles (63 km) of the cave's estimated 39 miles (63 km) length.

Visitors today take a 50-minute guided tour that descends six stories into spaces draped in stalactites and stalagmites. The tour is only half-a-mile in length, but requires descending and climbing 365 stairs. There are longer, more energetic tours available on Saturdays.

Colossal is a "dry cave" – it is no longer being shaped by water, and its ample air supply keeps the inside temperature at a comfortable 70°F (21°C). The cave is on the grounds of La Posta Quemada (Burned Station) Ranch, named for a Southern Pacific stagecoach station, which was destroyed by a fire in 1875.

**Helicopters at the Davis-Monthan air base, near Pima Air & Space Museum**

# Tucson: San Xavier del Bac Mission

San Xavier del Bac is the oldest and best-preserved mission church in the Southwest. An imposing landmark as it rises out of the stark, flat landscape of the surrounding Tohono O'odham reservation, its white walls dazzle in the desert sun. A mission was first established here by the Jesuit priest Father Eusebio Kino in 1700 *(see p39)*. The complex seen today was completed in 1797 by Franciscan missionaries.

Built of adobe brick, the mission is considered to be the finest example of Spanish Colonial architecture in the US *(see p20)*. The church also incorporates other styles, including several Baroque flourishes. In the 1990s its interior was extensively renovated, and five *retablos* (altarpieces) have been restored to their original glory.

**The Hill of the Cross, to the east of the mission, offering fine views**

**The bell tower's** elegant, white dome reflects the Moorish styles that are incorporated into San Xavier's Spanish Colonial architecture.

**★ Façade of the Church**
*The ornate Baroque façade is decorated with the carved figures of saints (although some are much eroded) including a headless St. Cecilia and an unidentifiable St. Francis, now a simple sand cone.*

**The mortuary chapel** contains a statue of the Virgin Mary, surrounded by candles.

**Stonework Detail**
*Over recent years the identity of the carved statues to the left of the entrance has changed. Long thought to be St. Catherine of Siena and St. Barbara, they have now been identified as St. Agatha of Catania and St. Agnes of Rome.*

**Painted Ceiling**
*On entering the church, visitors are struck by the dome's ceiling with its glorious paintings of religious figures. Vivid pigments of vermilion and blue were used to contrast with the stark white stone background.*

---

**STAR SIGHTS**

★ **Façade of the Church**

★ **Main Altar**

## ★ Main Altar
*The spectacular gold and red retablo mayor is decorated in Mexican Baroque style with elaborate columns. More than 50 statues were carved in Mexico, then brought to San Xavier where artists gilded and painted them with brightly colored glazes.*

**VISITORS' CHECKLIST**

**Road map** C5. 1950 W San Xavier Rd, 10 miles (16 km) south of Tucson on I-19. **(** (520) 294-2624. **⏰** 8am–5pm. **&** **▯** *booths selling Native American fry bread.* **▯** **w** www.sanxaviermission.org

### Altar Dome
*The dome and high transepts are filled with painted wooden statuary and covered with murals depicting scenes from the Gospels.*

**The patio** is closed to the public but can be seen from the museum.

### Chapel of Our Lady
*This statue is one of the church's three sculptures of Mary. Here she is shown as La Dolorosa or Sorrowing Mother.*

**The museum** includes a sheepskin psalter and photographs of other historic missions on the Tohono O'odham reservation.

**The shop entrance**

### 🚐 Sabino Canyon Tours

5900 N Sabino Canyon Rd. 📞 (520) 749-2861. ⏰ 8am–4:30pm Mon–Fri; 8:30am–4:30pm Sat–Sun. **Tram Tours:** 9am–4:30pm. 🎫 ♿ 🌐 www.sabinocanyon.com

The restless Sabino Creek began carving its way through Mount Lemmon, 13 miles (21 km) northeast of Tucson, five million years ago. The result was the lovely Sabino Canyon, with its towering rock walls and sparkling streams lined with cottonwood trees. Today, motorized trams take visitors on a 45-minute narrated trip into the canyon. Tourists can get off at one of several stops to hike on trails that range from easy to moderately difficult. Evening tram tours are also available at various times of the year.

### 🚐 Mount Lemmon

ℹ️ (520) 749-8700.

The highest peak in the Santa Catalina Mountains, standing at 9,157 ft (2,790 m), Mount Lemmon is located in the Coronado National Forest. During summer, thousands of visitors drive up on the weekends for rock climbing, hiking, camping, and fishing. A one-hour drive, beginning in the Tucson city limits and connecting to the Mount Lemmon Highway, takes visitors to the summit. The highway affords splendid vistas of the Tucson valley. There are around 150 miles (240 km) of hiking trails here, while a side road leads to the quaint resort village of Summerhaven. A forest fire in 2003 devastated parts of Mount Lemmon, resulting in road closures Monday to Thursday. Call for current road schedule.

Space Age buildings of the Biosphere 2 Center, north of Tucson

### 🏛 Biosphere 2 Center

5 miles (8 km) NE of jct of Hwys 77 & 79. 📞 (520) 838-6200. ⏰ 9am–4pm. ⬤ Thanksgiving, Dec 25. 🎫 ♿ 🅿️ 🌐 www.bio2.com

Biosphere 2 Center is a unique research facility that was set up in 1991. Eight people were sealed within a futuristic structure of glass and white steel furnished with five of the Earth's habitats: rainforest, desert, savanna, marsh, and an ocean with a living coral reef. Over a period of two years the effect of the people on the environment as well as the effect on them were studied.

Radio telescope at Kitt Peak

Today, there are no people living in the Biosphere, which is being used to explore the effect of increased carbon dioxide in the atmosphere. Visitors can take a two-hour guided tour. There are two tours of the interior, one of which incurs an additional charge.

### 🏛 Kitt Peak Observatory

Rte 86 to 386. 📞 (520) 318-8726. ⏰ 9am–3:45pm. ⬤ Jan 1, Thanksgiving, Dec 25. 🅿️ donation requested. 🅿️ 🌐 www.noao.edu/kpno/

Located 56 miles (90 km) southwest of Tucson, Kitt Peak boasts one of the largest and most diverse collection of astronomical observatories on the planet. It was established as a scientific center for the study of astronomy in 1952. Visitors can take a guided tour of the facility and get a close-up look at (but not through) several of the largest and most famous telescopes. To actually view the cosmos, you have to sign up (up to a month in advance) for nightly programs that allow you to scan the heavens through telescopes at the visitors' observatory. The guided program, which runs from September to mid-July, includes a sack dinner. Warm clothing is recommended.

Observatories at Kitt Peak in Southern Arizona

# Yuma ⓐ

**Road map** A4. ⓜ 65,000.
🚂 Amtrak, 291 Gila St. 🚌 Greyhound, 170 E 17th Place. ⓘ Yuma Convention & Visitors' Bureau, 377 S Main St, (800) 293-0071. Ⓐ
ⓦ www.visityuma.com

Yuma occupies a strategic position at the confluence of the Colorado and Gila Rivers in Arizona's far southwestern corner. Though noted by Spanish explorers in the 16th century, it was not until the 1850s that the town rose to prominence, when the river crossing became the gateway to California for thousands of gold seekers. Later, Yuma was a supply depot as riverboats steamed up and down the Colorado to link with the Sea of Cortez. In the early 20th century, Yuma was an important stop on the first ocean-to-ocean transcontinental road that ended in San Diego. Sadly, however, for much of the 20th century, Yuma was a dusty, bypassed border town.

Today, Yuma's hot, sunny winter climate has made it a magnet for "snowbirds" escaping the northern cold. Their swelling numbers have brought about a renaissance, as the town adds attractions, accommodations, restaurants, and services.

The town's first major construction project was Yuma Territorial Prison in 1876. Arizonans were more than delighted to finally

**Boats and watersports in the picturesque setting of Lake Yuma**

have a place to put away the growing numbers of train robbers, polygamists, murderers, and outlaws. Criminals, on the other hand, were less than thrilled, as Yuma Prison had a notorious reputation for stifling heat and brutal conditions. The prison's most famous inmate was John Swilling, sometimes called the "Father of Phoenix," who made big money selling real estate. He later tried robbing a stagecoach after falling on hard times. Visitors to the **Yuma Territorial Prison State Historic Park** can see the grounds and, in winter, take a guided tour to hear stories of the prison's famous and infamous inhabitants, guards, riots, and escapes.

Yuma's history as a crossroads is highlighted at the **Yuma Crossing State Historic Park**. It features several buildings reconstructed to their 1870s appearance, including a telegraph office and the Commanding

Officer's quarters, which dates back to 1855. As the town became an important junction for supplies, the military took an interest, and built Fort Yuma in 1851, now owned by the Quechan Indians. The **Quechan Indian Museum**, housed in an 1855 adobe building, has displays on the arrival of the Spanish missionaries, the 1781 Quechan uprising, and the history of Fort Yuma.

🏛 **Yuma Territorial Prison State Historic Park**
1 Prison Hill Rd. ⓒ (928) 783-4771.
⏲ 8am–5pm. ● Dec 25.
♿ 🄯 🄿

🏛 **Yuma Crossing State Historic Park**
201 North 4th Ave. ⓒ (928) 329-0471. ⏲ 9am–5pm. ● Dec 25.
🄯 ♿

🏛 **Quechan Indian Museum**
Across the river from Yuma, 350 Picacho Rd, Winterhaven, CA 92283. ⓒ (760) 572-0661. ⏲ 8am–noon & 1pm–5pm.
● major hols. 🄯 ♿

**Cell blocks at the historic, territorial prison in Yuma**

Rare cacti at the Organ Pipe Cactus National Monument

## Organ Pipe Cactus National Monument ❽

**Road map** B5. 📞 *(520) 387-6849*. 🕐 *visitor center 8am–5pm*. 🚫 *Dec 25.* 📷 ♿ 📷 🅰 🅆 www.nps.gov/orpi

THE ORGAN pipe is a Sonoran Desert species of cactus, which is a cousin to the saguaro *(see p90)* but with multiple arms branching up from the base, as its name suggests. The organ pipe is rare in the United States, growing almost exclusively in this large and remote area of land along the Mexican border in southwest Arizona. Many other plant and animal species flourish in this unspoiled desert wilderness, although a lot of animals, such as snakes, jackrabbits, and kangaroo rats, emerge only in the cool of the night. Other cacti such as the saguaro, the Engelmann prickly pear, and the teddy-bear cholla are best seen in the early summertime when they give their glorious displays of floral color.

There are two scenic drives through the park: the 21-mile (34-km) **Ajo Mountain Drive** and the longer 53-mile (85-km) **Puerto Blanco Drive**. The Ajo Mountain Drive takes two hours and winds through startling desert landscapes in

**Orange flowers of the barrel cactus**

the foothills of the mountains. The Puerto Blanco Drive takes around four hours and leads visitors through a range of landscapes from desert to the oasis at Quitobaquito Spring. A variety of hiking trails in the park range in difficulty from paved, wheelchair-accessible paths to wilderness walks. A visitor center offers exhibits on the park's flora and fauna, as well as maps and camping permits, and there are guided walks in winter. Be aware that the park is a good two-and-a-half- to three-hour drive from Tucson one way. If you want to explore this environment in any detail, plan to camp overnight. Ajo, 34 miles (55 km) to the north, has motels and services.

## Tubac ❾

**Road map** C5. 🔼 *150*.
ℹ️ *Tubac Chamber of Commerce, (520) 398-2704.* 🅆 www.tubacaz.com

THE ROYAL presidio (fortress) of San Ignacio de Tubac was built in 1752 to protect the local Spanish-owned ranches and mines, as well as the nearby missions of Tumacacori and San Xavier, from attacks by local Pima Indians. Tubac was also the first stopover on the famous overland expedition to colonize the San Francisco Bay area in 1776. The trek was led by the fort's captain, Juan Bautista de Anza *(see p39)*. Following his return, the garrison moved north to Tucson, and for the next 100 years, Tubac declined. Today, the town is a small but thriving art colony, with attractive shops, galleries, and restaurants lining the streets around the plaza.

Tubac's historical remains are displayed at the **Tubac Presidio State Historic Park**, which encompasses the foundations of the original presidio in an underground display, as well as several historic buildings, including the delightful Old Tubac Schoolhouse. The Presidio Museum, which is also situated here, contains artifacts covering over 100 years of Tubac's history, including painted altarpieces and colonial furniture.

**Mission church at Tumacacori National Historical Park near Tubac**

Block of bargain stores at Nogales, a border town

**ENVIRONS:** Just 3 miles (5 km) south of town lies **Tumacacori National Historical Park**, with its beautiful ruined mission. The present church was built in around 1800 upon the ruins of the original 1691 mission established by Jesuit priest Father Eusebio Kino *(see p39)*. The mission was abandoned in 1848, and today its weatherbeaten ochre façade, together with its brick columns, arched entry, and carved wooden door, is an evocative reminder of former times. The cavernous interior is wonderfully atmospheric, with patches of exposed adobe brick and faded murals on the sanctuary walls. A small museum provides an excellent background on the mission builders and Pima Indians. Weekend craft demonstrations, including tortilla-making, basketry, and Mexican pottery, are held September through June. During the first weekend in December, La Fiesta de Tumacacori *(see p33)*, which celebrates the cultural heritage of the upper Santa Cruz Valley, is held on the mission grounds.

**Mexican pottery found in Nogales**

🏛 **Tubac Presidio State Historic Park**
Burruel St & Presidio Dr.
📞 *(520) 398-2252.* ⏰ *8am–5pm.*
⬤ *Dec 25.* 📷 ♿ 📹
🏛 **Tumacacori National Historical Park**
📞 *(520) 398-2341.* ⏰ *8am–5pm.*
⬤ *Thanksgiving, Dec 25.* 📷 ♿ 📹
W *www.nps.gov/tuma*

## Nogales ❿

Road map C5. 🏃 *19,500.* 🚌 🚊
ℹ *123 W Kino Park, (520) 287-3685.*

NOGALES IS really two towns that straddle the US border with Mexico. This is a busy port of entry, handling huge amounts of freight, including 75 percent of all winter fruit and vegetables sold in North America. It attracts large numbers of visitors in search of bargains at shopping districts on both sides of the border. Decorative blankets, furniture, and crafts are good value. There is a profound contrast between the US side and the ramshackle houses across the border, and visitors should be aware that the Mexican Nogales can be crowded with continuous hustle from street vendors eager for business. Still, it is a popular day-trip and there are several good restaurants here. Visitors are advised to leave their cars on the US side, where attendants mind the parking lots, and to walk across the border. Those who drive across the border should check that their car insurance is valid in Mexico. Visas are required only for those traveling farther south than the town and for stays of more than 72 hours. US and Canadian citizens should carry a passport or birth certificate for identification. US dollars are accepted everywhere.

## Bisbee ⓫

Road map C5. 🏃 *6,500.* 🚌
ℹ *Bisbee Chamber of Commerce, 1 Main St, (520) 432-5421.*
W *www.bisbeearizona.com*

THIS IS ONE of the most atmospheric mining towns in the Southwest. The discovery of copper here in the 1880s sparked a mining rush, and by the turn of the century Bisbee was the largest city between St. Louis and San Francisco. Victorian buildings such as the landmark Copper Queen Hotel still dominate the historic town center, while attractive clusters of houses cling to the sides of the surrounding mountains.

Today, visitors can tour the mines that once flourished here, such as the deep underground Queen Mine or, a short drive south of town, the Lavender Open Pit Mine. Exhibits at the Bisbee Mining and Historical Museum illustrate the realities of mining and frontier life here.

The Victorian mining town of Bisbee

## Tombstone ⑫

Road map C5. 🚶 6,500. 🛈 Chamber of Commerce, 105 4th St, (520) 457-9317. ⓦ www.tombstone.org

THE TOWN of Tombstone is a living legend, forever known as the site of the 1881 gunfight at the OK Corral between the Earp brothers and the Clanton gang *(see p25)*. The town's historic streets and buildings form one of the most popular attractions in the Southwest.

Tombstone was founded by Ed Schieffelin, who went prospecting on Apache land in 1877 despite a warning that "all you'll find out there is your tombstone." He found a mountain of silver instead, and his sardonically named shanty town boomed with the ensuing silver rush. One of the wildest towns in the Wild West, Tombstone was soon full of prospectors, gamblers, cowboys, and lawmen. In its heyday, the town was larger than San Francisco. More than $37 million worth of silver was extracted from the mines between 1880 and 1887, when miners struck an aquifer and flooded the mine shafts.

In 1962 "the town too tough to die" became a National Historic Landmark, and, with much of its historic downtown immaculately preserved,

Re-enactment of the gunfight at the OK Corral, Tombstone

it attracts many visitors, all eager to sample the unique atmosphere. Allen Street, with its wooden boardwalks, shops, and restaurants, is the town's main thoroughfare. The **OK Corral** is preserved as a museum, and re-enactments of the infamous gunfight between the Earp brothers, Doc Holliday and the Clanton gang are staged daily at 2pm.

**Tombstone Courthouse** on Toughnut Street was the seat of justice for the county from 1882 to 1929, and is now a State Historic Site. It contains a museum featuring the restored courtroom, and many historical exhibits and artifacts,

Tombstone Courthouse in the town center, now a museum

including photographs of some of the town's famous characters. Toughnut Street used to be known as "Rotten Row" as it was once lined with miners' tents, bordellos, and more than 100 bars.

Among other buildings worth looking for in the downtown area is the **Rose Tree Inn Museum**, home of what is reputedly the world's largest rosebush. There is also the **Bird Cage Theater**, once a bawdy dance hall and bordello, and so-named for the covered "crib" compartments, or cages, hanging from the ceiling, from which ladies of the night plied their trade. Nearby is the once rowdy Crystal Palace Saloon, which is still a bar.

Just north of town, the well-known **Boothill Cemetery** is full of the graves of those who perished in Tombstone, peacefully or otherwise. This evocative place is not without the occasional spot of humor. Look for the marker lamenting the death of George Johnson, hanged by mistake in 1882, which reads: "He was right, we was wrong, but we strung him up, and now he's gone."

🏛 **OK Corral**
Allen St. 📞 *(520) 457-3456.*
🕘 *9am–5pm.* ⬛ *Dec 25.* 📷 ♿
ⓦ www.ok-corral.com

🏛 **Tombstone Courthouse**
219 E Toughnut St. 📞 *(520) 457-3311.* 🕘 *8am–5pm.* ⬛ *Dec 25.*
📷 ♿ ⓦ www.pr.state.az.us

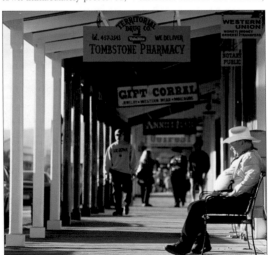
**Boardwalk in Tombstone**

# Kartchner Caverns State Park ⓭

**Road map** C5. ☎ *(520) 586-4100.* ◯ *7am–6pm (cave tours 8:30am–4:30pm by reservation).* ● *Dec 25.* ▨ ♿ ◪ *obligatory.* ⚠ ⓦ *www.pr.state.az.us*

THE KARTCHNER Caverns are one of Arizona's great natural wonders. Located in the Whetstone Mountains, the caves were discovered in 1974 when two cavers crawled through a sinkhole in a hillside that led them into 7 acres (3 ha) of caverns filled with colorful formations. Out of concern to protect the caves, they kept their discovery a secret for 14 years as they explored this wonderland of speleotherms, or cave formations, made of layers of calcite deposited by dripping or flowing water over millions of years. In 1988 the land was purchased by the state, but it took 11 years to complete the development that would allow public access while conserving the special conditions that enable these "wet" caves to continue growing.

Before entering the caves, visitors are introduced to the geology of the formations at the Discovery Center. Once inside, visitors must not touch the features, as skin oils stop their growth. Along with huge stalactites and stalagmites, there is an abundance of other types of formation such as the aptly named 21-ft (132-m) high soda straw, the turnip shields, and popcorn.

**Orange and white column formations at Kartchner Caverns**

# Amerind Foundation ⓮

☎ *(520) 586-3666.* ◯ *10am–4pm.* ● *Jun–Sep: Mon & Tue; public hols.* ▨ ⓦ *www.amerind.org*

THE AMERIND Foundation is one of the most important private archeological and ethnological museums in the country. The name Amerind is a contraction of "American Indian," and this collection contains tens of thousands of artifacts from different Native American cultures. All aspects of Native American life are shown here, with displays covering Inuit masks, Cree tools, and sculpted effigy figures from Mexico's Casas Grandes.

The adjacent Amerind Art Gallery has a fine collection of Western art by such prominent artists as William Leigh (1866–1955) and Frederic Remington (1861–1909). The delightful pink buildings, designed in the Spanish Colonial Revival style *(see p20),* are also of interest.

# Chiricahua National Monument ⓯

**Road map** D5. ☎ *(520) 824-3560.* ◯ *8am–4:30pm daily.* ● *Dec 25.* ▨ ♿ ◪ ⚠ ⓦ *www.nps.gov/chir*

THE CHIRICAHUA Mountains were once the homeland of a band of Apache people, and an impenetrable base from which they launched attacks on settlers in the late 1800s. This 12,000-acre (480-ha) area now preserves amazing rock formations, which were created by a series of volcanic eruptions around 27 million years ago. Massive rocks balanced on small pedestals, soaring rock spires, and enormous stone columns make up the bizarre landscape, viewed from the monument's scenic drive and hiking trails.

The nearby town of Willcox houses the intriguing **Rex Allen Arizona Cowboy Museum**, which is devoted to a native son who became a famous movie cowboy, starring in 19 films in the 1950s.

🏛 **Rex Allen Arizona Cowboy Museum**
155 N Railroad Ave. ☎ *(520) 384-4583.* ◯ *10am–4pm.* ● *public hols.* ▨ ♿

**Massive rock spires formed by million-year-old volcanic eruptions at Chiricahua National Monument**

# THE FOUR CORNERS

DOMINATED BY a Navajo reservation the size of Connecticut, and presenting sweeping panoramas of mesas, canyons, and vast expanses of high desert, the Four Corners is perfect for those wanting to experience Native culture and the real West.

Although it receives less than 10 in (25 cm) of rainfall per year, this arid land has supported life since the first Paleo-Indians arrived about 12,000 years ago. The Anasazi, today known as the Ancestral Puebloan peoples, lived here from about AD 500 until the 13th century. They are responsible for

the many evocative ruins found here, including those at Mesa Verde, Chaco Canyon, and Hovenweep National Monument. Their descendants include the Hopi, whose pueblos are said to be the oldest continuously occupied towns in North America. The Navajo arrived here in the 15th century and their spiritual center is Canyon de Chelly with its 1,000-ft (330-m) high red rock walls.

Monument Valley's impressive landscape has been used as a backdrop for countless movies and TV shows. The region is also popular for hiking, fishing, and whitewater rafting.

## SIGHTS AT A GLANCE

**Historic Towns & Cities**
Aztec **15**
Blanding **9**
Bluff **8**
Farmington **14**
Ganado & Hubbell
  Trading Post **5**
Tuba City **3**
Window Rock **6**

**National Parks & Monuments**
*Canyon de Chelly National Monument* **7**
*Chaco Culture National Historical Park* **13**
Four Corners Monument Navajo Tribal Park **12**

Hovenweep National
  Monument **10**
*Mesa Verde National Park* **17**
Navajo National Monument **2**

**Areas of Natural Beauty**
*Colorado Plateau Tour* **16**
*Monument Valley* **1**

**Indian Reservations**
Hopi Indian Reservation **4**
Ute Mountain Tribal
  Park **11**

**KEY**
- Interstate
- Major highway
- Highway
- Railroad
- State boundary

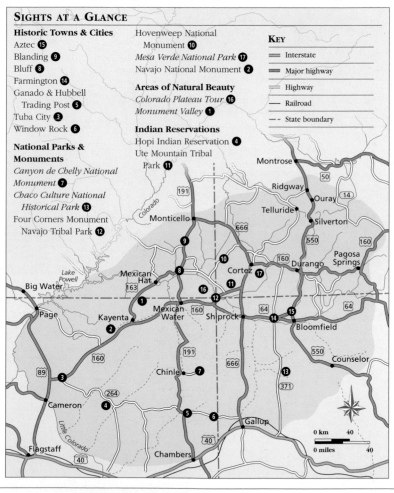

# Monument Valley ❶

FROM SCENIC HIGHWAY 163, which crosses the border of Utah and Arizona, it is possible to see the famous towering sandstone buttes and mesas of Monument Valley. These ancient rocks, soaring upward from a seemingly boundless desert, have come to symbolize the American West, largely because Hollywood has used these breathtaking vistas as a backdrop for hundreds of movies, TV shows, and commercials since the 1930s.

The area's visitor center sits within the boundary of Monument Valley Tribal Park, but many of the valley's spectacular rock formations and other sites are found just outside the park boundary.

**Guided Tours**
*A row of kiosks at the visitor center offers Navajo-guided 4WD tours of the valley. The marketing tactics can be aggressive, but the tours offer an excellent way to see places in the park that are otherwise inaccessible.*

**Three Sisters**
*The Three Sisters are one of several distinctive pinnacle rock formations at Monument Valley. Others include the Totem Pole and the "fingers" of the Mittens. The closest view of the sisters can be seen from John Ford's Point, and is one of the most photographed sights here.*

Left Mitten

**Art & Ruins**
*Petroglyphs such as this deer can be seen on Navajo-guided tours of rock art sites, which are dotted around the valley's ancient ruins.*

## EXPLORING THE VALLEY

The awe-inspiring beauty of Monument Valley's buttes and mesas can be viewed by travelers from Highway 163. Visitors can also pay a fee to travel on a 17-mile (27-km) self-guided drive along a well-marked dirt road. (Fees are collected at the visitor center.) Alternatively, Navajo guides may be hired for hiking, horseback, or 4WD tours to fascinating and less-visited parts of the valley.

Mitchell Butte

BLANDING

Left Mitten

Merrick Butte

Right Mitten

163

UTAH
ARIZONA

0 km 20

0 miles 20

MONUMENT VALLEY NAVAJO TRIBAL PARK

160

**KEY**

Major highway

Highway

Park boundary

State boundary

Visitor information

Kayenta

SHIPROCK

Gouldings Lodge

Elephant Butte

John Ford's Point

### John Ford's Point

*The most popular stop along the valley drive is John Ford's Point, which is said to be the film director's favorite view of the valley. Various stands offer a range of Navajo handicrafts. A nearby hogan (see p107) serves as a gift shop where Navajo weavers demonstrate their craft.*

(see p107)

**VISITORS' CHECKLIST**

Road map C2.
🛈 PO Box 360289, Monument Valley, (435) 727-5870.
🕒 sunrise–sunset. ⬤ Dec 25.
📷 ♿ visitor center only.
🚫 🅿 🍴 🏕
W www.navajonationparks.org

Right Mitten

Merrick Butte

**Navajo Weaver**

*Navajo women are usually considered to be the finest weavers in the Southwest. One rug can take months to complete and sells for thousands of dollars. Using the natural colors of the land, the weavers often add a "spirit line" to their work to prevent their spirit being "trapped" within the rug.*

## MONUMENT VALLEY

Monument Valley is not really a valley. The tops of the mesas mark what was once a flat plain. Millions of years ago, this plain was cracked by upheavals within the earth. The cracks widened and eroded, until all that is left today are the formations rising from the desert floor.

**Gouldings Lodge**

*The lodge offers accommodations, a restaurant, and guided bus tours of the valley. The original trading post is now a museum of the valley's cinematic history.*

Ancestral Puebloan ruins of Keet Seel at Navajo National Monument

# Navajo National Monument ❷

**Road map** C2. ☏ *(928) 672-2700.*
◻ *8am–5pm.* ● *Jan 1,*
*Thanksgiving, Dec 25.* ☐ ☒
🆆 *www.nps.gov/nava*

NAMED BECAUSE of its location on the Navajo Reservation, this monument is actually known for its Ancestral Puebloan ruins. The most accessible ruin here is the beautifully preserved, 135-room pueblo of Betatakin, which fills a vast, curved niche in the cliffs of Tsegi Canyon. An easy one-mile (1.6-km) trail from the visitor center leads to an overlook where Betatakin is clearly visible on the far side, near the canyon floor. This is a lovely hike through piñon pines and juniper trees. From late May to early September there are daily six-hour hiking tours to Betatakin, which allow a close look at the ruins of these ancient houses.

A much more demanding 17-mile (27-km) hike leads to **Keet Seel**, a more impressive ruin. Only a limited number

of permits to visit the ruin are issued each day. This hike requires overnight camping at a site with only the most basic facilities. Keet Seel was a larger and more successful community than Betatakin. Construction began on Keet Seel in about 1250, but the site is thought to have been abandoned by 1300.

These two sites are considered to mark the pinnacle of development of the area's Ancestral Puebloan people.

# Tuba City ❸

**Road map** C2. 🚶 *17,300.* ℹ *Tuba City Trading Post, (928) 283-5441.*

NAMED FOR TUUVI, a Hopi Indian who converted to the Mormon faith, Tuba City is best known for the 65-million-year-old dinosaur tracks found just off the main highway, 5 miles (8 km) southwest of the town. Beyond that, this is the largest community in the western section of the Navajo Reservation and is a good spot from which to explore both the Navajo National Monument and the Hopi Reservation.

# Hopi Indian Reservation ❹

**Road map** C3. 🚶 *10,000.*
ℹ *Hwy 264, Second Mesa,*
*(928) 734-2401.* ◻ *May–Sep:*
*6am– 9pm; Oct–Apr: 7am–8pm.*
● *Jan 1, Thanksgiving, Dec 25.*

ARIZONA'S ONLY Pueblo Indians, the Hopi *(see pp22–3)*, are believed to be direct descendants of the Ancestral Puebloan people, or Anasazi. The Hopi Reservation is surrounded by the lands of the Navajo. The landscape is harsh and barren, yet the Hopi have cultivated the land here for a 1,000 years. They worship, through the *kachina*, the living spirits of plants and animals, believed to arrive each year to stay with the tribe during the growing season. Most of the Hopi villages are located on or near one of three mesas, or flat-topped elevations named First, Second, and Third Mesa. The artisans on each of the mesas specialize in particular crafts: on First Mesa these are carved figures representing the *kachina* spirits and painted pottery; on Second Mesa, silver jewelry and coiled baskets are made; and on Third Mesa, craftspeople fashion wicker baskets and woven rugs.

**Kachina figure**

**Walpi**, the ancient pueblo on First Mesa, was first inhabited in the 12th century. To reach Walpi, visitors drive up to the Mesa from the Pollaca settlement in the village of Sichomovi. Nearby, the Ponsi Visitor Center is the departure

Historic pueblo town of Walpi on First Mesa at Hopi Indian Reservation

A range of merchandise in the general store at Hubbell Trading Post

point for the one-hour Walpi tours. Walpi was built to be easily defended, and straddles a dramatic knife edge of rock, extending from the tip of First Mesa. In places Walpi is less than 100 ft (33 m) wide with a drop of several hundred feet on both sides. The Walpi tour includes several stops where visitors can purchase *kachina* figurines and distinctive hand-crafted pottery, or sample the Hopi *piki* bread.

Those wishing to shop further can continue on to Second Mesa, where galleries and stores offer an array of Hopi arts and crafts. The Hopi Cultural Center is home to a restaurant *(see p141)* and the only hotel *(see p131)* for miles around, as well as a museum that has an excellent collection of photographs depicting scenes of Hopi life.

On Third Mesa, Old Oraibi pueblo, thought to have been founded in the 12th century, is of note only because of claims that it is the oldest continually occupied human settlement in North America.

**🏚 Walpi**
**ℹ** *(928) 737-2262. Walking tours available 9:30am–3pm.* 🖼

## Ganado & Hubbell Trading Post ❺

**Road map** D2. 🏚 *4,500.* **ℹ** *Hubbell Trading Post, Hwy 264, (928) 755-3475.*

A SMALL, BUSTLING town in the heart of the Navajo Reservation, Ganado's major attraction is the **Hubbell Trading Post National**

**Historic Site**. Established in the 1870s by John Lorenzo Hubbell, this is the oldest continually operating trading post in the Navajo Nation. Trading posts like this one were once the economic and social centers of the reservations. The Navajo traded sheep, wool, blankets, turquoise, and other items in exchange for tools, household goods, and food. The trading posts were also a resource during times of need. When a smallpox epidemic struck in 1886, John Lorenzo helped care for the sick, using his house as a hospital.

Today, the trading post still hums with traditional trading activities. One room is a working general store, the rafters hung with frying pans and hardware, and shelves stacked with cloth, medicines, and food. Another room is filled with beautiful hand-woven rugs, Hopi *kachina*

Navajo bracelet at
**Hubbell Trading Post**

dolls, and Navajo baskets. Another department has a long row of glass cases displaying an impressive array of silver and turquoise jewelry.

Visitors can tour Hubbell's restored home and view a significant collection of Southwestern art. At the visitor center Navajo women demonstrate rug weaving.

**🏚 Hubbell Trading Post National Historic Site**
A2264, near Ganado. **ℹ** *(928) 755-3254.* ◯ *May–Sep: 8am–6pm; Oct–Apr: 8am–5pm.* ● *Sun & public/tribal hols.* 🔲 *www.nps.gov/hutr*

## Window Rock ❻

**Road map** D2. 🏚 *4,500.* ▣
**ℹ** *Hwy 264, (928) 871-6436.*

THE CAPITAL OF the Navajo Nation, the town is named for the natural arch found in the sandstone cliffs located about a mile north of the main strip on Highway 12. The **Navajo Nation Museum** located here is one of the largest Native American museums in the US. Opened in 1997, the huge *hogan*-shaped building houses displays that cover the history of the Ancestral Puebloans and the Navajo.

**🏛 Navajo Nation Museum**
Hwy 264 & Post Office Loop Rd. **ℹ** *(928) 871-7941.* ◯ *8am–5pm Mon; 8am–8pm Tue–Fri; 9am–5pm Sat.*

Eroded sandstone opening of Window Rock, near Highway 12

# Canyon de Chelly National Monument ●

**Flowering cactus**

FEW PLACES IN North America can boast a longer or more eventful history of human habitation than Canyon de Chelly. Archeologists have found evidence of four periods of Native culture, starting with the Basketmaker people around AD 300, followed by the Great Pueblo Builders, who created the cliff dwellings in the 12th century. They were succeeded by the Hopi, who lived here seasonally for around 300 years, taking advantage of the canyon's fertile soil. In the 1700s, the Hopi left the area and moved to the mesas, returning to the canyon to farm during the summer months. Today, the canyon is the cultural and geographic heart of the Navajo Nation. Pronounced "d'Shay," de Chelly is a Spanish corruption of the Native name *Tsegi*, meaning Rock Canyon.

**Yucca House Ruin**
*Perched on the mesa top, this ruin of an Ancestral Puebloan house sits in a rock hollow, precariously overhanging a sheer drop to the valley floor.*

**Mummy Cave Ruin**
*These two pueblos, separated by a central tower, were built in the 1280s by Ancestral Puebloans, who had inhabited the caves for more than 1,000 years. An overlook provides a good view of this impressive ruin.*

**Stone and adobe** cliff dwellings were home to the Ancestral Puebloans from the 12th to the 14th centuries and were built to face south toward the sun, with cooler areas within.

**Navajo Fortress**
*This imposing rock tower was the site of a three-month siege in 1863–64, when a group of Navajos reached the summit via pole ladders to escape Kit Carson and the US army. The persistence of Carson and starvation led them to surrender and they were marched to a camp in New Mexico (see p109).*

**Canyon Landscape**
*The sandstone cliffs of Canyon de Chelly reach as high as 1,000 ft (300 m), towering above the neighboring meadows and desert landscape in the distance. The canyon floor around the cliffs is fringed with cottonwood bushes, watered by the Chinle Wash.*

**VISITORS' CHECKLIST**

**Road map** D2. 2 miles (3.5 km) east of Chinle & I-191. ℹ PO Box 588, Chinle, (928) 674-5500. ◯ 8am–5pm. ● Dec 25. ♿ partial. 📷 obligatory (except White House). 🍴 🚻 W www.nps.gov/cach

**The pale walls** of the White House cliff drop 550 ft (160 m) to the canyon floor.

***Hogan* Interior**
*The hogan is the center of Navajo family life. Made of horizontal logs, it has a smoke hole in the center to provide contact with the sky, while the dirt floor gives contact with the earth. A door faces east to greet the rising sun.*

## WHITE HOUSE RUINS

This group of rooms, tucked into a tiny hollow in the cliff, seems barely touched by time. The dwellings were originally situated above a larger pueblo, much of which has now disappeared. The only site within the canyon that can be visited without a Navajo guide, it is reached via a steep 2.5-mile (5-km) round-trip trail that winds to the canyon floor and offers magnificent views.

## MASSACRE CAVE

The canyon's darkest hour was in 1805, when a Spanish force under Lieutenant Antonio Narbona entered the area. The Spanish wanted to subdue the Navajo, claiming they were raiding their settlements. While some Navajo fled by climbing to the canyon rim, others took refuge in a cave high in the cliffs. The Spanish fired into the cave, and Narbona boasted that he had killed 115 Navajo including 90 warriors. Navajo accounts are different, claiming that most of the warriors were absent (probably hunting) and those killed were mostly women, children, and the elderly. The only Spanish fatality came when a Spaniard attempting to climb into the cave was attacked by a Navajo woman and both plunged over the cliff, gaining the Navajo name "Two Fell Over." The Anglo name is "Massacre Cave."

**Pictograph on a canyon wall showing invading Spanish soldiers**

# Exploring Canyon de Chelly

**Navajo ranger**

CANYON DE CHELLY is startlingly different from the sparse desert landscape that spreads from its rim. Weathered red rock walls, just 30-ft (9-m) high at the canyon mouth, rise to more than 1,000-ft (300-m) high within the canyon, creating a sheltered world. Navajo *hogans (see p107)* dot the canyon floor; Navajo women tend herds of sheep and weave rugs at outdoor looms, and everywhere Ancestral Puebloan ruins add to the canyon's appeal. Navajo-led 4WD tours along the scenic North and South Rims are a popular way to view the site.

**Antelope House Ruin**
*Named for a pictograph of an antelope painted by Navajo artists in the 1830s, Antelope House has ruins dating from AD 700. They can be seen from the Antelope House Overlook.*

**Canyon Vegetation**
*Within the canyon, cottonwood and oak trees line the river washes; the land itself is a fertile oasis of meadows, alfalfa and corn fields, and fruit orchards.*

0 km 3
0 miles 3

Chinle

64

Standing Cow Ruin

Ledge Ruin Overlook

Antelope House Overlook

Chinle Wash

White House Overlook

CANYON DE CHELLY

South Rim Drive

Shidin House Overlook

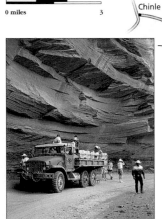

**Canyon Tour**
*Half- and full-day tours from Thunderbird Lodge carry passen-gers in open flatbed or large 6WD army trucks. Of varying length and difficulty, the tours are the best way to see ruins up close.*

**Tsegi Overlook**
*This high curve along the South Rim offers good general views of the farm-studded canyon floor and surrounding landscape.*

**Hiking in the Canyon**
*Canyon de Chelly is a popular destination for hikers, but only the White House Ruins Trail may be walked without a guide. The visitor center (see p107) offers Navajo-guided hikes on trails of varying lengths.*

### KEY

| | |
|---|---|
| ═══ | Highway |
| ◄ ■ ■ | Hiking route |
| Ⓐ | Campground/RV |
| 🅷 | Picnic area |
| 🛈 | Visitor information |
| ⚶ | Viewpoint |
| — | Park boundary |

TO TSAILE
WINDOW ROCK

North Rim Drive

⚶ Massacre Cave Overlook

⚶ Mummy Cave Overlook

Canyon del Muerto

Black Rock Canyon

Spider Rock Overlook ⚶

7

**Spider Rock**
*Rising more than 800 ft (245 m), this is where, according to Navajo legends, Spider Woman lived and gave them the skill of weaving.*

### KIT CARSON AND THE "LONG WALK"

In 1863, the US government sent Kit Carson under the command of General James A. Carlton to settle the problem of Navajo raids. To avoid outright slaughter Carson led his soldiers through the region, destroying villages and livestock as the Navajo fled ahead of them. In January 1864, Carson entered Canyon de Chelly, capturing the Navajo hiding there *(see p106)*. They were among 9,000 Navajo who were driven on the "The Long Walk," a forced march of 370 miles (595 km) from Fort Defiance to Bosque Redondo in New Mexico. There, in a pitiful reservation, more than 3,000 Navajo died before the US government accepted the resettlement as a failure and allowed them to return to the Four Corners.

**Fur trapper and soldier Kit Carson (1809–68)**

Dramatic mesas and buttes in the Valley of the Gods near Bluff

## Bluff ⑧

**Road Map** D1. 🏠 *300.* ℹ️ *Blanding Visitor Center, 12N Hwy 191, (435) 678-3662.* 🅰️

THE CHARMING TOWN of Bluff was settled in 1880 by Mormons who dynamited their way through Glen Canyon's rock walls along what is now called the Hole-in-the-Rock Road. Float trips along the San Juan River include stops at Ancestral Pueblo ruins that can be reached only by boat.

**ENVIRONS:** About 12 miles (20 km) north is a 17 mile (27 km) dirt road through the **Valley of the Gods**. Like Monument Valley *(see pp102–3)*, it features high rock spires, buttes, and mesas, but none of the crowds. On a quiet day, visitors may have the place all to themselves and imagine what it looked like to the first settlers.

## Blanding ⑨

**Road Map** D1. 🏠 *3,800.* ℹ️ *12N Hwy 191, (435) 678-3662.* 🆆 *www.blandingutah.org*

A TIDY MORMON town at the base of the Abajo Mountains, Blanding is home to the **Edge of Cedars State Park** *(see pp116–17)*. The park contains modest Ancestral Puebloan ruins, including a small *kiva*, or religious chamber. The park museum has well thought-out displays on the history of these ancient people and other cultures that have inhabited the region.

🏠 **Edge of Cedars State Park** ℹ️ *Park Museum, 660 W 400 N, (435) 678-2238.* ☉ *mid-May–mid-Sep: 9am–7pm; mid-Sep–mid-May: 9am–5pm.* ● *Thanksgiving, Dec 25.* 🅰️ 🆆 *www.stateparks.utah.gov*

## Hovenweep National Monument ⑩

**Road Map** D1. *East of Hwy 191.* ☎️ *(970) 562-4282.* ☉ *Oct 31–Apr 30: 8am–5pm; May 1–Oct 30: 8am–6pm.* ● *Jan 1, Thanksgiving, Dec 25.* 🅰️ 🆆 *www.nps.gov/hove*

ONE OF THE MOST mysterious Ancestral Puebloan sites in the Southwest, the Hovenweep ruins lie along the rim of a shallow canyon. These well-preserved ruins, which include unique round, square, and D-shaped towers, have neither been restored nor rebuilt. Indeed, they look much as they did when W.D. Huntington, leader of a Mormon expedition, first came upon the site in 1854. The site was named in 1874, after an

Ute word meaning "Deserted Valley." Little is known of the people who inhabited these ruins, and researchers have speculated that the towers at Hovenweep might have been defensive fortifications, astronomical observatories, storage silos, or the community's religious structures.

The six separate sets of ruins at Hovenweep can be visited by walking along either of the two self-guiding trails that link them.

## Ute Mountain Tribal Park ⑪

**Road Map** D2. ℹ️ *Junction of Hwys 160 & 666, (800) 847-5485.* ☉ *Apr–Oct: 8am–3:30pm daily; Nov–Mar: 8am–3pm Wed–Sat.* 🏃 *obligatory.*

THE RUINS of Ute Mountain Tribal Park are one of the better-kept secrets of the Southwest. The Ancestral Puebloan people first arrived here in about AD 400. They closely followed the Mesa Verde *(see pp118–19)* pattern of development, creating numerous magnificent cliff

Ancient brick tower at Hovenweep National Monument

dwellings, including the 80-room Lion House. These ruins have few visitors because of their inaccessibility. Visitors can use their own vehicles and join the tours led by local Ute guides, or pay an extra charge to be driven.

# Four Corners Monument Navajo Tribal Park ⑫

**Road Map** D2. Junction of Hwys 160 & 41. *(928) 871-6647.* ○ May–Aug: 7am–8pm; Sep–Apr: 8am–5pm. ● Thanksgiving, Dec 25. ⚐ ⚒ Ⓦ www.navajonationparks.org

THERE IS SOMETHING oddly compelling about being able to put one foot and hand in each of four states. It is the whole premise of the Four Corners Monument – the only place in the US where four states meet at one point.

# Chaco Culture National Historical Park ⑬

*See pp112–13.*

# Farmington ⑭

**Road Map** D2. ⚐ 40,000. ✕ ⊟ ℹ 3041 E Main St, (505) 326-7602. Ⓦ www.farmingtonnm.org

A DUSTY, HARD-WORKING ranch town, Farmington is a good base for exploring the surrounding monuments. It is home to one of the most unusual museums in the Southwest. The **Bolack Museum of Fish & Wildlife** covers over 30,000 sq ft (2,800 sq m) and houses the largest accumulation of mounted game animals in the world. It is divided into nine themed game rooms, including African, Asian, European, and Russian. The museum's newest addition is a 10,000 sq ft (929 sq m) display of electromechanical equipment that traces America's golden age of development in electrical power generation and TV and radio broadcasting.

The **Farmington Museum** focuses on the history and geology of the area. A new exhibit, "From Dinosaurs to Drillbits," features a simulated ride down inside an oil well. The museum also offers popular interactive displays for adults and children.

**ENVIRONS:** About 25 miles (40 km) west of Farmington is **Shiprock**, named for the spectacular 1,500-ft (457-m) rock peak that thrusts up from the valley floor about 5 miles (8 km) west of town. To the Navajo, this rock is sacred, and to early Anglo-American settlers it was a landmark that reminded them of a ship's prow. Now it is possible for sightseers to observe the peak only from the roadsides of Highways 64 or 33.

The **Salmon Ruins**, which once housed a Chaco settlement, are situated 8 miles (12 km) to the south. These ruins were protected from grave diggers by the Salmon family, who homesteaded here in the 1870s. As a result, a century later archeologists recovered more than a million artifacts, many of which are on display in the museum at the site.

## ⛫ Bolack Museum of Fish & Wildlife
3901 Bloomfield Hwy. *(505) 325-4275.* ○ 9am–3pm Mon–Sat, appointment only. ⚐ ⚒ ☑ obligatory. Ⓦ www.bolackmuseum.com

## ⛫ Farmington Museum
3041 E Main St. *(505) 599-1174.* ○ 8am–5pm Mon–Sat. ⚐ ⚒ ☑ Ⓦ www.farmingtonmuseum.org

## ⋔ Salmon Ruins
6131 Hwy 64. *(505) 632-2013.* ○ 8am–5pm Mon–Fri; Apr–Oct: 9am–5pm Sat & Sun; Nov–Mar: 9am–5pm Sat, noon–5pm Sun. ● Jan 1, Easter, Thanksgiving, Dec 25. ⚐ ⚒ ☑

**Interior of the Great Kiva at Ancestral Puebloan Salmon Ruins**

# Aztec ⑮

**Road Map** D2. ⚐ 6,000. ℹ 110 North Ash St, (505) 334-9551.

THE SMALL TOWN of Aztec was named for its ruins, which are Ancestral Puebloan and not Aztec as early settlers believed. Preserved as a National Monument, the site's 500-room pueblo was a flourishing settlement in the late 1200s. Visitors can look inside a rebuilt *kiva (see p36).*

## ⋔ Aztec Ruins National Monument
N of Hwy 516 on Ruins Rd. *(505) 334-6174.* ○ 8am–5pm daily (to 6pm May–Sep). ● Jan 1, Thanksgiving, Dec 25. ⚐ ⚒ ☑ Ⓦ www.nps.gov/azru

**The spectacular red peak of Shiprock near Farmington**

# Chaco Culture National Historical Park ⑬

**Arrowhead at Chaco Museum**

Chaco canyon is one of the most impressive cultural sites in the Southwest, reflecting the sophistication of the Ancestral Puebloan civilization (*see pp36–7*) that existed here. With its six "great houses" and many lesser sites, the canyon was once the political, religious, and cultural center for settlements that covered much of the Four Corners. At its peak during the 11th century, Chaco was one of the most impressive pre-Columbian cities in North America. Despite its size, it is thought that Chaco's population was small because the land could not have supported a larger community. Archeologists believe that the city was mainly used as a ceremonial gathering place, with a year-round population of less than 3,000. Probably the social elite, the inhabitants supported themselves largely by trading.

**Architectural Detail**
*Chaco's skilled builders had only stone tools to work with to create this finely wrought stonework.*

**The many *kivas*** here were probably used by visitors arriving for religious ceremonies.

## PUEBLO BONITO

Pueblo Bonito is an example of a "great house." Begun around AD 850, it was built in stages over the course of 300 years. This reconstruction shows how it might have looked, with its D-shaped four-story structure that contained more than 650 rooms.

**Chetro Ketl**
*A short trail from Pueblo Bonito leads to another great house, Chetro Ketl. Almost as large as Pueblo Bonito, at 3 acres (2 ha), Chetro Ketl has more than 500 rooms. The masonry used to build the later portions of this structure is among the most sophisticated found in any Ancestral Puebloan site.*

**Casa Rinconada**
*Also known as a great* kiva, *Casa Rinconada is the largest religious chamber at Chaco, measuring 62 ft (19 m) in diameter. It was used for spiritual gatherings.*

**Pueblo Alto**

*Pueblo Alto was built atop the mesa at the junction of several ancient Chacoan roads. Reaching the site requires a two-hour hike, but the views over the canyon are well worth it.*

### VISITORS' CHECKLIST

**Road map** D2. 3 miles (5 km) SE of Nageezi off US 550. 🛈 Chaco Culture Visitor Center (505) 786-7014. ◐ 8am–5pm. ● public hols. 🚫♿🚼 W www.nps.gov/chcu

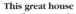

**This great house** was four stories high.

**Early Astronomers at Fajada Butte**

*Measurement of time was vital to the Chacoans for crop planting and the timing of ceremonies. A spiral petroglyph, carved on Fajada Butte, is designed to indicate the changing seasons through the shadows it casts on the rock.*

## EXPLORING CHACO

The site is accessed via a 16-mile (26-km) dirt road that is affected by flash floods in wet weather. Drivers can follow the paved loop road that passes several of Chaco's highlights. There is parking at all major sites. From the visitor center, a trail leads to Una Vida and the petroglyphs.

### KEY

━━ Highway

═══ Unpaved road

--- Hiking route

Ⓐ Campground/RV

🚻 Picnic area

🛈 Visitor information

━━ Park boundary

Kin Kletso

Pueblo Alto

Pueblo del Arroyo

Chetro Ketl

Una Vida

7950

Pueblo Bonito

Wijiji

Casa Rinconada

57

0 km    2

0 miles    2

Chaco Canyon

**Hundreds of rooms** within Pueblo Bonito show little sign of use and are thought to have been kept for storage or for guests arriving to take part in ceremonial events.

Totem Pole Rock at Monument Valley Navajo Tribal Park ▷

# Colorado Plateau Tour ⑯

T HE HAUNTING BEAUTY of the high plateau country, with its deep canyons and ancient, mysterious ruins, is the star of this tour, which follows some of the loneliest but loveliest roads in America. This area is very popular with hiking, mountain biking, river paddling, and 4WD enthusiasts. The plateau rises from around 2,000 ft (610 m) in elevation near Monument Valley to over 7,000 ft (2,134 m) at Monticello, Utah. The area is dotted with the ruins of the Ancient Puebloan civilization. Some, such as Hovenweep and Mesa Verde, were large complex towns, while others, for instance the ruins at Edge of Cedars State Park on a vast plain below the snowcapped Abajo Mountains, were small outposts.

**Bluff** ③
This appealing small town was founded by hardy Mormon pioneers in 1880. Today, it makes a great base for exploring the region, and is the starting point for rafting tours of the San Juan River *(see p151).*

**Valley of the Gods** ④
A 17-mile (27-km) long dirt road winds through this valley of eroded red rock spires. Recommended for high-clearance vehicles, this road presents the remote beauty of the Southwest that existed before modern roads were built.

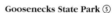

**Goosenecks State Park** ⑤
A set of incredibly tight switchbacks on the San Juan River give this overlook its name. The viewpoint is 1,500 ft (457 m) above the sinuous curves of the river, which travels 6 miles (9.7 km) to move 1.5 miles (2.4 km) forward.

*Mexican Hat*

A R I Z O N A

FLAGSTAFF

**Monument Valley** ⑥
Made famous through Western movies, the valley's buttes and bluffs were once ground level, before wind and water sculpted the landscape *(see pp102–3).*

**Hovenweep National Monument** ⑦
These evocative ruins are different from other Ancient Pueblo sites. Archeologists are still arguing the purpose of the round and square towers built along this canyon *(see p110).*

**Edge of Cedars State Park ②**
These small, well-preserved ruins are dwarfed by the surrounding high plateau. The park museum has a superb collection of Ancient Pueblo pottery and artifacts *(see p110)*.

**TIPS FOR DRIVERS**

*Tour length:* 290 miles (467 km).
*When to go:* Spring and fall. Snow in winter is a possibility.
*Stopping-off points:* The best bets for restaurants and accommodations are Bluff and Cortez.
*Note:* This route can be driven in either direction. There are long distances, up to 50 miles (80 km), without services, so fill up the gas tank, and review desert driving safety (see p160).

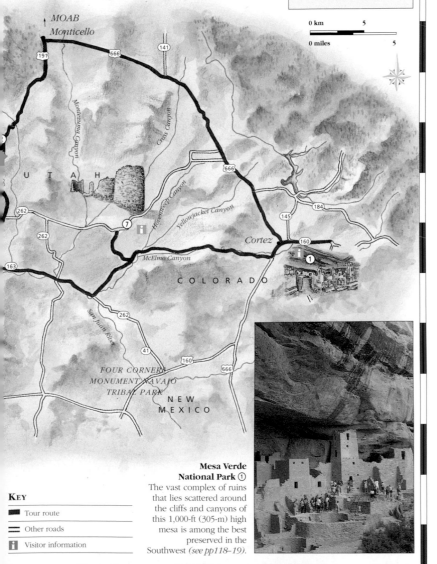

MOAB
Monticello

191
666
141

Montezuma Canyon
Cross Canyon

U T A H

666

Hovenweep Canyon
Yellowjacket Canyon

262

7

i

262

McElmo Canyon

Cortez

145

184

160

i ①

163

San Juan River

262

41

160

666

FOUR CORNERS
MONUMENT NAVAJO
TRIBAL PARK

COLORADO

NEW
MEXICO

**Mesa Verde National Park ①**
The vast complex of ruins that lies scattered around the cliffs and canyons of this 1,000-ft (305-m) high mesa is among the best preserved in the Southwest *(see pp118–19)*.

**KEY**

▬ Tour route

═ Other roads

i Visitor information

# Mesa Verde National Park ⑰

THIS HIGH, FORESTED mesa overlooking the Montezuma Valley was home to the Ancestral Puebloan people (see pp36–7) for more than 700 years. Within canyons that cut through the mesa are some of the best preserved and most elaborate cliff dwellings built by these people. Mesa Verde, meaning "Green Table," was a name given to the area by the Spanish in the 1700s, but the ruins were not widely known until the late 19th century. This site provides a fascinating record of these people from the Basketmaker period, beginning around AD 550, to the complex society that built the many-roomed cliff dwellings between 1000 and 1250. Displays at the Far View Visitor Center and the Chapin Mesa Museum provide a good introduction.

**Spruce Tree House**
*Tucked into a cliff niche, these three-story structures were probably home to as many as 100 people.*

**Guided Tours**
*Ranger-led tours give visitors a chance to actually enter the ruins and get a feel of the daily lives of these ancient people.*

### CLIFF PALACE
With 150 rooms, this is the largest Ancestral Puebloan cliff dwelling found anywhere, and is the site that most visitors focus on. The location and symmetry suggest that architecture was important to the builders. Begun around 1200, it was vacated around 1275.

HWY 160

Morefield Village

Far View Visitor Center

Spruce Tree House

Wetherill Mesa

Chapin Mesa Museum

Cliff Palace

Balcony House

### EXPLORING THE PARK
Most visitors start at Chapin Mesa, which has the highest concentration of sites. A paved scenic drive leads around the mesa and overlooks offer excellent views.

**KEY**

━━ Scenic route

ℹ Visitor information

🏃 Ranger station

━ Park boundary

0 km      5

0 miles      5

### Balcony House
*Possibly built for defense, Balcony House could not be seen from above, and access was (and still is) difficult. Visitors on tours must climb three ladders high above the canyon floor, then crawl through an access tunnel.*

**Towers** were probably used for signaling or as lookouts for defense.

### Square Tower House
*Early cowboys named this ruin for the prominent, tower-like central structure, which was actually a vertical stack of rooms that was once surrounded by other rooms. It may have been used as a dwelling or for ceremonial purposes.*

**The 23 *kivas*** or religious rooms at this site are thought to indicate that at least 23 clans lived here at various times.

### Wetherill Mesa Long House
*A scenic 12-mile (17-km) drive on a winding mountain road leads to Wetherill Mesa, named for the local rancher, Richard Wetherill, who found Cliff Palace in the 1880s. Two cliff dwellings here, Step and Long houses, are open to visitors.*

DRINK
**Coca-Cola**

# JOE & AGGIE

ROUTE
**66**

OPEN

MEXICAN & AMERICAN
**FOOD**

Free PARKING IN REAR of CAFE

# TRAVELERS' NEEDS

# WHERE TO STAY

Arizona has a long history of hospitality that is reflected in the wide variety of accommodations available. From lavish five-star resorts to simple rustic lodges, there is a wealth of options for visitors. You can choose modern or historic hotels, cozy bed-and-breakfasts, inns, convenient motels, or fully equipped apartments. For those seeking Western-style adventure, there are dude ranches, many of which provide luxurious lodgings with horseback riding and outdoor activities.

**Weatherford Hotel
sign in Flagstaff**

Accommodations in all price categories usually offer private bathrooms in addition to clean, comfortable rooms. Historic hotels provide a glimpse into Arizona's early, pioneering years, and the lobby areas of these impressive hotels are worth a visit even when staying elsewhere.

Hotel prices in the region tend to vary according to season. The listings provided on pages 124–31 recommend places in all price ranges, each representing the best of their kind for that area.

Teepees at the Wigwam Motel along Route 66 in Holbrook, Arizona

## HOTEL CLASSIFICATIONS

The tourist industry throughout Arizona is recognized for quality lodgings. A guideline to travelers is the diamond rating system of the American and Canadian Automobile Associations (AAA and CAA). Every accommodation, from the one-diamond motel to the five-diamond resort hotel, is rated for service, cleanliness, and the facilities offered. AAA members also benefit from discounts when they book in advance.

## TAXES

Accommodation tax varies across the region as it is charged by both state and city or county governments. Expect to pay between 10 and 14 percent of the room price in tax. Prices given for hotels in this book include taxes.

## LUXURY HOTELS

In Arizona, hotels come in every shape and size, including historic showplaces, such as Grand Canyon's El Tovar (see p125), originally built to impress East Coast investors and prove that the Southwest was an exciting tourist destination. Today, some of the most lavish hotels in Arizona are large resort hotels located in the Scottsdale and Phoenix area. A prime example is the Boulders Resort and Golden Door Spa in Scottsdale (see p129) with its two championship 18-hole golf courses, tennis courts, and gourmet dining. The areas around Sedona, Phoenix, and Tucson are famous for both luxury health spas and golf resorts. Small, independently owned "boutique" hotels offer opulent facilities combined with an intimate atmosphere and attentive service.

There are also many hotels aimed specifically at business travelers, offering weekly rates, and computer and fax outlets in rooms, although these services are now available in a range of hotels.

## CHAIN HOTELS & MOTELS

For the most part, you can count on efficient service, moderate prices, and comfortable (if bland) surroundings at a chain hotel. The most popular chains include **Holiday Inn**, **Comfort Inn**, **Best Western**, **Ramada Inns**, **Econolodge**, and **Super 8**. Particularly good value are suite hotels, such as **Country Inn and Suites** and **Embassy Suites**, which offer living rooms and kitchenettes for little more than the cost of a basic hotel room. Chain hotels also offer central reservation systems that can help you find a room at peak times. Motels provide rooms that are usually accessible from the parking area. They are often the only option in remote areas, and can vary from nostalgic Route 66 places (see pp28–9) to such bargain lodgings as Motel 6.

**A hotel in the Best
Western chain**

Jeanette's Bed-&-Breakfast in Flagstaff

## HISTORIC INNS & BED-&-BREAKFASTS

THERE ARE hundreds of excellent inns, and bed-and-breakfasts located throughout Arizona. Generally, inns are larger, with more spacious public areas and a dining room. Bed-and-breakfast establishments tend to be more homey. Both inns and bed-and-breakfasts may be found in restored or reconstructed historic buildings, and many are located in charming Victorian houses in historic towns. These lodgings pride themselves on providing a warm welcome and friendly service. For bookings, contact **Arizona Association of Bed & Breakfast Inns**, **Arizona Trails Bed & Breakfast Reservation Service**, and **Mi Casa Su Casa**.

## WESTERN HOTELS & DUDE RANCHES

IF YOU'VE EVER wanted to indulge your "Wild West" fantasies, there are plenty of historic hotels in which to do so. Between 1880 and 1920, Western towns gained prestige through the quality and grandeur of their hotels, and many boast extravagantly ornate decor. Today, many of them have been restored and offer great settings for a vacation. Prescott's Hassayampa Inn *(see p126)*, for example, with its grand lobby and attractive rooms, is both a historic hotel and an oasis for a relaxing, pampered stay.

Dude ranches offer visitors the chance to experience Western life. They first appeared in the 1920s – the name "dude" is a colloquialism meaning "a city-dweller unfamiliar with life on the range." Choices range from relaxing vacations that include leisurely horseback rides to working ranches where you participate in such activities as cattle roundups. Meals, accommodations, and horses are usually included in the price. Arizona has a **Dude Ranch Association** to help you find the perfect Western vacation.

Barbecue on the Lazy K Dude Ranch near Tucson

## CAMPGROUNDS & RV PARKS

CAMPGROUNDS FOR both tents and RVs (recreational vehicles) are found all over Arizona, and are especially popular in the national parks. The **National Forest Service** provides information on forest campgrounds, which range from extremely basic to those with running water and limited RV hookups.

# Choosing a Hotel

HOTELS HAVE BEEN selected for good value, excellent facilities, or location. This chart lists them by region in the same order as the guide. The color codes of each region are shown on the thumb tabs. Entries are alphabetical within price category. Prices given are in-season rates but always enquire as rates can vary from week to week and between weekdays and weekends.

| | NUMBER OF ROOMS | RESTAURANT | CHILDREN'S FACILITIES | GARDEN/TERRACE | SWIMMING POOL |
|---|---|---|---|---|---|
| **GRAND CANYON & NORTHERN ARIZONA** | | | | | |
| **BOULDER CITY:** *El Rancho Boulder Motel* $$ <br> 725 Nevada Way, NV 89005. ☎ *(702) 293-1085.* <br> With its 1940s architecture, the El Rancho Boulder Motel has clean rooms and is within walking distance of the town center. 🚐 TV P 🗑 | 38 | | | | ● |
| **CAMP VERDE:** *Camp Verde Comfort Inn* $$ <br> 340 N Goswick Way, AZ 86322. ☎ *(928) 567-9000, (866) 302-2300.* <br> FAX *(928) 567-1828.* W *www.comfortinn.com* A straightforward but well-kept chain motel, near several of the state's most interesting sights. 🚐 TV 🚻 P 🗑 | 85 | | | | ● |
| **CAMP VERDE:** *Hacienda de la Mariposa Bed & Breakfast* $$$$ <br> 3875 Stagecoach Rd, AZ 86322. ☎ *(928) 567-1490, (888) 520-9095.* <br> W *www.lamariposa-az.com* Lovely resort on Beaver Creek near Montezuma Castle, with large guest rooms in a Santa Fe-style building. <br> 🚐 TV P 📶 ⛱ 1 🏊 🗑 | 5 | | | ■ | |
| **COTTONWOOD:** *Best Western Cottonwood Inn* $$ <br> 993 S Main St, AZ 86326. ☎ *(928) 634-5575, (877) 377-6415.* FAX *(928) 634-5576.* <br> W *www.cottonwoodinn-az.com* The Best Western group has built a pleasant, spacious hotel here, with comfortable rooms. 🚐 TV 🚻 P 🗑 | 77 | ■ | ● | | ● |
| **FLAGSTAFF:** *Hotel Monte Vista* $$ <br> 100 N San Francisco St, AZ 86001. ☎ *(928) 779-6971, (800) 545 3068.* <br> FAX *(928) 779-2904.* W *www.hotelmontevista.com* Many rooms in this 1920s hotel are named after famous guests who stayed here, such as Bob Hope. <br> 🚐 TV P 🗑 | 50 | ■ | | | |
| **FLAGSTAFF:** *Hotel Weatherford* $$ <br> 23 N Leroux St, AZ 86001. ☎ *(928) 779-1919.* FAX *(928) 773-8951.* <br> W *www.weatherfordhotel.com* The 1890s Weatherford is one of Flagstaff's most distinctive hotels. Its rooms are decorated in antique style. 🚐 P 🗑 | 10 | ■ | | | |
| **FLAGSTAFF:** *Arizona Mountain Inn* $$$ <br> 4200 Lake Mary Rd, AZ 86001. ☎ *(928) 774-8959, (800) 239-5236.* FAX *(928) 774-8837.* <br> W *www.arizonamountaininn.com* Set amid ponderosa pines south of town this inn provides B&B suites and rustic cabins. Many rooms offer views of the pines. 🚐 🚻 P 📶 1 ⛰ 🏊 🗑 | 20 | | | | |
| **FLAGSTAFF:** *Hilton Garden Inn* $$$ <br> 350 W Forest Meadows St, AZ 86001. ☎ *(928) 226-8888, (800) 548-8690.* <br> FAX *(928) 556-9059.* W *www.hilton.com* This modest, medium-sized establishment provides everything from an ironing board to a microwave in each of the rooms. 🚐 TV 🚻 P 🍽 🗑 | 90 | | | | ● |
| **FLAGSTAFF:** *Little America Hotel* $$$ <br> 2515 E Butler Ave, AZ 86004. ☎ *(928) 779-2741, (800) 865-1401.* <br> FAX *(928) 779-7983.* W *www.flagstaff.littleamerica.com* This comfortable resort complex is set among pine trees, to the east of downtown Flagstaff. <br> 🚐 TV 🚻 P 🍽 🗑 | 247 | ■ | ● | ■ | ● |
| **FLAGSTAFF:** *Starlight Pines Bed-&-Breakfast* $$$ <br> 3380 E Lockett Rd, AZ 86004. ☎ *(800) 752-1912.* <br> This appealing B&B in a Victorian-style house has antique-filled rooms. A gourmet breakfast is included in the room price. 🚐 P 🗑 | 4 | | | | |
| **FLAGSTAFF:** *Sled Dog Inn* $$$ <br> 10155 Mountainaire Rd, AZ 86001. ☎ *(928) 525-6212, (800) 754-0664.* <br> FAX *(928) 525-1855.* W *www.sleddoginn.com* Modern mountain lodge in ponderosa pine woods south of Flagstaff. The full breakfast is served family-style. 🚐 🚻 P 📶 📶 1 ⛰ 🏊 🗑 | 10 | | | | |

| | Number of Rooms | Restaurant | Children's Facilities | Garden/Terrace | Swimming Pool |
|---|---|---|---|---|---|
| **Price categories** for a standard double room per night, inclusive of service charges, and any additional taxes:<br>⑤ under US$50<br>⑤⑤ US$50–$100<br>⑤⑤⑤ US$100–$150<br>⑤⑤⑤⑤ US$150–$200<br>⑤⑤⑤⑤⑤ US$200 plus<br><br>**RESTAURANT** Hotel restaurant or dining room usually open to non-residents unless otherwise stated.<br>**CHILDREN'S FACILITIES** Cribs and a baby-sitting service available. Some hotel restaurants have children's portions and high chairs.<br>**GARDEN/TERRACE** Hotels with a garden, courtyard, or terrace.<br>**SWIMMING POOL** Hotel with an indoor or outdoor swimming pool. | | | | | |
| **FLAGSTAFF:** *Inn at 410*  ⑤⑤⑤⑤<br>410 N Leroux St, AZ 86001. **(** (800) 774-2008. **FAX** (928) 774-6354.<br>**W** www.inn410.com Distinctive rooms in a restored 1907 Craftsman-style bungalow. Most rooms have fireplaces. | 9 | | | ■ | |
| **FLAGSTAFF:** *Radisson Woodlands Hotel Flagstaff*  ⑤⑤⑤⑤<br>1175 W Route 66, AZ 86001. **(** (928) 773-8888, (800) 333-3333.<br>**FAX** (928) 773-0597. One of the best chain hotels in town, this well-equipped establishment has excellent health and fitness facilities. | 183 | ■ | | | ● |
| **GRAND CANYON:** *Bright Angel Lodge*  ⑤⑤<br>Grand Canyon South Rim, AZ 86023. **(** (303) 297-2757, (888) 297-2757. **FAX** (303) 297-3175. **W** www.grandcanyonlodges.com Popular with hikers, it offers frugal rooms in its 1930s lodge, as well as appealing log cabins. | 89 | ■ | | ■ | |
| **GRAND CANYON:** *Best Western Grand Canyon Squire Inn*  ⑤⑤⑤<br>Hwy 64, AZ 86023. **(** (928) 638-2681, (800) 622-6966. **FAX** (928) 638-2782.<br>**W** www.grandcanyonsquire.com Large modern rooms and many activities, including bowling, tennis, whirlpool, and sauna. | 250 | ■ | ● | | ● |
| **GRAND CANYON:** *Phantom Ranch*  ⑤⑤⑤<br>Grand Canyon, AZ 86023. **(** (303) 297-2757, (888) 297-2757. **FAX** (303) 297-3175. **W** www.grandcanyonlodges.com Among the cottonwoods down in the canyon are a central lodge and timber cabins in a stunning setting. | 40 | ■ | | | |
| **GRAND CANYON:** *Grand Canyon Quality Inn & Suites*  ⑤⑤⑤⑤<br>SR 64, AZ 86023. **(** (928) 638-2673, (800) 221-2222. **FAX** (928) 638-9537.<br>**W** www.grandcanyonqualityinn.com This Southwest-style inn has spacious rooms, most of which have patios. The large atrium has a lounge, trees, flowers, and a restaurant. | 232 | ■ | ● | ■ | ● |
| **GRAND CANYON:** *Grand Hotel*  ⑤⑤⑤⑤<br>SR 64, AZ 86023. **(** (928) 638-3333. **FAX** (928) 638-3131. **W** www.visitgrandcanyon.com Comfortable, modern hotel with rustic flair. Rooms are tastefully decorated, and some have balconies. | 121 | ■ | | | ● |
| **GRAND CANYON (NORTH RIM):** *Grand Canyon Lodge*  ⑤⑤<br>Bright Angel Point, Grand Canyon, AZ 86052. **(** (303) 297-2757, (888) 297-2757.<br>**FAX** (928) 638-2554. **W** www.grandcanyonnorthrim.com The only in-park accommodation on the North Rim, this lodge has cabins and a few modern rooms. Advance reservations are essential. ● Oct–May. | 205 | ■ | | | |
| **GRAND CANYON (NORTH RIM):** *Kaibab Lodge*  ⑤⑤<br>Arizona 67, AZ 86003. **(** (928) 638-2389. **W** www.kaibab.org<br>The lodge is located in the pine and aspen woods beside a meadow in the Kaibab National Forest, just five miles from the entrance to the North Rim. Cabins are rustic with wood floors. ● Nov–mid-May. | 29 | ■ | | | |
| **GRAND CANYON VILLAGE:** *Maswik Lodge*  ⑤⑤⑤<br>Grand Canyon South Rim, AZ 86023. **(** (303) 297-2757, (888) 297-2757.<br>**FAX** (303) 297-3175. **W** www.grandcanyonlodges.com Popular with families, it is located at the west end of the village near the South Rim. | 278 | ■ | ● | | |
| **GRAND CANYON VILLAGE:** *Thunderbird & Kachina Lodges*  ⑤⑤⑤<br>Grand Canyon South Rim, AZ 86023. **(** (303) 297-2757, (888) 297-2757. **FAX** (303) 297-3175. **W** www.grandcanyonlodges.com The two modern lodges offer deluxe accommodation very close to the South Rim. | 100 | | | ■ | |
| **GRAND CANYON VILLAGE:** *Yavapai Lodge*  ⑤⑤⑤<br>Grand Canyon South Rim, AZ 86023. **(** (303) 297-2757, (888) 297-2757. **FAX** (303) 297-3175. **W** www.grandcanyonlodges.com Motel-style rooms in the pine and juniper woods beside the visitor center. ● Nov–Mar. | 358 | ■ | ● | ■ | |

For key to symbols see back flap

**Price categories** for a standard double room per night, inclusive of service charges, and any additional taxes:

$ under US$50
$$ US$50–$100
$$$ US$100–$150
$$$$ US$150–$200
$$$$$ US$200 plus

**RESTAURANT**
Hotel restaurant or dining room usually open to non-residents unless otherwise stated.

**CHILDREN'S FACILITIES**
Cribs and a baby-sitting service available. Some hotel restaurants have children's portions and high chairs.

**GARDEN/TERRACE**
Hotels with a garden, courtyard, or terrace.

**SWIMMING POOL**
Hotel with an indoor or outdoor swimming pool.

| | Price | Number of Rooms | Restaurant | Children's Facilities | Garden/Terrace | Swimming Pool |
|---|---|---|---|---|---|---|
| **GRAND CANYON VILLAGE:** *El Tovar Hotel*<br>Grand Canyon South Rim, AZ 86023. (303) 297-2757, (888) 297-2757. FAX (303) 297-3175. W www.grandcanyonlodges.com  This Edwardian hotel offers the most sumptuous accommodation in Grand Canyon National Park. Some rooms have panoramic views of the canyon. | $$$$ | 78 | ■ | ● | ■ | |
| **HOLBROOK:** *Wigwam Village Motel*<br>811 W Hopi Dr, AZ 86025. (928) 524-3048. Wigwam architecture has made this motel a Route 66 icon. Cozy interiors and original hickory furniture. | $ | 15 | | | | |
| **HOLBROOK:** *Ramada Limited*<br>2608 E Navajo Blvd, AZ 86025. (800) 272 6232. W www.ramada.com  Modern rooms in a standard Ramada motel. | $$ | 42 | | | | ● |
| **JEROME:** *Ghost City Inn*<br>541 N Main St, AZ 86331. (928) 634-4678, (888) 634-4678. W www.ghostcityinn.com  In a handsome Victorian villa, this well-maintained inn has tastefully decorated bedrooms and fabulous views. | $$$ | 6 | | | ■ | |
| **KINGMAN:** *Best Western A Wayfarer's Inn*<br>2815 E Andy Devine Ave, AZ 86401. (928) 753-6271, (800) 548-5695. FAX (928) 753-9608. This well-kept hotel is up to the chain's usual high standards, with a pool and indoor spa. Buffet breakfast is included. | $$ | 100 | | | | ● |
| **KINGMAN:** *Hotel Brunswick*<br>315 E Andy Devine Ave, AZ 86401. (928) 718-1800. FAX (928) 718-1801. W www.hotel-brunswick.com  Built in 1909, this restored hotel offers rooms decorated with quilts and antiques. | $$ | 24 | ■ | | | |
| **LAKE HAVASU CITY:** *Ramada Inn*<br>271 S Lake Havasu Ave, AZ 86403. (928) 855-1111, (800) 528-5169. FAX (928) 855-6228. W www.ramada.com  Recently revamped, this hotel offers spacious elegant rooms and is a short walk from London Bridge. | $$ | 193 | ■ | ● | | ● |
| **LAKE HAVASU CITY:** *Island Inn*<br>1300 McCulloch Blvd, AZ 86403. (928) 680-0606, (800) 243-9955. FAX (928) 680-4218. W www.havasumotels.com  Located on the island less than a mile from London Bridge, it offers standard rooms and a heated swimming pool and whirlpool. | $$$ | 117 | | | | ● |
| **LAKE HAVASU CITY:** *Nautical Inn Resort & Conference Center*<br>1000 McCulloch Blvd, AZ 86403. (928) 855-2141, (800) 892-2141. FAX (928) 855-8460. W www.nauticalinn.com  Spread along Lake Havasu's shore, it appeals to both family vacationers and conference organizers. Watersports are available. | $$$ | 139 | | | ■ | ● |
| **LAKE HAVASU CITY:** *Sands Vacation Resort*<br>2040 Mesquite Ave, AZ 86403. (928) 855-1388. FAX (928) 453-1802. W www.sands-resort.com  Standard rooms, outdoor swimming pool, whirlpool and exercise room. | $$$ | 42 | | | | ● |
| **PRESCOTT:** *Hotel St. Michael*<br>205 W Gurley St, AZ 86301. (928) 776-1999, (800) 678-3757. FAX (928) 776-7318. W www.stmichaelhotel.com  This 1900s hotel is located on Whiskey Row, a street of saloons in 1900. Clean, old fashioned rooms have a charming back-in-time style. Coffee shop onsite. | $$ | 69 | ■ | | | |
| **PRESCOTT:** *Hassayampa Inn*<br>122 E Gurley St, AZ 86301. (928) 778-9434, (800) 322-1927. FAX (928) 445-8590. W www.hassayampainn.com  This sophisticated, elegant hotel opened in 1927, and remains one of the best places to stay in Prescott. | $$$$ | 67 | ■ | | | |

**SEDONA:** *Star Motel*  $$  11
295 Jordan Rd, AZ 86336. 【 *(928) 282-3641.*
Conveniently located in the center of Sedona, this unassuming motel offers some of the most reasonably priced rooms in town. 🛏 TV P 🅿

**SEDONA:** *Cozy Cactus B&B*  $$$  5
80 Canyon Circle Dr, AZ 86351 【 *(928) 284-0082, (800) 788-2082.* FAX *(928) 284-4210.* W *www.cozycactus.com* Excellent family lodgings at this affordable, scenic ranch house B&B on the southern outskirts of Sedona. 🛏 P 🅿

**SEDONA:** *Sky Ranch Lodge*  $$$  94
1105 Airport Rd, AZ 86339. 【 *(928) 282-6400, (888) 708-6400.* FAX *(928) 282-7682.* W *www.skyranchlodge.com* Located at the top of Airport Mesa, this lodge offers a variety of rooms with great views. 🛏 TV P ▤ ❄ 1 ♨ ≋ 🅿

**SEDONA:** *Apple Orchard Inn*  $$$$  7
656 Jordan Rd, AZ 86336. 【 *(928) 282-5328, (800) 663-6968.* FAX *(928) 204-0044.* W *www.appleorchardbb.com* Beautiful and luxurious rooms, in varying Wild West decor. Gourmet breakfast is included, and a cooling pool and spa are available. 🛏 TV P ▤ ❄ 1 ♨ ≋ 🅿

**SEDONA:** *Enchantment Resort*  $$$$$  238
525 Boynton Canyon Rd, AZ 86336. 【 *(928) 282-2900, (800) 826-4180.* FAX *(928) 282-9249.* W *www.enchantmentresort.com* A ritzy complex of adobe-style houses, hidden away in the beautiful Boynton Canyon. 🛏 TV & P 🚻 🅿

**WILLIAMS:** *Canyon Country Inn*  $$  12
442 W Rte 66, AZ 86046. 【 *(928) 635-2349, (877) 405-3280.* W *www.thegrandcanyon.com/canyoncountryinn/* Located downtown, this inn has homey rooms with private baths, and serves a Continental breakfast. 🛏 TV P ▤ 1 ♨ ≋ 🅿

**WILLIAMS:** *Mountainside Inn*  $$  96
642 E Rte 66, AZ 86046. 【 *(928) 635-4431, (800) 462-9381.* FAX *(928) 635-2292.* Tucked away among pine trees, the Mountainside Inn offers tidy rooms, and is a convenient base for Grand Canyon. 🛏 TV & P 🅿

**WILLIAMS:** *Grand Canyon Railway Hotel*  $$$  297
235 N Grand Canyon Blvd, AZ 86046. 【 *(928) 635-4010, (800) 843-8724.* FAX *(928) 635-2180.* W *www.thetrain.com* This elegant hotel, next to the terminus of the Grand Canyon Railway, has a stately wood-beamed hall. 🛏 TV & P 🚻 🅿

**WINSLOW:** *La Posada*  $$$  37
303 E 2nd St (Route 66), AZ 86047. 【 *(928) 289-4366.* FAX *(928) 289-3873.* W *www.laposada.org* Great railroad-era hotel built in 1930 offers distinctive rooms with private baths. 🛏 TV & P ▤ 1 ♨ ≋ 🅿

## PHOENIX & SOUTHERN ARIZONA

**APACHE JUNCTION:** *Express Inn*  $$  40
1101 West Apache Trail, AZ 85220. 【 *(480) 982-9200.* FAX *(480) 671-6183.* Convenient for the Apache Trail, this small and intimate hotel has views of the Superstition Mountains, and serves a lavish breakfast. 🛏 TV & P 🅿

**BISBEE:** *Shady Dell*  $$  10
1 Douglas Rd, AZ 85603. 【 *(520) 432-3567.* Unique accommodation in vintage 1950s aluminum trailers, set in a 1927 trailer park. Original decor includes black-and-white TVs. P

**BISBEE:** *Bisbee Grand Hotel*  $$$  16
61 Main St, AZ 85603. 【 *(520) 432-5900, (800) 421-1909.* FAX *(520) 432-5900.* W *www.bisbeegrandhotel.com* This romantic restored Wild West-style hotel has a pressed-tin ceiling in the saloon. All rooms have private baths, but some are across the hallway. 🛏 TV P ▤ ❄ 1 ≋ 🅿

**BISBEE:** *Copper Queen Hotel*  $$$  48
11 Howell Ave, AZ 85603. 【 *(520) 432-2216.* FAX *(520) 432-4298.* W *www.copperqueen.com* Atmospheric, late 19th-century hotel, decorated in period style. A list of sightings of resident ghosts is available. 🛏 TV & P 🅿

**DOUGLAS:** *The Gadsden Hotel*  $$  160
1046 G Ave, AZ 85607. 【 *(520) 364-4481.* FAX *(520) 364-4005.* W *www.theriver.com/gadsdenhotel/* Opened in 1907, this historic hotel has sumptuously decorated rooms and public areas. 🛏 TV & P 🅿

**Price categories** for a standard double room per night, inclusive of service charges, and any additional taxes:
$ under US$50
$$ US$50–$100
$$$ US$100–$150
$$$$ US$150–$200
$$$$$ US$200 plus

**RESTAURANT**
Hotel restaurant or dining room usually open to non-residents unless otherwise stated.

**CHILDREN'S FACILITIES**
Cribs and a baby-sitting service available. Some hotel restaurants have children's portions and high chairs.

**GARDEN/TERRACE**
Hotels with a garden, courtyard, or terrace.

**SWIMMING POOL**
Hotel with an indoor or outdoor swimming pool.

| | Number of Rooms | Restaurant | Children's Facilities | Garden/Terrace | Swimming Pool |
|---|---|---|---|---|---|
| **DRAGOON:** *Triangle T Guest Ranch* $$ <br> I-10 exit 318, Dragoon Rd, AZ 85609. & FAX *(520) 586-7533.* <br> W *www.triangletguestranch.com* Historic ranch in Texas Canyon close to Kartchner Caverns and Tombstone. Comfortable cabins. | 8 | ■ | | | ● |
| **GREEN VALLEY:** *Best Western Green Valley* $$ <br> 111 S La Cañada, AZ 85614. *(520) 625-2250, (800) 344-1441.* FAX *(520) 625-0215.* <br> W *www.bestwestern.com* A great base for exploring San Xavier mission and Madera Canyon. Heated pool and spa. | 108 | ■ | | ■ | ● |
| **MESA:** *Saguaro Lake Ranch Resort* $$$ <br> 13020 Bush Hwy, AZ 85206. *(480) 984-2194.* FAX *(480) 380-1489.* <br> W *www.saguarolakeranch.com* Rustic resort with quaint, well-maintained rooms, swimming pool, and hiking and riding trails. Provides a great base for outdoor activities. ● *late May–Sep.* | 25 | ■ | ● | ■ | ● |
| **PHOENIX:** *Ramada Inn Downtown* $$ <br> 401 North 1st St, AZ 85004. *(602) 258-3411, (800) 272-6232.* FAX *(602) 258-3171.* <br> W *www.ramada.com* Situated in the downtown core near the convention center, the rooms here are stylish, brisk, and business-like. | 163 | ■ | | ■ | ● |
| **PHOENIX:** *Sunshine Hotel & Resort* $$ <br> 3600 N 2nd Ave, AZ 85031. *(602) 248-0222.* FAX *(602) 265-6331.* <br> W *www.sunshinehotel-az.com* Extensive facilities including a well-equipped gym, four pools, and a spa. | 274 | ■ | ● | ■ | ● |
| **PHOENIX:** *Best Western Central Phoenix Inn* $$$ <br> 1100 N Central Ave, AZ 85004. *(602) 252-2100, (800) 528-1234.* FAX *(602) 252-2731.* W *www.bwcpi.com* In the heart of the downtown business area, this chic hotel provides a free airport shuttle. | 107 | ■ | | | ● |
| **PHOENIX:** *Econo Lodge & Suites* $$$ <br> 202 E McDowell Rd, AZ 85004. *(602) 528-9100.* FAX *(602) 258-7259.* <br> W *www.econolodge.com* An inexpensive option, this simple, downtown hotel is within easy walking distance of the Heard Museum. | 48 | | | | ● |
| **PHOENIX:** *Hotel San Carlos* $$$ <br> 202 N Central Ave, AZ 85004. *(602) 253-4121, (866) 253-4121.* FAX *(602) 253-6668.* <br> W *www.hotelsancarlos.com* Located at the heart of downtown Phoenix, this designated historic hotel has rooms decorated in tasteful style. | 133 | | | | ● |
| **PHOENIX:** *Hyatt Regency Phoenix* $$$$$ <br> 122 N 2nd St, AZ 85004. *(602) 252-1234, (800) 233-1234.* FAX *(602) 254-9472.* <br> W *www.hyatt.com* This downtown hotel has modern rooms decorated in Southwest style, with an atrium lobby, revolving restaurant, swimming pool, and whirlpool. | 712 | ■ | ● | | ● |
| **PHOENIX:** *Pointe At South Mountain Resort* $$$$$ <br> 7777 S Pointe Parkway, AZ 85044. *(602) 438-9000, (877) 800-4888.* FAX *(602) 431-6535.* W *www.pointesouthmtn.com* In the hills south of Phoenix, this resort offers every amenity, including golf and four restaurants. | 640 | ■ | ● | ■ | ● |
| **PHOENIX:** *Ritz-Carlton Hotel* $$$$ <br> 2401 E Camelback Rd, AZ 85016. *(602) 468-0700, (800) 241-3333.* <br> FAX *(602) 468-0793.* W *www.ritzcarlton.com* This hotel occupies a modern tower with Neo-Classical flourishes. Large, comfortable rooms. | 281 | ■ | | | ● |
| **PHOENIX:** *Arizona Biltmore Resort & Spa* $$$$$ <br> 2400 E Missouri Ave, AZ 85016. *(602) 955-6600, (800) 950-0086.* <br> FAX *(602) 381-7600.* W *www.arizonabiltmore.com* Designed by Frank Lloyd Wright, this 1930s hotel has excellent facilities and grounds. | 746 | ■ | ● | ■ | ● |

**PHOENIX:** *Royal Palms Hotel*    $$$$$    117
5200 E Camelback Rd, AZ 85018. ☎ (602) 840-3610, (800) 672-6011.
FAX (602) 840-6927. w www.royalpalmshotel.com Spanish Mediterranean hotel
with a restful atmosphere, courtyards, and gardens. 🛏 24 TV ⅃ P ♈ 🈂 📶 🍽 ◼ ✉

**PHOENIX:** *The Wigwam Resort*    $$$$$    331
300 E Wigwam Blvd, AZ 85251. ☎ (623) 935-3811, (800) 327-0396. FAX (623) 535-
1309. w www.wigwamresort.com The resort boasts three 18-hole golf courses,
two pools, and a choice of fabulous restaurants. 🛏 24 TV ⅃ P 🍽 ✉

**PINETOP-LAKESIDE:** *Lake of the Woods*    $$$    35
2244 W White Mountain Blvd, AZ 85929. ☎ (928) 368-5353.
w www.privatelake.com Cabins are located near the resort's private lake.
Canoes are available for touring the lake. 🛏 ⅃ P 🈂 🈂 📶 🍽 ✉

**SCOTTSDALE:** *Ramada–Scottsdale*    $$$    92
6935 5th Ave, AZ 85251. ☎ (480) 994-9461, (800) 553-2666. FAX (480) 947-1695.
w www.ramada.com Spacious rooms in a standard motel centrally located
near the Fifth Avenue shopping district. 🛏 TV P ◼ 1 🈂 📶 🍽 ✉

**SCOTTSDALE:** *Hyatt Regency Scottsdale Resort at Gainey Ranch*    $$$$$    494
7500 E Doubletree Ranch Rd, AZ 85258. ☎ (800) 554-9288, (480) 991-3388.
FAX (480) 483-5550. w www.scottsdale.hyatt.com Contemporary architecture, lush
gardens, and ten swimming pools. 🛏 24 TV ⅃ P 🍽 ✉

**SCOTTSDALE:** *Boulders Resort and Golden Door Spa*    $$$$$    215
34631 N Tom Darlington Dr, AZ 85377. ☎ (480) 488-9009, (800) 553-1717.
FAX (480) 488-4118. w www.wyndham.com Luxurious golf and spa
resort with hiking and jogging trails. 🛏 TV ⅃ P ♈ ◼ 📶
🈂 ✉ 1 🈂 📶 🍽 ✉

**SCOTTSDALE:** *The Phoenician*    $$$$$    654
6000 E Camelback Rd, AZ 85251. ☎ (480) 941-8200, (800) 888-8234. FAX (480) 947-
4311. w www.thephoenician.com An extravagant resort complex, with golf
course, tennis courts, and nine swimming pools. 🛏 24 TV ⅃ P 🍽 ✉

**SCOTTSDALE:** *Scottsdale Princess*    $$$$$    651
7575 E Princess Dr, AZ 85255. ☎ (480) 585-4848, (800) 441-1414. FAX (480) 585-0086.
w www.fairmont.com A first-rate resort-hotel in a handsome setting with all
amenities, and several award-winning restaurants. 🛏 24 TV ⅃ P 🍽 ✉

**SHOW LOW:** *Best Western Paint Pony Lodge*    $$$    50
581 W Deuce of Clubs Ave, AZ 85901. ☎ (928) 537-5773. FAX (928) 537-5766.
Standard rooms, some with whirlpool tubs. 🛏 TV ⅃ P ◼ 1 🈂 📶 ✉

**SHOW LOW:** *Holiday Inn Express*    $$$    71
151 W Deuce of Clubs Ave, AZ 85901. ☎ (928) 537-5115, (800) 465-4329.
FAX (928) 537-2929. The usual multifloor motel with standard rooms and
suites, a few with whirlpool tubs. 🛏 TV ⅃ P ◼ 1 🈂 📶 🍽 ✉

**TOMBSTONE:** *Silver Nugget Bed & Breakfast*    $$    4
520 E Allen St, AZ 85638. ☎ (520) 457-9223. FAX (520) 457-3471.
w www.tombstone1880.com/silvernugget/ A friendly B&B with a different
Western theme in each of the rooms. P ✉

**TOMBSTONE:** *Tombstone Boarding House*    $$    6
108 N 4th St, AZ 85638. ☎ (520) 457-3716, (877) 225-1319.
w www.tombstoneboardinghouse.com Country inn furnished with antiques
and collectibles from the 1880s. 🛏 P ♈ 🈂 📶 ✉

**TOMBSTONE:** *Best Western Lookout Lodge*    $$$    40
Hwy 80 W, AZ 85638. ☎ (520) 457-2223, (877) 652-6772. FAX (520) 457-3870.
w www.bestwestern.com Large rooms look out over the desert and the
mountains. Complimentary full breakfast. 🛏 TV P 🈂 ✉

**TUCSON:** *Sam Hughes Inn Bed & Breakfast*    $$    4
2020 E 7th St, AZ 85719. ☎ (520) 861-2191. w www.samhughesinn.com
This California mission-style inn located in the National Historic District of
Tucson has Southwestern decor and a superb breakfast. 🛏 P ◼ 🈂 📶 ✉

**TUCSON:** *El Presidio Bed & Breakfast Inn*    $$$    4
297 N Main Ave, AZ 85701. ☎ (800) 349-6151, (520) 623-6151. FAX (520) 623-3860.
Restored Victorian adobe mansion set around a pretty courtyard.
Delicious breakfasts included. 🛏 TV P

*For key to symbols see back flap*

**Price categories** for a standard double room per night, inclusive of service charges, and any additional taxes:

- $ under US$50
- $$ US$50–$100
- $$$ US$100–$150
- $$$$ US$150–$200
- $$$$$ US$200 plus

**RESTAURANT**
Hotel restaurant or dining room usually open to non-residents unless otherwise stated.

**CHILDREN'S FACILITIES**
Cribs and a baby-sitting service available. Some hotel restaurants have children's portions and high chairs.

**GARDEN/TERRACE**
Hotels with a garden, courtyard, or terrace.

**SWIMMING POOL**
Hotel with an indoor or outdoor swimming pool.

| | NUMBER OF ROOMS | RESTAURANT | CHILDREN'S FACILITIES | GARDEN/TERRACE | SWIMMING POOL |
|---|---|---|---|---|---|
| **TUCSON:** *Windmill Suites* $$$ <br> 4250 N Campbell Ave, AZ 85718. ☎ (520) 577-0007, (800) 547-4747. FAX (520) 577-0045. W www.windmillinns.com Located in an upscale shopping plaza, this hotel is great value. It offers complimentary breakfast. | 122 | | | | ● |
| **TUCSON:** *Hacienda del Sol Guest Ranch Resort* $$$$ <br> 5601 N Hacienda del Sol Rd, AZ 85718. ☎ (800) 728-6514, (520) 299-1501. FAX (520) 299-5554. W www.haciendadelsol.com Overlooking desert landscape, this luxury retreat in the hills above town has been popular since the 1940s when stars such as Katherine Hepburn used to visit. | 30 | ■ | | ■ | ● |
| **TUCSON:** *Lodge on the Desert* $$$$ <br> 306 N Alvernon Way, AZ 85711. ☎ (520) 325-3366, (800) 456-5634. FAX (520) 327-5834. W www.lodgeonthedesert.com A tranquil hideaway featuring adobe-style buildings with charming rooms amid pretty desert gardens. | 35 | ■ | | ■ | ● |
| **TUCSON:** *Arizona Inn* $$$$$ <br> 2200 E Elm St, AZ 85719. ☎ (520) 325-1541, (800) 993-1093. FAX (520) 881-5830. W www.arizonainn.com This pink stucco resort hotel, opened in 1930, features spacious rooms in lush grounds. | 86 | ■ | | ■ | ● |
| **TUCSON:** *Canyon Ranch Health Resort–Tucson* $$$$$ <br> 8600 E Rockcliff Rd, AZ 85710. ☎ (520) 749-9000, (800) 742-9000. FAX (520) 749-7755. W www.canyonranch.com Spa with four-nights minimum stay. Three healthy meals a day, spa, activities, and wellness services are included in the package. | 180 | | | ■ | ● |
| **TUCSON:** *Lazy K Bar Guest Ranch* $$$$$ <br> 8401 N Scenic Dr, AZ 85743. ☎ (520) 744-3050. FAX (520) 744-7628. W www.lazykbar.com An authentic ranch offering desert trail rides and dance lessons as part of the package. | 24 | ■ | ● | ■ | ● |
| **TUCSON:** *Tanque Verde Guest Ranch* $$$$$ <br> 14301 E Speedway Blvd, AZ 85748. ☎ (520) 296-6275, (800) 234-3833. FAX (520) 721-9426. W www.tvgr.com This Southwestern-style resort offers horseback riding, hiking, and nature walks. Located in the Sonoran Desert near Saguaro National Park. | 74 | ■ | | ■ | ● |
| **YUMA:** *Best Western InnSuites* $$$ <br> 1450 Castle Dome Ave, AZ 85365. ☎ (928) 783-8341, (888) 986-2784. FAX (928) 783-1349. W www.innsuites.com Large suites and standard rooms. Breakfast buffet is included, and there are tennis and basketball courts and a whirlpool. | 166 | ■ | ● | | ● |
| **YUMA:** *La Fuente Inn & Suites* $$$ <br> 1513 E 16th St, AZ 85365. ☎ (928) 329-1814, (800) 841-1814. FAX (928) 343-2671. W www.lafuenteinn.com Complimentary Continental breakfast is available daily, and early evening cocktails with complimentary appetizers are served Monday through Thursday. | 97 | | | ■ | ● |
| **THE FOUR CORNERS** | | | | | |
| **AZTEC:** *Step Back Inn* $$ <br> 103 W Aztec Blvd, NM 87410. ☎ (505) 334-1200. FAX (505) 334-9858. Aztec's newest hotel is clean, comfortable, and close to the amenities of the downtown area. | 39 | | | | |
| **BLUFF:** *Desert Rose Inn* $$ <br> 701 W Highway 191, UT 84512. ☎ (435) 672-2303, (888) 475-7673. FAX (435) 672-2217. W www.desertroseinn.com Located on the west side of Bluff, the wood exterior lodge has 30 modern rooms, each uniquely decorated in a Southwest mode. | 36 | | | | |

**Bluff:** *Recapture Lodge*  $$  26
Hwy 191, UT 84512. ( (435) 672-2281. FAX (435) 672-2284.
W www.recapturelodge.com  This country lodge hosts regular speakers on local geology and archeology, and offers adventure tours.

**Cameron:** *Cameron Trading Post*  $$  66
Rte 89, AZ 86020. ( (928) 679-2231, (800) 338-7385. FAX (928) 679-2350.
W www.camerontradingpost.com  This working trading post has a delightful garden and fine Native arts gallery. The rooms are comfortable.

**Chinle:** *Holiday Inn, Canyon de Chelly*  $$  108
Garcia Trading Post, Canyon de Chelly, AZ 86503. ( (928) 674-5000, (800) 465-4329. FAX (928) 674-8264. W www.holiday-inn.com  A hotel complex, it houses the Garcia Restaurant *(see p140)*. Tours of Canyon de Chelly can be arranged.

**Chinle:** *Thunderbird Lodge*  $$$  73
Canyon De Chelly, AZ 86503. ( (928) 674-5841, (800) 679-2473.
FAX (928) 674-5844. W www.tbirdlodge.com  Part of the excellent complex at the mouth of Canyon de Chelly. Rooms are tastefully decorated.

**Cortez:** *Kelly Place*  $$  11
14663 Rd G, CO 81321. ( (800) 745-4885. FAX (970) 565-3540.
W www.kellyplace.com  This quiet country retreat is set among contrasting landscapes of fruit orchards and red rock canyons, and offers group workshops on local Native culture and archeology.

**Farmington:** *Best Western Inn at Farmington*  $$$  192
700 Scott Ave, NM 87401. ( (505) 327-5221, (800) 528-1234. FAX (505) 327-1565.
W www.bestwestern.com  This good-value and dependable chain hotel has a pool, which is very inviting in summer.

**Mesa Verde National Park:** *Far View Motor Lodge*  $$$  150
Mile Marker 15, Mancos, CO 81328. ( (800) 449-2288. FAX (970) 533-7831.
W www.visitmesaverde.com  Away from the bustle of the park, this modern hotel has great views across the mesa and Montezuma Valley.
● Oct 15–Apr.

**Mexican Hat:** *Valley of the Gods Bed & Breakfast*  $$$  4
Valley of the Gods Rd, UT 84531. ( (970) 749-1164.
W www.valleyofthegods.cjb.net  As "away from it all" as you can get, this pleasant house is the only building in the Valley of the Gods.

**Monument Valley:** *Gouldings Lodge*  $$$$  62
Off Hwy 163, UT 84536. ( (435) 727-3231, (800) 874-0902.
FAX (435) 727-3344. W www.gouldings.com  This famous inn has hosted movie stars and directors from almost every movie made here. Each room has a balcony with a superb view of Monument Valley. A museum features the cabin John Wayne used in an early movie.

**Page:** *Best Western Arizona Inn*  $$  103
716, Rim View Dr, AZ 86040. ( (928) 645-2466, (800) 826-2718.
FAX (928) 645-2053. This inn has modern rooms, many of which offer panoramic views of Lake Powell.

**Page:** *Lake Powell Resort*  $$$  350
100 Lakeshore Dr, AZ 86040. ( (928) 645-2433, (800) 528-6154. FAX (928) 645-1031. W www.visitlakepowell.com  Lakeside lodging on the shore of Lake Powell with resort-style amenities. Powerboat and houseboat rentals are available.
● mid-Nov–mid-Mar.

**Second Mesa, Hopi Reservation:** *Hopi Cultural Center Hotel*  $$  33
Rte 264, AZ 86043. ( (928) 734-2401. FAX (928) 734-6651.
W www.hopiculturalcenter.com  This renovated hotel with an adobe look and pastel interior is the best accommodation for miles around.

**Window Rock:** *Quality Inn*  $$  56
48 W Hwy 264, AZ 86515. ( (928) 871-4108, (800) 662-6189. FAX (928) 871-5466.
W www.navajonationinn.com  This attractive, comfortable hotel is one of the Navajo reservation's showpieces. Rooms are immaculately clean, with private bathrooms.

For key to symbols see back flap

# WHERE TO EAT

As well as offering high quality and top-class regional cusine, Arizona offers an exciting range of eating experiences, especially in its larger cities. Phoenix, Scottsdale, Tucson, and Sedona rival any city in the United States for the quality of ingredients and variety of cuisine available, with ambiences ranging from rustic to romantic. In keeping with its newly-acquired, international status, Southwestern cuisine is served in a growing number of casual but stylish

**Pub sign in Flagstaff**

cafés. Steakhouses, too, abound in this region. Local restaurants usually serve the best Mexican food, and there are also restaurants with a cowboy or Mexican theme, where one can get an inexpensive meal and great entertainment. In small towns, the best food is served in swish restaurants in hotels.

The restaurants on pages 134–41 have been chosen for their quality, location, and good value. Some typical Mexican dishes available in Arizona are shown in the box at the bottom of this section.

## PRICES & TIPPING

EATING OUT in Arizona is very reasonable, and even expensive restaurants offer good value. Light meals in cafés and diners usually cost under $10, while chain restaurants serve complete dinners for under $15. Mexican restaurants offer combination plates for $8–$12. At finer restaurants, dinner entrées range from $15 to $30, and diners can still buy a three-course meal, excluding wine, for under $50.

The standard tip is 15 percent of the cost of the meal. However, leave up to 20 percent if the service is good. Sales tax is not shown on the menu and will add around 5–7 percent to the cost of a meal.

**A tortilla and bean stall at Tumacacori, Southern Arizona**

## TYPES OF FOOD & RESTAURANTS

DINING ESTABLISHMENTS in Arizona range from small and friendly diners and cafés, offering hearty burgers and snacks, to gourmet restaurants that serve the latest Southwestern and fusion

cuisine, to lavish dining rooms in the top-class and upscale resorts found in and around Phoenix, Scottsdale, and Tucson.

Starting at the lower end of the scale, fast food is a way of life throughout the state, and a string of outlets such as McDonald's, Burger King, Wendy's, and Arby's are found along the main strips of most towns in the state. They serve the usual inexpensive variations of burgers, fries, and soft drinks. Chains such as Applebee's and Denny's offer more variety, with soups, salads, sandwiches, meals, and desserts. These are generally good value, but the quality varies from one establishment to the next. Pizza chains are also ubiquitous in the region. Mid-range eating places can

## AN INTRODUCTION TO SOUTHWESTERN FOOD

Southwestern food reflects the region's strong Hispanic and Native cultures. Mexican food and its more refined cousin, Southwestern cuisine, enjoy a following around the globe. One of the pleasures of a visit to Arizona is discovering the great variety of restaurants that serve dishes made with the freshest ingredients, and cooked with expertise. The chili pepper is at the heart of Southwestern cuisine, and some pack a powerful bite, but there are other milder varieties that add flavor without heat. Most menus in restaurants frequented by tourists provide an explanation of the dishes, and friendly staff offer advice. The region's other great staple is beef, and there is no shortage of good steaks and burgers in most areas.

**Red and green chilis**

**Huevos rancheros**
*Fried egg on a soft tortilla, served with chili sauce, melted cheese, and refried beans, is a favorite for breakfast.*

include a range of ethnic cuisine such as Italian, Greek, Chinese, Japanese, and Indian. Many good restaurants that fall into this category can be found in shopping malls.

Native American food is found in many areas of the state, especially on reservations, and is reasonably priced. Frybread forms the base of many meals, and is often topped with meat, beans, cheese, lettuce, and tomatoes.

Steakhouses serving mesquite barbecue, steaks, and ribs are found across Arizona in a wide variety of price ranges. Some of these restaurants also serve fresh mountain-trout and seafood, and provide live Western-style entertainment.

Mexican restaurants are popular and proliferate in the state. They vary from roadside stands and snack bars to upscale restaurants, where the food is complemented by the ambience of adobe-style buildings with lush interior courtyards that provide a romantic atmosphere.

"Southwestern" cuisine is a fusion of Native American, Hispanic, and international influences, and is increasingly showcased in Arizona's finest restaurants. This cuisine creates flavorful dishes using traditional Southwest ingredients such as corn, chilis, beans, cilantro, tomatillos, and pine nuts.

Southwestern decor at the Two Micks Cantina Grill in Tucson

## VEGETARIAN

SOUTHWESTERN cuisine is largely meat based. Vegetarians may not find much variety outside the larger cities and resorts. However, salad bars are available everywhere, from fine restaurants to fast food chains. Salads can be a complete meal as they often come with meat and seafood, but vegetarian orders are usually accommodated. Many fast food chains now serve salads, soups, or baked potatoes to cater to the more health-conscious customer.

The more expensive restaurants, and those affiliated with hotels, are usually willing to provide vegetarian meals on request when they have the ingredients. It is a good idea to phone ahead.

## DISABLED FACILITIES

RESTAURANTS ARE required to provide wheelchair access and a ground-level restroom by law, but check with older places in advance.

## ALCOHOL

BEER, PARTICULARLY the many kinds of *cervezas* imported from Mexico, is the most popular drink in the region. Arizona has a growing brew-pub and microbrewery industry as well. Wine and other alcoholic drinks are also available throughout the state, except on Native reservations.

The finer restaurants usually serve a wide variety of alcoholic beverages. Visitors need to be 21 to buy alcohol. Be sure to carry ID, as it is often requested before you are served.

**Margarita cocktail**

**Enchiladas**
*Rolled corn tortillas, filled with cheese, beef or chicken, and usually topped with a red chili sauce and melted cheese.*

**Tacos with guacamole**
*A popular snack food. Tortillas folded in half and filled with ground beef, beans, onions, tomatoes, lettuce, and grated cheese.*

**Chili relleno**
*A whole green chili is stuffed with cheese, dipped in a light egg batter, and deep fried. The chili is sometimes stuffed with rice or meat.*

# Choosing a Restaurant

THE RESTAURANTS in this guide have been selected across a wide range of price categories for their exceptional food, good value, or interesting location. Entries are listed by region, in alphabetical order within price category. The thumb tabs on the pages use the same color-coding as the corresponding regional chapters in the main section of this guide.

| | Outdoor Eating | Vegetarian Specialties | Bar Area | Fixed-Price Menu | Children's Facilities |
|---|---|---|---|---|---|
| **GRAND CANYON & NORTHERN ARIZONA** | | | | | |
| **CAMP VERDE:** *The Ranch House* $$<br>N Montezuma Ave, AZ 86322. 🕻 *(928) 567-4492.*<br>Located next to the Beaver Creek golf course at Lake Montezuma, this restaurant offers an extensive menu of steak, prime ribs, seafood, and homemade desserts. 🕭 ▤ ✂ 🎵 🎵 | ■ | | ■ | | |
| **FLAGSTAFF:** *Charly's Pub & Grill* $<br>23 N Leroux, AZ 86001. 🕻 *(928) 779-1919.*<br>This fast-moving restaurant is popular for its enticing range of steaks, seafood, burgers, and sandwiches, as well as Mexican specialties. 🕭 🕭 | | ● | ■ | | ■ |
| **FLAGSTAFF:** *Downtown Diner* $<br>7 E Aspen Ave, AZ 86001. 🕻 *(928) 774-3492.*<br>An atmospheric spot, the diner serves inexpensive, filling American meals from early morning. 🕭 | | ● | | | |
| **FLAGSTAFF:** *San Felipe's Cantina* $<br>103 N Leroux, AZ 86001. 🕻 *(928) 779-6000.*<br>A popular and lively spot, offering an excellent range of Baja-style Mexican dishes. The fish tacos are especially tasty. 🕭 🕭 | | ● | ■ | | ■ |
| **FLAGSTAFF:** *Black Bart's* $$<br>2760 E Butler Ave, AZ 86001. 🕻 *(928) 779-3142.*<br>Enjoy great steaks and seafood in this appealing Western atmosphere. Waiting staff sing Broadway songs, showtunes, and old favorites. 🕭 🕭 | | | ■ | | ■ |
| **FLAGSTAFF:** *Cottage Place Restaurant* $$$<br>126 W Cottage Ave, AZ 86001. 🕻 *(928) 774-8431.*<br>One of Flagstaff's best restaurants, the menu includes vegetarian dishes and a good selection of seafood and meats. ● *L; Mon.* 🕭 🍷 🕭 | | ● | | | |
| **FLAGSTAFF:** *Pasto* $$$<br>19 E Aspen, AZ 86001. 🕻 *(928) 779-1937.*<br>A busy, downtown restaurant, it offers excellent Italian cuisine. Vegetarian and wheat-free dishes are also served. ● *L Sat & Sun.* 🕭 🕭 | | ● | | | ■ |
| **GRAND CANYON:** *Bright Angel Restaurant* $$<br>Bright Angel Lodge, AZ 86023. 🕻 *(928) 638-2631.*<br>This café-restaurant serves light meals and salad, as well as full meals. 🕭 🕭 | | ● | | | ■ |
| **GRAND CANYON:** *Canyon Star Restaurant* $$<br>SR 64, AZ 86023. 🕻 *(928) 638-3333.*<br>Located in the Grand Hotel *(see p125)*, the restaurant features a dinner theater with Native American programs and cowboy songs. 🕭 ▤ ✂ 🎵 🕭 | | ● | ■ | | ■ |
| **GRAND CANYON:** *Grand Canyon Lodge* $$<br>North Rim, AZ 86023. 🕻 *(928) 638-2611, (888) 297-2757.*<br>Though remote, this lodge *(see p125)* manages to sustain a good restaurant, where American dishes are the order of the day.<br>● *Mid-Oct–mid-May.* 🕭 *Partial.* 🕭 | | ● | ■ | | |
| **GRAND CANYON:** *Grand Canyon Quality Inn & Suites Restaurant* $$<br>SR 64, AZ 86023. 🕻 *(928) 638-2673.*<br>Enjoyable setting with choice of buffet or à la carte. Large selection of salads and fruit, as well as steak and seafood choices. 🕭 ▤ ✂ 🕭 | | ● | ■ | | |
| **GRAND CANYON:** *Phantom Ranch* $$<br>Grand Canyon, AZ 86023. 🕻 *(888) 297-2757.*<br>Situated on the canyon floor and accessible only by hiking or mule trail, Phantom Ranch *(see p125)* has a canteen providing meals by advance reservation only. The house specialty is the "Hiker's Stew." 🕭 | ■ | ● | | | |

**Price categories** include a three-course meal for one, a glass of house wine, and all unavoidable extra charges including tax:
$ under US$25
$$ US$25–$35
$$$ US$35–$50
$$$$ US$50–$70
$$$$$ over US$70

**OUTDOOR EATING**
Some tables on a patio or terrace.
**VEGETARIAN SPECIALTIES**
One menu always includes a selection of vegetarian dishes.
**BAR AREA**
There is a bar area or cocktail bar within the restaurant, available for drinks and/or bar snacks.
**FIXED-PRICE MENU**
A fixed-price menu available at a good rate, for lunch, dinner or both, usually with three courses.
**CHILDREN'S FACILITIES**
Small portions and/or high chairs available on request.

| | OUTDOOR EATING | VEGETARIAN SPECIALTIES | BAR AREA | FIXED-PRICE MENU | CHILDREN'S FACILITIES |
|---|---|---|---|---|---|
| **GRAND CANYON:** *Coronado Room*  $$$ <br> Hwy 64, AZ 86023. ( *(928) 638-2681.* <br> Located in the Grand Canyon Squire Inn, it serves prime ribs, steaks, barbecue ribs, seafood, pasta, and Mexican dishes. <br> ● *L.* & ▤ ⚡ 🗐 | ● | | ■ | | ■ |
| **GRAND CANYON (NORTH RIM):** *Kaibab Lodge Restaurant*  $$ <br> Arizona 67, AZ 86003. ( *(928) 638-2389.* <br> Located in the main lodge, which also has a comfortable sitting area and stone fireplace, the restaurant serves a limited menu of simple, basic food. ● *Nov–mid-May.* ▤ ⚡ 🗐 | | | | | |
| **GRAND CANYON VILLAGE:** *Maswik Cafeteria*  $ <br> Grand Canyon South Rim, AZ 86023. ( *(928) 638-2631.* <br> Maswik Lodge *(see p125)* offers this inexpensive, self-service café, with Mexican food as its specialty. There is also a cocktail lounge. & 🗐 | ● | | ■ | | ■ |
| **GRAND CANYON VILLAGE:** *El Tovar Hotel*  $$$$ <br> Grand Canyon South Rim, AZ 86023. ( *(928) 638-2631.* <br> El Tovar has a large dining room overlooking the South Rim. The menu is wide-ranging, and reservations for dinner are essential. & 💺 🗐 | ● | | ■ | | |
| **HOLBROOK:** *Butterfield Stage Co.*  $ <br> 609 W Hopi Dr, AZ 86025. ( *(928) 524-3447.* <br> This rustic steakhouse serves barbecue ribs and steaks. ● *L.* ▤ ⚡ 🗐 | | | ■ | | |
| **HOLBROOK:** *Mesa Italianna Restaurant*  $$ <br> 2318 Navajo Blvd, AZ 86025. ( *(928) 524-6696.* <br> Fine Italian cuisine includes veal, chicken, shrimp, pasta, and pizza. Chicken Jerusalem in a butter, garlic, shrimp, and lemon sauce is popular. A children's menu is available. ● *Sat & Sun L.* & ▤ ⚡ 🗐 | ● | | ■ | | ■ |
| **JEROME:** *English Kitchen*  $ <br> 119 Jerome Ave, AZ 86331. ( *(928) 634-2132.* <br> This café serves standard but well-prepared meals in premises that served as an opium den in Jerome's wild past. ● *D; Mon.* 🗐 | | ■ | ● | | |
| **JEROME:** *Flatiron Café*  $ <br> 416 N Main St, AZ 86331. ( *(928) 634-2733.* <br> Great salads are a specialty of this amiable café in the center of Jerome. Also try the tasty scrambled eggs at breakfast. ● *D.* 🗐 | | ■ | ● | | |
| **KINGMAN:** *Mr D'z Route 66 Diner*  $ <br> 105 E Andy Devine, AZ 86401. ( *(928) 718-0066.* <br> Painted pink and peppermint green, there is no missing this cheerful diner, which is crammed with Route 66 memorabilia. & 🗐 | | | | | ■ |
| **KINGMAN:** *Hubb's Café*  $$ <br> 315 E Andy Devine Ave, AZ 86401. ( *(928) 718-1800.* Ⓦ *www.hotel-brunswick.com* <br> Located in the restored 1909 Hotel Brunswick *(see p126)*, the restaurant serves excellent French cuisine, steak, and Southwestern dishes. <br> ● *Sun.* & ▤ ⚡ 🎵 🗐 | ● | | ■ | | |
| **LAKE HAVASU CITY:** *Krystal's Fine Dining*  $ <br> 460 El Camino Way, AZ 86403. ( *(928) 453-2999.* <br> Fine dining in a casual atmosphere. Specialties are steaks, ribs, and seafood. ● *L; Dec 25.* & ▤ ⚡ 🗐 | ● | | ■ | | |
| **LAKE HAVASU CITY:** *Mudshark Brewing Co.*  $$ <br> 210 Swanson Ave, AZ 86403. ( *(928) 453-2981.* Ⓦ *www.mudsharkbrewingco.com* <br> American and Southwest food including steak, ribs, pork and seafood. The creative entrées, salads, and pizzas exceed the usual pub fare. 🎵 ▤ ⚡ 🗐 | ■ | | ● | ■ | |

**Price categories** include a three-course meal for one, a glass of house wine, and all unavoidable extra charges including tax:
$ under US$25
$$ US$25–$35
$$$ US$35–$50
$$$$ US$50–$70
$$$$$ over US$70

**OUTDOOR EATING**
Some tables on a patio or terrace.
**VEGETARIAN SPECIALTIES**
One menu always includes a selection of vegetarian dishes.
**BAR AREA**
There is a bar area or cocktail bar within the restaurant, available for drinks and/or bar snacks.
**FIXED-PRICE MENU**
A fixed-price menu available at a good rate, for lunch, dinner or both, usually with three courses.
**CHILDREN'S FACILITIES**
Small portions and/or high chairs available on request.

| Restaurant | Price | Outdoor Eating | Vegetarian Specialties | Bar Area | Fixed-Price Menu | Children's Facilities |
|---|---|---|---|---|---|---|
| **LAKE HAVASU CITY:** *Shugrue's*<br>1425 McCulloch Blvd, AZ 86403. ☎ *(928) 453-1400.* The restaurant has a view of the London Bridge. Garlic crusted halibut and five-star pepper steak are popular dishes. ● *Dec 25.* ♿ ▤ ♫ ✍ | $$$ | | | ■ | | |
| **PRESCOTT:** *Murphy's*<br>201 N Cortez St, AZ 86301. ☎ *(928) 445-4044.* Housed in a historic 1890 building, this restaurant serves mesquite-broiled steak, prime-rib, and seafood. ● *Day after Labor Day & Dec 25.* ♿ ▤ ♫ *(Tue only)* ✍ | $$$ | ● | | ■ | | ■ |
| **PRESCOTT:** *The Palace*<br>120 S Montezuma St, AZ 86301. ☎ *(928) 541-1996.* Ⓦ *www.historicpalace.com* Wild West atmosphere, serving steak, seafood, and pasta with soups and salads. Dinner theater some Monday nights with Western entertainment. ● *Dec 25.* ♿ ▤ ✍ ♫ ✍ | $$$ | ■ | ● | ■ | | ■ |
| **PRESCOTT:** *Peacock Room*<br>122 E Gurley St, AZ 86301. ☎ *(928) 778-9434.* Ⓦ *www.hassayampainn.com* This luxurious restaurant features a varied menu of American and Continental choices, including daily specials. ♿ ▤ ✍ ♫ ✍ | $$$ | | ● | ■ | | ■ |
| **PRESCOTT:** *Rose*<br>234 S Cortez St, AZ 86303. ☎ *(928) 777-8308.* Intimate dining in a restored Victorian house from the late 1890s. The menu includes a wide variety of Continental dishes that are cooked-to-order. ● *L; Mon, Tue.* ♿ ▤ ✍ ✍ | $$$ | ■ | ● | ■ | | |
| **SEDONA:** *Black Cow Café*<br>229 N Hwy 89A, AZ 86336. ☎ *(928) 203-9868.* Bright and breezy, this café makes an excellent pit stop, serving filling sandwiches, cakes, and pastries. The homemade ice cream is irresistible. ♿ | $ | | ● | | | |
| **SEDONA:** *Dahl & Diluca Ristorante Italiano*<br>2321 W Hwy 89A, AZ 86336. ☎ *(928) 282-5219.* The food is inspired by Tuscan cuisine. Its claim that guests can "dine in Italy without leaving Sedona" is entirely justifiable. ● *L.* ♿ ✍ | $$ | ■ | ● | ■ | | |
| **SEDONA:** *El Rincon Restaurante Mexicano*<br>Tlaquepaque Mall, 336 S Hwy 179, AZ 86336. ☎ *(928) 282-4648.* This restaurant specializes in Mexican and Navajo-influenced dishes. ♿ ✍ | $$ | ■ | ● | | | ■ |
| **SEDONA:** *Oaxaca Restaurante & Cantina*<br>321 N Hwy 89A, AZ 86336. ☎ *(928) 282-4179.* An appealing café-restaurant, it serves Southwestern and Mexican food. ♿ ✍ | $$ | ■ | ● | ■ | | ■ |
| **SEDONA:** *Takashi Japanese Restaurant*<br>465 Jordan Rd, AZ 86336. ☎ *(928) 282-2334.* Traditional Japanese cuisine is available at this friendly restaurant. Dishes include tempura, teriyaki, and sushi. ● *Sat & Sun L.* ♿ ✍ | $$ | ■ | ● | ■ | | |
| **SEDONA:** *Cowboy Club*<br>241 N Hwy 894, AZ 86336. ☎ *(928) 282-4200.* This has Wild West decor and features High Desert cuisine, including steak, ribs, seafood, rattlesnake, buffalo, and vegetarian dishes. ● *Thanksgiving, Dec 25.* ▤ ✍ ✍ | $$$ | | ● | ■ | | |
| **SEDONA:** *Shugrue's Hillside Grill*<br>Hillside Courtyard, 671 Hwy 179, AZ 86336. ☎ *(928) 282-5300.* Arguably the best steaks in town can be enjoyed at this brisk, modern restaurant. The service is excellent – both efficient and courteous. ♿ ✍ | $$$ | ■ | ● | ■ | | ■ |
| **SHOW LOW:** *Branding Iron Steak House*<br>1261 E Deuce of Clubs, AZ 85901. ☎ *(928) 537-5151.* Friendly atmosphere, and a menu that includes prime ribs, steak, seafood, and chicken, along with a soup and salad bar. ● *L; Sat, Sun.* ♿ ▤ ✍ ✍ | $ | | ● | ■ | | ■ |

**WILLIAMS:** *Miss Kitty's Steakhouse* $
Mountainside Inn, 642 E Rte 66, AZ 86046. ( *(928) 635-4431.*
A local tradition, Miss Kitty's offers tasty steaks, ribs, and more at good
prices. There is live music and dancing most nights of the week. ♿ ♫ 🖘

**WILLIAMS:** *Twisters Soda Fountain & The Route 66 Place* $
417 E Route 66, AZ 86046. ( *(928) 635-0266.*
One of the few of the town's old diners that has survived, Twisters
is furnished with colorful retro American memorabilia. ♿ 🖘

**WILLIAMS:** *Cruiser's Café 66* $$
233 W Route 66, AZ 86046. ( *(928) 635-2445.*
A 1930s former gas station that serves thick, juicy burgers, barbecued ribs,
vegetarian fajitas, pasta, and sandwiches. ● *Mon–Fri L.* 🗔 🍴 🖘

**WILLIAMS:** *Max & Thelma's* $$
235 N Grand Canyon Blvd, AZ 86046. ( *(928) 635-8970.*
Next to the Grand Canyon Railway Depot, the restaurant is named for the
couple that brought the railway back. Serves American-style food, including
steak, barbecue, seafood, and pasta. 🗔 🍴 🖘

**WILLIAMS:** *Rod's Steak House* $$
301 E Rte 66, AZ 86046. ( *(928) 635-2671.*
Established in 1946, this steakhouse has long been a Route 66 landmark.
The food is well prepared and service is first-rate. ● *Sun.* 🖘

**WINSLOW:** *Turquoise Room* $$$
303 E 2nd St, AZ 86047. ( *(928) 289-2888.*
The menu changes frequently, and features steak, prime ribs, lamb,
chicken, seafood, pasta, and Southwestern entrées. 🗔 🍴 🖘

## PHOENIX & SOUTHERN ARIZONA

**APACHE JUNCTION:** *Mammoth Steakhouse & Saloon* $
3650 N Mammoth Mine Rd, AZ 85220. ( *(480) 983-6402.*
Steakhouse with live entertainment on some nights. All tables allow
smoking. ♿ 🗔 ♫ 🖘

**APACHE JUNCTION:** *Mining Camp Restaurant & Trading Post* $
6100 E Mining Camp St, AZ 85217. ( *(480) 982-3181.*
This well-established restaurant, in a modern version of a miners' canteen,
offers tasty traditional American dishes at affordable prices. ● *Jul–Sep.* 🖘

**GLOBE:** *Chalo's* $
902 E Ash St, AZ 85501. ( *(928) 425-0515.*
This restaurant is a local favorite. The interior is simple with linoleum floors
and vinyl booths, but the Mexican food, which includes huge servings of enchiladas smothered in homemade sauces, is delicious. ● *Jan 1, Dec 25.* ♿ 🖘

**GLOBE:** *La Luz del Dia* $
304 N Broad St, AZ 85001. ( *(928) 425-8400.*
For something distinctive, try this Mexican bakery and coffee shop. A good
place to fill up before exploring this attractive town and its surroundings.

**NOGALES:** *La Roca Restaurant* $$
Calle Elias 91, Nogales, Mexico 84000. ( *(011-52) 631-312-4686.*
This spacious restaurant is built into a rocky outcrop. The interior has
Spanish Colonial decor and folk art. Superb margaritas. ♿ 🖘

**PHOENIX:** *Arcadia Farms* $
Heard Museum, 2301 N Central Ave, AZ 85004. ( *(602) 252-8848.*
Full lunch restaurant serving Southwestern salads, sandwiches and
complete meals. ● *D.* ♿ 🖘

**PHOENIX:** *Fast Eddie's Diner* $
3422 West Glendale Ave, AZ 85016. ( *(602) 242-2288.*
This 1950s-style diner serves breakfast, lunch and dinner. Fare includes
steaks, burgers, pot roast, meatloaf, and Friday night fish-fry. ♿ 🗔 🍴 🖘

**PHOENIX:** *Sam's Café* $
2566 E Camelback Rd, AZ 85016. ( *(602) 954-7100.*
This casually upscale restaurant has a friendly Tex-Mex flavor with hand-
crafted specialties such as applewood smoked pecan salmon or chili-
rubbed shrimp with pineapple-mango salsa. ♿ 🗔 🍴 🖘

**Price categories** include a three-course meal for one, a glass of house wine, and all unavoidable extra charges including tax:

$ under US$25
$$ US$25–$35
$$$ US$35–$50
$$$$ US$50–$70
$$$$$ over US$70

**OUTDOOR EATING**
Some tables on a patio or terrace.
**VEGETARIAN SPECIALTIES**
One menu always includes a selection of vegetarian dishes.
**BAR AREA**
There is a bar area or cocktail bar within the restaurant, available for drinks and/or bar snacks.
**FIXED-PRICE MENU**
A fixed-price menu available at a good rate, for lunch, dinner or both, usually with three courses.
**CHILDREN'S FACILITIES**
Small portions and/or high chairs available on request.

| | OUTDOOR EATING | VEGETARIAN SPECIALTIES | BAR AREA | FIXED-PRICE MENU | CHILDREN'S FACILITIES |
|---|---|---|---|---|---|
| **PHOENIX:** *Aunt Chilada's at Squaw Peak* $$<br>7330 N Dreamy Draw Dr, AZ 85020. ( (602) 944-1286.<br>Mexican food is the specialty of this popular restaurant, which occupies an imaginatively modernized, 19th-century general store.<br>● *Thanksgiving, Dec 25.* | ■ | ● | ■ | | ■ |
| **PHOENIX:** *Avanti Restaurant* $$$<br>2728 E Thomas Rd, AZ 85016. ( (602) 956-0900.<br>With justification, the Avanti bills itself as a Valley tradition – it has been serving up first-rate Italian cuisine for nearly 30 years. | ■ | ● | ■ | | |
| **PHOENIX:** *Rustler's Rooste* $$$<br>Pointe South Mountain Resort, 7777 S Pointe Pkwy, AZ 85044.<br>( (602) 431-6474. Those with a hankering for Western country-style fixings can enjoy delicious mesquite-grilled steak and ribs.<br>● *L Mon–Sat.* | | ● | ■ | | ■ |
| **PHOENIX:** *Arizona Kitchen* $$$$<br>Wigwam Resort, 300 Wigwam Blvd, Litchfield Pk, AZ 85340.<br>( (623) 935-3811. Diners can watch Southwestern cuisine being prepared in this charming open-plan restaurant.<br>● *Mon D.* | | ● | ■ | | |
| **PHOENIX:** *Vincent's on Camelback* $$$$$<br>3930 E Camelback Rd, AZ 85251. ( (602) 224-0225.<br>This classy restaurant offers an imaginative menu that blends French and Southwestern cuisine. Advance reservations are recommended.<br>● *mid-May–Sep: Mon & Sun.* | | ● | ■ | | |
| **PINETOP-LAKESIDE:** *Christmas Tree* $$<br>455 N Woodland Rd, AZ 85929. ( (928) 367-3107.<br>This eatery's good home-style cooking is a favorite with locals and visitors alike. Beef, chicken, and seafood entrées are served with homemade cinnamon rolls. The house specialty is chicken and dumplings. ● *L; Mon–Tue D; Nov 1–Thanksgiving.* | ■ | ● | ■ | | ■ |
| **PINETOP-LAKESIDE:** *Charlie Clark's Steakhouse* $$$$<br>1701 E White Mountain Blvd, AZ 85935. ( (928) 367-4900.<br>Established in 1938, this informal Western-style restaurant is very popular. Entrées include prime ribs, seafood, and mesquite-broiled steak. | | ● | ■ | | |
| **SCOTTSDALE:** *Ristorante Sandolo* $$$<br>Hyatt Regency at Gainey Ranch, 7500 E Doubletree Ranch Rd, AZ 85258.<br>( (480) 483-5574. The singing servers offer a serenade that precedes – if you book it – a gondola ride on the canal behind the hotel. ● *L.* | ■ | ● | ■ | | |
| **SCOTTSDALE:** *The Squash Blossom* $$$<br>Hyatt Regency at Gainey Ranch, 7500 E Doubletree Ranch Rd, AZ 85258.<br>( (480) 991-3388. The emphasis of this excellent café is on Southwest cuisine with such delicacies as fajitas and adobo, a marinated steak. | ■ | ● | ■ | | ■ |
| **SCOTTSDALE:** *Compass Restaurant* $$$$<br>Hyatt Regency, 122 N 2nd St, AZ 85004. ( (602) 440-3166.<br>Phoenix's only revolving restaurant has fabulous views across the city. The food is first-rate too, featuring regional American dishes. | | ● | ■ | | |
| **SCOTTSDALE:** *Ruth's Chris Steakhouse* $$$$<br>7001 N Scottsdale Rd, AZ 85253. ( (480) 991-5988.<br>One of the best steakhouses in town, noted for its corn-fed and aged US prime beef. Chicken and seafood dishes are also available. | ■ | ● | ■ | | |

**SCOTTSDALE:** *La Hacienda* ⑤⑤⑤⑤⑤
Scottsdale Princess, 7575 E Princess Dr, AZ 85255. *(480) 585-4848.*
This top-flight restaurant offers Mexican dishes and is ideal for a leisurely evening. Strolling Mariachis serenade guests while they eat.

**SCOTTSDALE:** *Mary Elaine's* ⑤⑤⑤⑤⑤
The Phoenician, 6000 E Camelback Rd, AZ 85251. *(480) 941-8200.*
One of the city's smartest restaurants, Mary Elaine's focuses on contemporary French cuisine. The location offers fine views over the valley. Men are required to wear jackets when dining here.

**SUPERIOR:** *Buckboard City* ⑤
1111 Hwy 60, AZ 85273. *(520) 689-5800.* W *www.worldssmallestmuseum.com*
The "World's Smallest Museum" boasts a restaurant serving desserts, hamburgers, salads, sandwiches, and breakfast specials. *D.*

**TOMBSTONE:** *Big Nose Kate's* ⑤
417 E Allen St, AZ 85638. *(520) 457-3107.*
This restaurant has a great old-fashioned saloon atmosphere, with an original cowboy bar and loads of Western memorabilia. *D.*

**TOMBSTONE:** *O.K. Café* ⑤
3rd & Allen Sts, AZ 85638. *(520) 457-3980.*
Charbroiled buffalo, emu, and ostrich burgers are the main dishes at this historic café, along with soups, salads, daily lunch specials, and tasty desserts. The service is fast and friendly. *D.*

**TOMBSTONE:** *The Lamplight Room* ⑤
108 N 4th St, AZ 85638. *(520) 457-3716, (877) 225-1319.*
This fine restaurant serves traditional steak, pork, chicken, and fish, as well as Mexican dishes. Sauces and bread are prepared onsite.

**TOMBSTONE:** *The Longhorn Restaurant* ⑤
501 E Allen at Fifth, AZ 85638. *(520) 457-3405.*
Family dining in a historical setting, serving barbecued smoked pork and beef ribs, steak and prime ribs. Also Mexican specialties and burgers.
*Thanksgiving, Dec 25.*

**TUCSON:** *El Charro Café* ⑤
311 N Court Ave, AZ 85701. *(520) 622-1922.*
Tucson's oldest Mexican restaurant is critically acclaimed as serving some of the best traditional Mexican food in the country. Try the famous *carne seca* – beef that is sun-dried onsite – a Tucson specialty.

**TUCSON:** *La Cocina* ⑤
Old Town Artisans, 201 N Court Ave, AZ 85701. *(520) 622-0351.*
Dine outdoors in the lush shady courtyard, or indoors surrounded by art for sale. Southwest Mexican specials, salads and burgers. *D.*

**TUCSON:** *Li'l Abner's Steakhouse* ⑤
8500 N Silverbell Rd, AZ 85743. *(520) 744-2800.*
An outdoor mesquite grill is located in the eatery's popular patio dining area. Savory steaks, chicken, and ribs with large portions. A live cowboy band performs Friday and Saturday evenings. *L.*

**TUCSON:** *Schlotzsky's Deli* ⑤
3270 E Valencia Blvd, AZ 85706. *(520) 741-2333.*
This exceptional chain serves healthy and delicious sandwiches, salads, and pizzas. Try the "Original" sandwich that made them famous.

**TUCSON:** *Café Poca Cosa* ⑤⑤
88 E Broadway, AZ 85701. *(520) 622-6400.*
A friendly restaurant serving fine authentic Mexican cuisine, with dishes from several regions. Vibrant Mexican-style decor. *Sun.*

**TUCSON:** *El Corral* ⑤⑤
2201 E River Rd, AZ 85718. *(520) 299-6092.*
This steakhouse is set in an old adobe hacienda with wood beams, fireplaces, and stone floors. The specialty is prime rib. *L.*

**TUCSON:** *La Fuente Restaurant* ⑤⑤
1749 N Oracle Rd, AZ 85705. *(520) 623-8659.*
Serving Tucson for 40 years, this restaurant specializes in authentic Mexican cuisine with a live Mariachi band most nights.

For key to symbols see back flap

| | | OUTDOOR EATING | VEGETARIAN SPECIALTIES | BAR AREA | FIXED-PRICE MENU | CHILDREN'S FACILITIES |
|---|---|---|---|---|---|---|

**Price categories** include a three-course meal for one, a glass of house wine, and all unavoidable extra charges including tax:

$ under US$25
$$ US$25–$35
$$$ US$35–$50
$$$$ US$50–$70
$$$$$ over US$70

**OUTDOOR EATING**
Some tables on a patio or terrace.
**VEGETARIAN SPECIALTIES**
One menu always includes a selection of vegetarian dishes.
**BAR AREA**
There is a bar area or cocktail bar within the restaurant, available for drinks and/or bar snacks.
**FIXED-PRICE MENU**
A fixed-price menu available at a good rate, for lunch, dinner or both, usually with three courses.
**CHILDREN'S FACILITIES**
Small portions and/or high chairs available on request.

---

**TUCSON:** *The Grill*    $$$
5601 N Hacienda del Sol Rd, AZ 85718. ( *(520) 529-3500, (800) 728-6514.*
The Grill offers American regional cooking at its finest. Fresh ingredients and inspired combinations make the menu truly memorable. Only lodging guests are served lunch, while dinner is open to all.

| OUTDOOR EATING | VEGETARIAN SPECIALTIES | BAR AREA | FIXED-PRICE MENU | CHILDREN'S FACILITIES |
|---|---|---|---|---|
| ■ | ● | ■ | | ■ |

**TUCSON:** *Janos*    $$$$$
Westin La Paloma, 3770 E Sunrise Dr, AZ 85718. ( *(520) 615-6100.*
One of Tucson's most elegant restaurants, Janos blends French cooking techniques with Southwestern ingredients. The menu changes seasonally and the extensive wine list is chosen to match. ● *Sun & public hols.*

| ■ | ● | ■ | | ■ |
|---|---|---|---|---|

**TUMACACORI:** *Wisdom Café*    $
1931 Frontage Rd, AZ 85640. ( *(520) 398-2397.*
Serving outstanding Mexican fare based on old family recipes, this café is famous for its crispy *chimichangas* and fruit-filled burros. ● *Sun.*

| ■ | ● | ■ | | ■ |
|---|---|---|---|---|

**YUMA:** *Garden Café*    $
250 Madison Ave, AZ 85364. ( *(928) 783-1491.*
Located on an old family estate near the Century House Museum, this café has a European feel. Everything is homemade. Entrées include marinated chicken and tri-tip steak, soups, sandwiches, quiche, salads, and desserts. ● *D; Mon L; Jul–Sep.*

| ■ | ● | | | |
|---|---|---|---|---|

**YUMA:** *Julieanna's Patio Café*    $$
1951 W 25th St, AZ 85364. ( *(928) 317-1961.*
Colorfully decorated dining room and large outdoor patio where seafood, prime ribs, lamb, pasta, steak, and chicken dishes are served with homemade soups. ● *Sat & Sun L; Sun D; Dec 25.*

| ■ | ● | ■ | | ■ |
|---|---|---|---|---|

## THE FOUR CORNERS

**BLUFF:** *Cottonwood Steakhouse*    $
Hwy 191, UT 84512. ( *(435) 672-2282.*
Guests can eat inside or around the outdoor barbecue pit under a giant cottonwood tree. The grilled steaks are substantial.
● *Nov–Feb.*

| ■ | | | | |
|---|---|---|---|---|

**BLUFF:** *Twin Rocks Café*    $
Navajo Twins Dr, UT 84512. ( *(435) 672-2341.*
Located below the twin sandstone pillars that gave the place its name, it serves sandwiches and Southwest Native American dishes.

| ■ | ● | | | ■ |
|---|---|---|---|---|

**BLUFF:** *Cow Canyon Trading Post*    $$
Intersection of Hwy 191 & Hwy 163, UT 84512. ( *(435) 672-2208.*
This former trading post and gas station is now a delightful small restaurant and gift shop. The limited but innovative menu changes regularly to use the best fresh ingredients.
● *L; Tue & Wed.*

| | ● | | | |
|---|---|---|---|---|

**CAMERON:** *Cameron Trading Post*    $
Route 89, AZ 86020. ( *(928) 679-2231.*
Hearty breakfasts and dinners feature standard but tasty versions of chicken, steak, and fish, as well as the ubiquitous Navajo taco.

| | | | | ■ |
|---|---|---|---|---|

**CHINLE:** *Garcia's Restaurant*    $
Garcia Trading Post, Canyon de Chelly, AZ 86503. ( *(928) 674-5000.*
Classic Southwestern dishes, as well as Native and Mexican specialties, such as fajitas and the marinated cowboy sirloin, are served here.
● *Sat & Sun L.*

| | | | | ■ |
|---|---|---|---|---|

**CHINLE:** *Thunderbird Lodge*                                 $
Canyon De Chelly, AZ 86503. (928) 674-5841.
This cafeteria-style restaurant serves large portions of classic
American diner food from breakfast through dinner. Excellent value
and tasty.

**CORTEZ:** *Homesteaders*                                      $$
45 E Main Cortez, CO 81321. (970) 565-6253.
Barbecued pork ribs and steaks are served with homemade bread and
pies amid a stylish country decor of antiques and old license plates.
Sun.

**FARMINGTON:** *Clancy's Pub*                                  $$$
2701 E 20th St, NM 87401. (505) 325-8176.
A friendly, oak-and-fern type bar with better-than-average sandwiches,
steaks, and lots of cold imported beer. major hols.

**GREY MOUNTAIN:** *Anasazi Restaurant*                         $
Grey Mtn Trading Post, Grey Mountain, AZ 86016. (928) 679-2203.
A typical regional restaurant featuring Mexican, Native, and American
dishes with lots of frybread, hamburgers, and tacos. Nov–Mar.

**KAYENTA:** *Amigo Café*                                       $
Hwy 163, AZ 86033. (928) 697-8448.
The simple but delicious Mexican food offered by this restaurant is a
welcome treat in the remote northern Four Corners region. Efficient and
cheerful service. Sun.

**MONUMENT VALLEY:** *Stagecoach Dining Room*                   $$
Goulding's Lodge, UT 84536. (435) 727-3231.
This large, touristy restaurant serves standard American fare. The
highlight here is the stunning view of Monument Valley.

**PAGE:** *Italia Family Buffet*                                $
810 N Navajo Dr, AZ 86040. (928) 645-2706.
A family oriented restaurant with indoor and patio dining, it
serves traditional Italian dishes and pizza. With homemade
soups, salad bar, and desserts. major hols.

**PAGE:** *Ken's Old West*                                      $
718 Vista Ave, AZ 86040. (928) 645-5160.
Live country and Western music nightly in summer with Western-style
dinners of steak, barbecued ribs, prime ribs, chicken, and seafood.
Mon–Wed in winter; Jan 1, Dec 25.

**PAGE:** *Dam Bar & Grill*                                     $$$
644 N Navajo Dr, AZ 86040. (928) 645-2161.
The eclectic industrial-dam decor of this pub and eatery complements
the contemporary steak and pasta dishes served. Dec–Mar: Sun.

**PAGE:** *Rainbow Room*                                        $$$
Lake Powell Resort, Lakeshore Dr, UT 86040. (928) 645-1162.
This elegant lodge offers innovative takes on classic steak,
pasta, and seafood dishes, and has sweeping views of
Lake Powell. mid-Nov–mid-Mar.

**SECOND MESA, HOPI RESERVATION:** *Hopi Cultural Center Restaurant*  $$
Rte 264, AZ 86043. (928) 734-2401.
Try traditional dishes like Hopi stew, which can be interesting, though
standard Mexican and American fare is also served. Thanksgiving,
Dec 25.

**TUBA CITY:** *Hogan Restaurant*                               $
PO Box 247, AZ 86045. (928) 283-5260.
Located next to the Quality Inn, Hogan's offers a full Mexican/American
menu, which is a cut above the average diner fare.

**WINDOW ROCK:** *Navajo Nation Inn Dining Room*               $
48 W Hwy 264, AZ 86515. (928) 871-4108.
This is the place where Navajo businessmen and politicians eat.
Traditional dishes are served in a room decorated with Native art.
Sat & Sun D.

For key to symbols see back flap

# SHOPPING IN ARIZONA

WITH SUCH AN EXCITING range of Native American, Hispanic, and Anglo-American products, shopping in Arizona is a cultural adventure. Native crafts, including rugs, jewelry, and pottery, top the list of things that people buy. The Southwest is also known as a center for the fine arts, with Scottsdale *(see p80)* and Sedona *(see p68)* famous for their many galleries, selling everything from Arizona-inspired landscapes and the latest contemporary work, to kitsch bronze sculptures of cowboys and Indians.

Chili-shaped pot

Across the state, specialty grocery stores and supermarkets stock a range of Southwestern products from hot chili sauces to blue corn tortilla chips. Western wear, including boots, hats, and belts are found in shops across the state. In the major cities, there is a choice of glamorous fashion districts, usually situated in air-conditioned, landscaped malls. Phoenix and Scottsdale rank shopping among their top attractions, and themed malls and boutique shopping areas attract hundreds of thousands of visitors each year.

## WESTERN WEAR

AMONG THE most popular souvenirs of Arizona are hand-tooled cowboy boots, cowboy hats, and decorative leather belts. Western wear is made to high standards throughout the region. Phoenix is a famous center for cowboy clothes. **Az-Tex Hats** of Scottsdale has the largest selection of cowboy hats in the Southwest, while **Saba's Western Store** has been outfitting customers in Western fashions since 1927. **Bacon's Boots & Saddles**, which is located in the historic mining town of Globe *(see p85)*, is owned by craftsman Ed Bacon who has been making fine boots and saddles for more than 50 years. **Sheplers** is a major Western-wear store, and kids as well as grown-ups are catered for with mini hats, spurs, and toys.

Chili peppers hanging from a cart in Sedona

## REGIONAL FOOD

ARIZONANS ARE proud of their Southwestern cuisine, and in most shopping areas you will find grocery stores and specialty shops selling an array of Arizona-made sauces, salsas, dips, and gourmet food items. Many of these foods are chili based, ranging from the mild jalapeño to the super-hot habañero peppers. The mesquite-smoked jalapeño pepper, known as *chipotle*, is medium hot and has a smoky flavor. Salsa is a condiment made from tomatoes, chilli, garlic, and cilantro.

Farmers' markets are another good source of local produce, and usually stock a range of dried chili strings, known as *ristras*. Several companies have websites where you can order such regional gourmet foods as

handmade corn tortillas, chili-stuffed olives, hot-spiced microwave popcorn, mesquite bean candy, and prickly pear jam.

A large number of bookstores and shops offer a variety of cookbooks with recipes on Arizonan and Southwestern cuisine, from easy-to-prepare dishes to traditional and fusion recipes using all the favorite ingredients.

## GEMS & MINERALS

WITH ARIZONA'S fascinating geology and long mining history *(see pp26–7)*, it is not surprising to find glittering gems and minerals on display in shops across the state. Rock shops and museum shops, such as the shop in the

Typical Southwestern boots and hats on sale in Phoenix

Cut stones on display during the Tucson Gem & Mineral Show

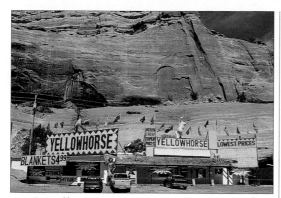

Typical Route 66 souvenir shop, on the Arizona-New Mexico border

The association's gift shop offers books, videos, and souvenirs on the road. **Route 66 Roadworks**, located in Winslow, carries Harley Davidson, Burma Shave, and other memorabilia of the era. In Williams, **The Route 66 Place** provides Route 66 information and mementos, including T-shirts, jackets, vests, and signs and shields, as well as Coca-Cola, John Deere, Betty Boop, and 1950s memorabilia.

## ANTIQUES

ANTIQUES, AND especially those that evoke memories of the Wild West, are very popular in Arizona. Western, Native and cowboy antiques include saddles, hats, spurs, badges, Navajo rugs, silver and turquoise jewelry, as well as lanterns and wagon wheels.

In the Phoenix area, the **Old Towne Shopping District** in downtown Glendale is the main antiques district, with more than 80 antiques shops and specialty stores. Arizona's largest collector's show, the **Phoenix Fairgrounds Antique Market**, is held at the Arizona State Fairgrounds six times a year.

Prescott is known for its antiques shops, many of which are located in the central town square area of downtown Prescott. In Tucson, the Fourth Avenue shopping district has antiques stores between 4th and 7th Streets.

**Arizona Mining & Mineral Museum** in Phoenix, provide reasonably priced and beautiful minerals such as turquoise, azurite, and malachite, quartz crystals of varied shapes and sizes, and gold and silver. The staff in these shops are usually knowledgable and enjoy talking about Arizona's minerals and geology. The Sleeping Beauty Mine in Globe is Arizona's largest source of turquoise, and its retail shop, **True Blue Jewelry & Gift Shop**, offers turquoise jewelry, tumbled nuggets, and rough turquoise. **Tucson Mineral & Gem World** carries a large selection of both Arizonan and other minerals and crystals for novices and collectors alike. **Ramsey's Fine Jewelry & Minerals** in Sedona specializes in making custom jewelry using Arizona gemstones, as well as quality gemstones and minerals from every corner of

the globe, and offers an eye-dazzling array of colorful crystals, minerals, and fossils.

Besides shopping, Arizona hosts two of the world's largest gems and minerals shows during January and February each year in Quartzsite and Tucson *(see p33)*. Rockhounds, gem and mineral dealers and enthusiasts from around the world are known to gather in Arizona for these shows.

## ROUTE 66 MEMORABILIA & TOURIST KITSCH

MEMORIES, memorabilia, kitsch, and souvenirs can be found in shops all along Arizona's Route 66. The **Historic Route 66 Association of Arizona** in Kingman is a non-profit corporation that is dedicated to the preservation, promotion, and protection of Route 66 and its memories.

Shopkeeper stands among the varied collectibles in his antiques store near Prescott

Outside view of Scottsdale's El Pedregal Festival Marketplace

## FLEA MARKETS

ACROSS THE state, flea markets offer everything Arizonan and much more. Flea markets are usually open on weekends, and sometimes on Fridays or other weekdays. Advertised as the largest open-air flea market in the Southwest, **Phoenix Park 'n Swap** in Phoenix offers a broad range of products, from tools, clothing and jewelry, to furniture, luggage, and athletic footwear. **Mesa Market Place Swap Meet** features 1,600 booths filled with new and used items, antiques, home furnishings, clothing, jewelry, toys, and food products. In Tucson, 800 vendors at the **Tanque Verde Swap Meet** flea market sell antiques and collectibles, fresh produce, Southwestern crafts, and coins and stamps. **Peddler's Pass** of Prescott Valley features antiques and collectibles, plus clothing, crafts, and fresh produce. Quartzsite has more than a dozen festive flea markets from November to March, including the **Main Event** in January.

## MALLS

SOUTHERN ARIZONA has some of the most stunning malls in the US, featuring air conditioning, plant-filled atriums, and fine restaurants. The largest of these is Phoenix's **Metrocenter**, with more than 200 stores. Large department stores such as Neiman Marcus can be found at the **Scottsdale**

**Fashion Square**. Phoenix's **Biltmore Fashion Park** offers Gucci, Cartier, and Saks Fifth Avenue, and has some of the best dining options in town.

Themed malls are abundant in the region. **Borgata of Scottsdale** is styled as a 14th-century Italian village with medieval courtyards. The Arizona Center in Phoenix has restaurants and shops set among gardens, fountains, and a waterfall. The **El Pedregal Festival Marketplace** in Scottsdale has a festive Moroccan atmosphere with 25 boutique shops and a branch of the Heard Museum store.

Tucson has several large shopping malls, including one of the largest in the state, **Tucson Mall** with over 200 stores. **El Con Mall** has a great selection of department and specialty stores.

## ART GALLERIES

ARIZONA HAS a vibrant artistic tradition with skilled artists and numerous galleries across the state displaying works of art that reflect the unique colors, light, and landscapes of the Southwest. Scottsdale is Arizona's premier fine art center. It has over a 100 galleries that stock the works of internationally recognized artists in many disciplines. The popular Thursday evening **Scottsdale ArtWalk** features special exhibits and artist receptions in the galleries.

The downtown area of Tucson is home to over 40 art galleries. **Old Town Artisans** houses eight distinctive galleries and shops that display the arts and crafts of hundreds of local and regional artists. Sedona has an active art scene, and Western art can be found in 40 galleries in the city. **Tlaquepaque** is a small art village in Spanish Colonial style with courtyards and gardens, offering primarily Southwestern and Native art. Tubac, Bisbee, and Jerome all have galleries and craft shops, many of which display the work of emerging artists.

## ONE-OF-A-KIND SHOPS

ARIZONA-STYLE independence and creativity have created unique products that go beyond the expected. Part of the delight of shopping in Arizona is finding shops such as **Poisoned Pen**, one of the country's largest mystery books' store. Traveling mystery buffs can browse through 15,000 titles, and appreciate the special events and talks given by authors.

Architect Paolo Soleri built Arcosanti, the experimental town in the high desert of Arizona *(see p81)*, to the north of Phoenix. **Cosanti Originals**, located in the town, offers unique, one-of-a-kind Soleri sculptures in the form of windbells, and their sales help fund research into alternative living.

Paintings and drawings on adobe walls at DeGrazia Gallery in Tucson

## DIRECTORY

### WESTERN WEAR

**Az-Tex Hats**
3903 N Scottsdale Rd,
Scottsdale, AZ 85251.
( (800) 972-2116,
(480) 481-9900.
W www.aztexhats.com

**Bacon's Boots
& Saddles**
290 N Broad St,
Globe, AZ 85501.
( (928) 425-2681.

**Saba's Western
Store**
3965 N Brown Ave,
Scottsdale, AZ 85251.
( (877) 342-1835,
(480) 947-7664.
W www.sabas
westernwear.com

**Sheplers**
2643 E Broadway,
Mesa, AZ 85204.
( (480) 827-8244.
W www.sheplers.com

### GEMS &
### MINERALS

**Arizona Mining &
Mineral Museum**
1502 W Washington St,
Phoenix, AZ 85007.
( (602) 255-3777.
W www.admmr.
state.az.us.

**Ramsey's Fine
Jewelry & Minerals**
150 Hwy 179 Suite #6,
Sedona, AZ 86339.
( (928) 204-2075.
W www.
ramseysedona.com

**True Blue Jewelry
& Gift Shop**
200 N Willow St,
Globe, AZ 85501.
( (928) 425-7625,
(888) 425-7698.
W www.sbturquoise.com

**Tucson Mineral &
Gem World**
2801 S Kinney Rd,
Tucson, AZ 85735.
( (520) 883-0682.
W www.tucson
mineral.com

### ROUTE 66
### MEMORABILIA &
### TOURIST KITSCH

**Historic Route 66
Association of
Arizona**
120 W Andy Devine
Ave, Kingman,
AZ 86401.
( (928) 753-5001.
W www.azrt66.com

**Route 66
Roadworks**
101 W Second St,
Winslow, AZ 86047.
( (928) 289-5423.
W www.
route66roadworks.com

**The Route
66 Place**
417 E Route 66,
Williams, AZ 86046.
( (928) 635-0266.
W www.route66place.com

### ANTIQUES

**Old Towne
Shopping
District**
East of 59th Avenue,
Glendale, AZ 85308.
( (877) 800-2601.

**Phoenix
Fairgrounds
Antique Market**
Arizona State Fairgrounds.
( (623) 587-7488,
(602) 717-7337.
W www.
azantiqueshow.com

### FLEA MARKETS

**Main Event**
PO Box 2801, Quartzsite,
AZ 85346.
( (928) 927-5213.
W www.quartzsite.com

**Mesa Market Place
Swap Meet**
10550 E Baseline,
Mesa, AZ 85212.
( (480) 380-5572.
W www.mesamarket.com

**Peddler's Pass**
6201 E Hwy 69,
Prescott Valley,
AZ 86314.
( (928) 775-4117.

**Phoenix Park
'n Swap**
3801 E Washington St,
Phoenix, AZ 85034.
( (800) 772-0852.
W www.
americanparknswap.com

**Tanque Verde
Swap Meet**
4100 S Palo Verde Rd,
Tucson, AZ 85714.
( (520) 294-4252.

### MALLS

**Biltmore Fashion
Park**
2502 Camelback Rd,
Phoenix,
AZ 85016.
W www.westcor.com

**Borgata of
Scottsdale**
6166 N Scottsdale Rd,
Scottsdale, AZ 85253.
W www.westcor.com

**El Con Mall**
3601 E Broadway
Blvd, Tucson,
AZ 85701.
( (520) 795-9958.

**El Pedregal
Festival
Marketplace**
34505 N Scottsdale Rd,
Scottsdale, AZ 85251.
( (480) 488-1072.

**Metrocenter**
9617 Metro Parkway,
Phoenix, AZ 85051.
( (602) 997-2641.

**Scottsdale Fashion
Square**
7014 E Camelback Rd,
Scottsdale, AZ 85251.
( (480) 990-7800.
W www.westcor.com

**Tucson Mall**
4500 N Oracle Rd,
Tucson, AZ 85701.
( (520) 293-7330.
W www.tucsonmall.com

### ART GALLERIES

**Old Town Artisans**
201 N Court Ave,
Tucson, AZ 85701.
( (520) 623-6024.

**Scottsdale Arts
District & ArtWalk**
Scottsdale, AZ 85251.
( (480) 421-1004.

**Tlaquepaque**
336 Hwy 179,
Sedona, AZ 86351.
( (928) 282-4838.

**Tucson Arts District
Partnership**
125 S Arizona Ave,
Tucson, AZ 85701.
( (520) 624-9977.

### ONE-OF-A-
### KIND SHOPS

**Cosanti Originals**
6433 E Doubletree Ranch
Rd, Paradise Valley,
AZ 85253.
( (800) 752-3187.

**Poisoned Pen**
4014 N Goldwater Blvd,
Suite 101, Scottsdale,
AZ 85251.
( (888) 560-9919.

### NATIVE ARTS
### & CRAFTS

**Cameron Trading
Post**
Highway 89,
Cameron,
AZ 86020.
( (928) 679-2231.

**Heard Museum
Shop**
2301 N Central Ave,
Phoenix, AZ 85004-1323.
( (800) 252-8344,
(602) 252-8344.

**Hopi House**
Main St,
Grand Canyon,
AZ 86023.
( (928) 638-2631.

**Hubbell Trading
Post**
Highway 264,
Ganado, AZ 86505.
( (928) 755-3254.
W www.nps.gov/hutr

**Sewell's Indian
Arts**
7087 5th Ave,
Scottsdale, AZ 85251.
( (480) 945-0962.

# Shopping for Native Arts & Crafts

**Pottery**

ONE OF THE MOST rewarding parts of a trip to Arizona is shopping for Native arts and crafts *(see pp18–19)*. Now valued as collectors' items, many modern crafts, such as pottery and basket-making, can trace their history to centuries-old tribal life. There is intense competition between Native artisans, and the quality of traditional arts continues to be high. At the same time, a new wave of Native artists are successfully blending traditional art with modern media and styles from around the world.

Whether shopping in trading posts, art galleries, or museum shops *(see p145)*, a skillful eye can result in bargains. Purchasing work from Native artists offers the bonus of possible new friendships.

*Rug-making is practiced by the Navajo. A large rug created by a master weaver can fetch thousands of dollars.*

## TRADING POSTS

The Cameron Trading Post and the Hubbell Trading Post originated in the mid-1800s, and are thriving Native arts and crafts centers today. Trading posts are classic middlemen. They benefit the tribes by nurturing Native artists and offering a ready market for their work. For visitors, they provide advice and a generous variety of crafts for comparison shopping.

**Basket-making** *is one of the oldest Native American crafts, dating back over a 1,000 years. Virtually all tribes in Arizona practice basket-making, but the baskets of the Apache and the Hopi are particularly refined.*

**Silverwork**, *often with turquoise arrays, has been produced by Navajo, Zuni, and Hopi peoples for centuries. Since the mid-19th century, Navajo jewelers have incorporated Spanish styles. Hopi and Zuni silver is different, with an intricate overlay process that has raised silver patterns against a dark background.*

**Pottery** *is practiced by many tribes, but Hopi pottery is considered to be the best. Made from local clays, it features both contemporary and traditional designs, many taken from nature, with names such as "birdwing," "dragonfly," "hummingbird," or "rain."*

Navajo sand painting showing abundant crops

## GALLERIES & MUSEUMS

Some of the very best traditional and contemporary Native art can be found in fine art galleries and museum shops, such as **Hopi House** at the Grand Canyon or the **Heard Museum Shop**. Prices in these shops tend to be higher, but careful shopping can still result in bargains. These galleries and museum shops often have long-established relationships with some of the very best Native artisans, and can provide shoppers with information on art trends, investment considerations, and provenance (documented information on the artist, and background and history of the artwork).

## BUYING DIRECTLY FROM NATIVES

One of the most gratifying shopping experiences is purchasing crafts directly from Native artisans, who are found at the major tourist destinations. These craftsmen are either beginners or mid-level artisans, and the prices are usually very reasonable.

- Exercise normal caution. Look for flaws such as uneven edges or curling in rugs, and lopsidedness in pottery.
- Do not purchase expensive articles if you do not know how to determine quality. Avoid making large purchases from unknown vendors.
- Don't be too aggressive while bargaining. A good price is usually 70 to 80 percent of the originally offered price.
- Remember Native etiquette. Speak softly and clearly. Don't point, and if you shake hands, do so gently.
- If you want a photograph of the artist, they may ask for money ($2–$10 is normal).

Navajo weaver working outdoors

***Carvings*** *are primarily represented by* kachina *or* katsina *dolls – beautifully painted, ornate representations of the* kachina *spirits of the Hopi and the Pueblo peoples. Although popular with tourists, they have deep significance for the Hopis, and should be handled and treated with respect. Other tribes occasionally make kachina-like dolls for the tourist trade.*

# ENTERTAINMENT IN ARIZONA

ARIZONA'S LIVELY BLEND of cultures and increasing population have made it a thriving center for arts and entertainment. The large cities of Phoenix and Tucson have vibrant artistic communities, and offer opera, ballet, classical music, and major theatrical productions. Sedona is famous for its resident painters and sculptors, and regularly hosts prestigious touring

**Museum Club sign**

productions, as well as regional theater, dance, and musical events. Also, almost every city and major town has a lively nightlife that includes popular music such as country, jazz, and rock, and dinner theater and standup comedy.

Sport is a popular pastime in Arizona, and fans can find major league and college football, baseball, and basketball teams playing across the state.

**Bull riding, a popular rodeo event in Arizona**

## INFORMATION

THE BEST information source on entertainment and events are local newspapers. Phoenix's *The Arizona Republic* and Tucson's *Daily Star* are useful, and they also have websites with up-to-date information. Several magazines also review events and nightlife. Most hotels offer magazines, such as *Where* and *Key*, that feature dining, attractions, and entertainment. **Jazz in Arizona**'s website details upcoming events. You can book tickets for most events through **Ticketmaster** outlets, or at www.ticketmaster.com, their online booking service.

## RODEOS & WILD WEST SHOWS

SINCE BUFFALO BILL'S first Wild West show in the 1880s, Arizona has been a mecca for Western-style entertainment. Traditional

cowboy skills, like roping steers and breaking wild mustangs, are now rodeo contests that offer substantial money prizes. Rodeo is the Spanish word for round-up, harking back to the 19th century when herds of cattle crossed the Southwest on their way to California. Today's rodeo circuit is very competitive and dangerous, attracting full-time professionals whose high pay reflects this risky career. Some of the most popular rodeos in Arizona are Tucson's Fiesta de los Vaqueros Rodeo, The Payson Rodeo, The Summer Rodeo Series in Williams, and Frontier Days Rodeo in Prescott.

Arizona offers plenty of opportunities to sample the Wild West atmosphere, either

**Baseball player**

in the many ghost towns or in historic frontier towns such as **Tombstone** *(see p98)*, which stages mock-gunfights. Western towns that were built as film studios, such as **Old Tucson Studios** *(see p90)*, offer tours of their working movie sets. Similar entertainment can be found at **Rawhide**, north of Scottsdale, which has a museum, an old-fashioned ice cream parlor, and a famous music venue. Goldfield, near Apache Junction, which was once the richest gold mining town in America, offers a train tour of the original gold mine site, a working saloon, and a bordello museum.

## SPORTS

THE THREE most popular spectator sports in Arizona, as in the rest of the country, are football, baseball, and basketball. The state's largest concentration of major teams is in the Phoenix area. The **Arizona Cardinals**, who play their home games at the Sun Devil Stadium, are the state's only major league football team, and the oldest continually operating NFL football team in the country. The Arizona Diamondbacks baseball team joined the major league in 1998 and is based at the $275-million **Bank One Stadium** in

Phoenix. Professional basketball is represented by the Phoenix Suns, who share the **America West Arena** with a football team, the Arizona Rattlers.

While tickets may be hard to obtain for league games, it is relatively easy to gain entrance to the many college games in any sport throughout the region. Phoenix's warm climate also attracts the Cactus League, a series of training games for seven major league baseball teams in February and March.

## CLASSICAL MUSIC, BALLET & OPERA

IN PHOENIX, both the excellent Phoenix Symphony and Arizona Opera perform at the **Phoenix Symphony Hall** building. The city's $14-million refurbishment of the Spanish Baroque-style **Orpheum Theater** has created the state's top venue for big name Broadway shows, and a stunning addition to more than 20 major venues for arts, sports, and entertainment in and around Phoenix. Arizona Theater Company and Actors Theater occupy the **Herberger Theater Center**, offering a regular program of performances. With more than 20 theater companies in Phoenix, there is an impressive array of plays to choose from, as well as touring stage shows and big name entertainers.

In Tucson, the **Arizona Opera** begins its productions at Convention Center Music Hall, which is also home to the award-winning **Tucson Symphony Orchestra**.

Dancing couple at The Museum Club in Flagstaff, Arizona

## NIGHTLIFE

IN ALMOST EVERY town in Arizona, there are restaurants, bars, and nightclubs that offer country music and dancing. Among the most famous country music venues is the Wild West theme-town of Rawhide in Scottsdale, where a large number of well-known bands play. **The Museum Club** in Flagstaff is a legendary Route 66 *(see p29)* roadhouse that has hosted such top country music names as Hank Williams and Willy Nelson, and still offers a lively selection of Southwestern bands.

The major cities of the state have virtually every type of evening entertainment on offer. For instance, jazz bars and cafés are gaining in popularity, and standup comedy and rock music are available in countless venues. In Tucson, The Rialto brings a wide variety of live entertainment – from punk rock to salsa – to the stage of this renovated 1918 playhouse. Clubs and arenas based in Phoenix and Tucson are regular stops for big stars on US tours.

Phoenix Symphony Hall, home to Phoenix Symphony and Arizona Opera

# SPECIALTY VACATIONS & ACTIVITIES

Wᴵᵀʜ ʜᴜɴᴅʀᴇᴅꜱ of miles of deep rock canyons, spectacular deserts, and towering, snow-capped mountains, Arizona offers a wide and tempting array of outdoor adventure activities. Much of the state's wilderness is protected by the federal government in national parks, national recreation areas, and lands administered by the National Forest Service and the Bureau of Land Management. An increasing numbers of visitors are being drawn to the region, and it is now a magnet for

Powerboating near Parker Dam in Arizona

climbers, mountain bikers, hikers, and 4WD enthusiasts. The range of organized tours includes whitewater rafting and horseback riding, as well as cultural heritage tours of the many ancient Native American sites. Wildlife enthusiasts, particularly birdwatchers, can spot rare species on the spring and fall migration routes that cross the Southwest. The region is also a center for sports activities, especially for golfers *(see pp154–5)*, who can choose from over 300 courses, some of which are the world's finest.

## GENERAL INFORMATION

Tʜᴇ ᴍᴀɪɴ centers for outdoor activities in the region are Phoenix *(see pp76–83)*, Tucson *(see pp88–94)*, Flagstaff *(see pp64–6)*, and Sedona *(see p68)*. These towns have excellent equipment shops and visitor information centers.

Hikers and campers exploring national park backcountry will need permits from the National Park Service as well as detailed maps, which can be obtained from the **USDA Forest Service**, or the **US Geological Survey (USGS)**. National parks have excellent, well-marked trails, and fascinating ranger-led hikes that focus on the local flora, fauna, and geology. Advice on trails, permits, and weather conditions at most attractions can be obtained at both the state and local tourist offices. Anyone exploring desert or canyon country should be aware of the potential for flash floods, and should check weather reports daily, especially during the summer months of July and August.

## HIKING

Tʜᴇ ꜱɪɴɢʟᴇ most popular outdoor activity in Arizona is hiking. Day hikes and longer trips draw large

**Hikers on the trail to Pueblo Alto at Chaco Canyon**

numbers of residents and visitors, who feel that this is the best way to see the region's stunning scenery.

Popular hiking areas include Mount Lemmon *(see p94)* outside Tucson, Camelback Mountain *(see p81)* and the Superstition Mountains *(see pp84–5)* outside Phoenix, Oak Creek Canyon *(see p69)* near Sedona, and the vast desert expanses of Glen Canyon Recreation Area *(see pp62–3)*.

For low-effort hiking and driving tours, contact **Walk Softly Tours**, which offers single- and multi-day

adventures in the Sonoran Desert and Four Corners areas. Utah-based **Nichols Expeditions** offers five-day hiking tours to the Canyon de Chelly National Monument *(see pp106–9)*, in the midst of the Navajo Reservation.

To explore Arizona's south, get in touch with **Southern Arizona Adventures**, which takes visitors to the unique Sky Islands *(see pp16–17)*, and Kartchner Caverns caves and Chiricahua National Monument *(see p99)*.

## ROCK CLIMBING

Aʀɪᴢᴏɴᴀ'ꜱ ᴅʀʏ, sunny climate and extensive mountains, canyons, and sheer rock faces make it one of America's most popular climbing destinations.

There are excellent, and often busy, climbing locations near each city, and nearly all the major cities have first-rate climbing shops and schools. **Arizona White Knuckle Adventures**, in Scottsdale, provides full- and half-day climbs across the state, for groups as well as individuals.

One of the oldest rock climbing resources in Arizona is the **Rocky Mountain Climbing School** in Tucson, which offers professional climbing instruction and guiding for both beginners and intermediate climbers.

**Mountain biking on red rock in Coconino National Forest, Sedona**

## MOUNTAIN BIKING & FOUR-WHEEL DRIVING

WITH SO MUCH wilderness crisscrossed by trails and jeep tracks, mountain biking and 4WD touring are two of the fastest growing sports in Arizona. Casual riders will find plenty of thrills in Phoenix's Papago Park *(see p82)*. In Tucson, there are numerous trails in the Mount Lemmon area.

**Bikeapelli Adventure Tours** offers single- and multi-day adventures on rough desert single-tracks and slickrock rides. Sedona is also a hotbed for 4WD adventures, and local legend **Pink Jeep Tours** offers guided 4WD tours. Monument Valley *(see pp102–3)* is a prime location for 4WD tours, which are often led by Navajo guides from **Goulding's Lodge Monument Valley Tours**. Glenn Canyon National Recreation Area's miles of trails and dirt roads make it a hotspot for both mountain bikers and 4WD enthusiasts.

**A Pink Jeep in Sedona**

## WHITEWATER RAFTING & KAYAKING

WHEN PEOPLE think of whitewater rafting in Arizona, they often dream of the 16-day run through Grand Canyon *(see pp48–61)*. But, as incredible as this trip is, it requires time, and up to a year of advance planning. When time is short, Arizona offers plenty of other whitewater and flatwater rafting choices. If you want to see the Grand Canyon, several operators, including **Tour West**, offer three- to five-day trips through the lower Grand Canyon, beginning at Diamond Creek on Hualapai reservation and ending at Lake Mead. The Salt River is a raging torrent in the White Mountains, where **Far Flung Adventures** offers one- to five-day rafting trips. On the Colorado Plateau, **Wild River Expeditions** offers a gentle one-day float through the canyons of the San Juan River that includes stops to see petroglyphs and Ancestral Puebloan ruins.

## OTHER WATERSPORTS

ARTIFICIAL LAKES along the Colorado River – formed because of the damming of the river – offer a variety of watersports, including powerboating and jetskiing. Lake Powell is famous for houseboat cruises, which showcase remote beaches, canyons, and the desert beauty for which the lake is known. **Lake Powell Resorts & Marinas** rents out houseboats and powerboats.

At **Lake Mead** *(see p72)*, shops rent fishing boats and jetskis, and offer waterskiing lessons. All kinds of equipment, from waterskis to tubes, can be taken on rent from **Fun Time Boat Rentals**, which is near Lake Havasu *(see p73)*.

## FISHING

LAKES MEAD, Powell, and Havasu are also noted as fishing destinations. The lakes are well stocked with game fish during the fishing season, which runs from March to November. River anglers can also fish for salmon and trout. Fishing licenses are required almost everywhere, and catch and release is the rule in many areas. Information about licenses, tournaments, and tours can be obtained from marinas, outdoor equipment stores, local gas stations, and The **Arizona Game and Fish Department**.

## HOT AIR BALLOONING

COOL, STILL mornings, dependable sunshine, and steady breezes have made Arizona one of the top hot air ballooning destinations in America. Around Phoenix, several operators, including **Hot Air Expeditions**, offer Champagne flights over the Sonoran Desert. You can also drift gently over the canyons of Sedona with **Northern Light Balloon Expeditions**.

**Whitewater rafting trip on the Colorado River**

## BIRDWATCHING

WITH MORE than 200 species of birds, including many rare breeds, birdwatching is a popular pastime in Arizona, particularly in spring, early summer, and fall. These are the peak migration seasons for many species such as warblers and flycatchers, and for shorebirds.

**Cibola National Wildlife Refuge** is home to nesting waders, ducks and a winter population of snow geese, and more than 1,000 sandhill cranes. Several habitats across the region suit desert birds such as the roadrunner and elf owl; Saguaro National Park *(see p90)*, located in the Sonoran Desert, is a notable example. Southern Arizona is also home to America's greatest variety of hummingbirds. The **Southeastern Arizona Bird Observatory**, a non-profit organization, offers educational tours in the region.

## LEARNING VACATIONS

SOME OF ARIZONA'S most interesting learning vacations focus on Native cultures and ancient civilizations. Two organizations, **The Crow Canyon Archeological Center** and **The Four Corners School**, offer vacation courses on geography, flora and fauna, ancient ruins, and Native arts. Most programs last between four and ten days, and visitors are housed either in college campuses or in motels. Several of Arizona's top museums offer a variety of learning vacations. The **Smithsonian Institution** also offers popular programs such as the past and present arts of the Hopi and Navajo tribes.

## SPA VACATIONS

ARIZONA'S WARM winter weather and spectacular outdoors have resulted in the blossoming of high-end spas in Phoenix, Tucson, and

Telemark turns on San Francisco Peaks, near Flagstaff

Sedona *(see p68)*. These spas offer everything from posh pampering to serious diet and fitness programs, and a host of New Age wellness experiences.

Tucson's **Canyon Ranch**, considered one of the world's finest destination spas, offers a stunning array of programs incorporating tennis, hiking, biking, yoga, tai chi, and meditation. Nearby, **Miraval** is famous for its blend of pampering and physical regimen, offering over 100 facial and body treatment options, including acupuncture, Shiatsu, and Trager. The spa's immaculate grounds feature waterfalls, tennis courts, stables, and a Zen garden.

**Broad-billed hummingbird**

## SKIING & WINTER SPORTS

FEATURING 2,300 ft (700 m) of vertical drop and a network of superb trails serviced by five chairlifts, the 12,600-ft (3,840.48-m) **Arizona Snowbowl** *(see p65)*, which lies just north of Flagstaff, is the undisputed champion of downhill ski resorts in

Arizona. Another major resort, **Sunrise Park**, in the White Mountains, features ten lifts and 65 runs, and is a favorite with visitors, particularly snowboarders. Also growing in popularity is the southernmost ski resort in the country, **Mount Lemmon Ski Valley**, which is located just outside Tucson. The Grand Canyon's North Rim is particularly sought after by cross-country skiing enthusiasts.

## HORSEBACK RIDING

HORSEBACK riding is synonymous with Arizona. Even large cities have stables that offer trail rides through the desert. **OK Corral Stables**, at Apache Junction near Phoenix, offers horseback trail camping trips for one to five days. Cooler summer locations, such as Sedona and Pinetop-Lakeside, are also popular. Dude ranches offer a range of experiences, from pampered luxury with daytime trail rides, to real cattle ranches that offer visitors the chance to live and work as a cowboy. The **Arizona Dude Ranch Association** can help plan a dude ranch vacation.

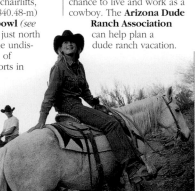
Horseback riding through the desert near Tuscon, Arizona

## DIRECTORY

### INFORMATION

A wealth of information on using and enjoying public lands is available at www.recreation.gov

**USDA Forest Service**
333 Broadway SE, Albuquerque, NM 87102.
☎ (505) 842-3898.

**USGS**
12201 Sunrise Valley Dr, Reston, VA 20192.
☎ (703) 648-4748.
W www.usgs.gov

### HIKING

**Nichols Expeditions**
497 N Main St, Moab, UT 84532.
☎ (800) 648-8488.
W www.nicholsexpeditions.com

**Southern Arizona Adventures**
PO Box 1032, Bisbee, AZ 85603.
☎ (520) 432-9058.
W www.arizonatour.com

**Walk Softly Tours**
PO Box 5510, Scottsdale, AZ 85261-5510.
☎ (480) 473-1148.
W www.walksoftlytours.com

### ROCK CLIMBING

**Arizona White Knuckle Adventures**
10401 McDowell Mountain Ranch Rd, #A2-112, Scottsdale, AZ 85253.
☎ (480) 342-9669.
W www.arizona-adventures.com

**Rocky Mountain Climbing School**
260 S Pantano Rd, #251, Tucson, AZ 85710.
☎ (520) 721-6751.
W www.climbarizona.com

### MOUNTAIN BIKING & 4WD

**Bikeapelli Adventure Tours**
1695 W Hwy 89a, Sedona, AZ 86336.
☎ (928) 282-1312.

**Goulding's Lodge Monument Valley Tours**
Hwy 163, Goulding, UT 84536.
☎ (435) 727-3231.

**Pink Jeep Tours**
PO Box 1447, Sedona, AZ 86339.
☎ (928) 282-5000, (800) 873-3662.
W www.pinkjeep.com

### WHITEWATER RAFTING & KAYAKING

**Far Flung Adventures**
PO Box 1550, Vista, CO 81211.
☎ (800) 231-7238.
W www.inaraft.com

**Tour West**
PO Box 333, Orem, UT 84059.
☎ (800) 453-9107.
W www.twriver.com

**Wild River Expeditions**
PO Box 118/101, Main St, UT 84512-0118.
☎ (435) 672-2244.
W www.riversandruins.com

### OTHER WATER-SPORTS

**Fun Time Boat Rentals**
1685 Industrial Blvd, Lake Havasu City, AZ.
☎ (928) 680-1003, (800) 680-1003.
W www.funtimeboatrentals.com

**Lake Mead Visitor Center**
601 Nevada Hwy, Boulder City, NV 89005.
☎ (702) 293-8906/8907.

### Lake Powell Resorts & Marinas
PO Box 1597, Page, AZ 86040.
☎ (928) 645-2433, (602) 278-8888, (800) 528-6154.
W www.lakepowell.com

### FISHING

**Arizona Game & Fish Department**
2222 Greenway Rd, Phoenix, AZ 85023.
☎ (602) 942-3000.

### HOT AIR BALLOONING

**Hot Air Expeditions**
2243 E Rose Garden Loop, Phoenix, AZ 85024.
☎ (480) 502-6999, (800) 831-7610.

**Northern Light Balloon Expeditions**
PO Box 1695, Sedona, AZ 86339.
☎ (928) 282-2274, (800) 230-6222.

### BIRDWATCHING

**Cibola National Wildlife Refuge**
Rte 2, Box 138, Cibola, AZ 85328.
☎ (928) 857-3253.

**Southeastern Arizona Bird Observatory**
PO Box 5521, Bisbee, AZ 85603.
☎ (520) 432-1388.
W www.sabo.org

### LEARNING VACATIONS

**The Crow Canyon Archeological Center**
23390 County Road K, Cortez, CO 81321.
☎ (970) 565-8975.

**The Four Corners School**
Box 1028, Monticello, UT 84535.
☎ (435) 587-2859.

### Smithsonian Institution
1000 Jefferson Dr SW, MRC702, Washington DC 20560.
☎ (202) 357-4700.

### SPA VACATIONS

**Canyon Ranch**
8600 E Rockcliff Rd, Tucson, AZ 85750.
☎ (520) 749-9655, (800) 742-9000.
W www.canyonranch.com

**Miraval**
5000 E Via Estancia, Catalina, AZ 85739.
☎ (800) 232-3969.
W www.miravalresort.com

### SKIING & WINTER SPORTS

**Arizona Snowbowl**
PO Box 40, Flagstaff, AZ 86002.
☎ (928) 779-1951.
W www.arizonasnowbowl.com

**Mount Lemmon Ski Valley**
10300 Ski Run Rd, Mt. Lemmon, AZ 85619.
☎ (520) 576-1321.

**Sunrise Park Ski Resort**
PO Box 117, Greer, AZ 85927.
☎ (928) 735-7669, (800) 772-7669.
W www.sunriseskipark.com

### HORSEBACK RIDING

**Arizona Dude Ranch Association**
PO Box 603, Cortaro, AZ 85652.
W www.azdra.com

**OK Corral Stables**
2665 E Whiteley St, Apache Junction, AZ 85219-8981.
☎ (480) 982-4040.
W www.okcorrals.com

# Golfing in Arizona

**Golfer Casey Martin**

Boasting over 300 golf courses, many of which are among the world's finest, Arizona is a golfer's paradise. With so many courses, golf enthusiasts have a dazzling array of terrains and levels of challenge to choose from. Green fees can range from nominal to expensive. Private courses are open to club members exclusively, and to those with reciprocal memberships. Semi-private courses are reserved for members, but do accept paying guests at certain times. Public courses are open to all, but golf resorts prefer guests staying with them, though they are opened to the public occasionally. The legendary Boulders Club, near Phoenix, rotates access to its two world-class courses between resort guests, private members, and the public.

**A private golf course in the cooler climes of Flagstaff**

## FLAGSTAFF & NORTHERN ARIZONA

Golf on the Colorado Plateau, at elevations between 5,000 ft (1,524 m) and 7,000 ft (2,134 m), is played throughout the year, although some courses close in winter.

In summer, the northern courses usually bustle as they are cooler by 15°F, on an average, than courses in Phoenix. Busy is relative, however, and seldom will the Northern Arizona courses be as crowded as their southern cousins.

In Sedona, the Gary Pranks-designed course at **Sedona Golf Resort** is one of Northern Arizona's must-play venues. Regularly featured in lists of the state's best courses, this par 71 course features lush greens and stunning views of the surrounding red rock canyons.

Surrounded by pine-covered mountains, Prescott is one of the busiest golf regions in Northern Arizona. One of the best deals can be found at **Antelope Hills Golf Course**. For a modest fee of about

$55, players can choose from the 50-year-old, 18-hole North Course, with its towering elm trees, classic layout, and challenging doglegs, or the links-style South Course, opened in 1992. In nearby Prescott Valley, the par 72 **Stoneridge Golf Course** is one of Northern Arizona's bright new stars with a visually stunning and physically challenging links-style course that features over 350 ft (107 m) of vertical rise and fall across its 18 holes.

**Golfer Charlotta Sorenstam at a golf resort in Phoenix**

## PHOENIX & CENTRAL ARIZONA

The Valley of the Sun has perhaps more golf courses per capita than anywhere in the world, 180 and counting, including some of the world's very best. Since this is a spot that must satisfy not only its residents, but also over a million visiting golfers every year, it's no surprise that many of the courses are public or resort courses with generous public access.

Golf is big business here, particularly in Scottsdale, a town virtually synonymous with the concept of luxurious golf resorts such as **The Boulders Club** and **Troon North**, which offer some of the best courses in the world. In fact, the Tom Weiskopf-designed course at Troon North is a desert golfer's dream, and is rated No. 1 public golf course in Arizona by *Golf Digest*. Like many Scottsdale courses, the amenities and services at Troon North are

## PGA TOUR

Arizona's sunshine and warm winter temperatures make it a favorite of the Professional Golfer's Association (PGA), which holds two important tournaments here early in the year. In late January, the FBR Open (formerly the Phoenix Open) attracts huge crowds to the Tournament Players Club of Scottsdale. The club's unusual layout allows for virtually unlimited viewing, and as many as 400,000 people have attended a single tournament. A month later, The PGA Chrysler Classic, with its purse of $3 million, attracts golf fans by the thousands from all over the world to the beautiful Omni Tucson National Golf Resort.

**Tiger Woods hits a tee shot during the Phoenix Open**

Randolph Park in Tuscon – one of the top ten public golf courses in Arizona

top-notch, but all this comes at a steep price, at up to $295 a round. In Phoenix, there is the **Wildfire Golf Club**, which features two first-class courses, a classic Arnold Palmer Signature course, and the desert-style Faldo Championship Course.

Those wanting to opt for a public course can head east to **Gold Canyon Resort**, which has the Sidewinder and Dinosaur Mountain courses, both top-rated public courses since they opened. Both courses are visually stunning and among the best value in this land of golf and sunshine.

## TUCSON & SOUTHERN ARIZONA

SET IN THE VERDANT Sonoran Desert, surrounded by stunning landscape and boasting over 350 days of sunshine every year, Tucson is one of America's best golf destinations. The city has fantastic offerings, including **Ventana Canyon Resort**, whose Tom Fazio-designed Mountain Course offers immaculate greens. Listed among North America's best courses, it offers enough challenge to keep even the

most experienced golfers focused. Another rewarding course is the classic **Randolf Park**, with its broad water hazards and towering eucalyptus trees. A popular PGA venue in the 1980s, Randolf Park now hosts LPGA events.

South of Tucson, the suburbs of Green Valley have some of the finest courses in Southern Arizona. One of these is **Torres Blancas**, a Lee Trevino-designed course with a monster 484-yard (442-m), par 4 signature 17th hole that gives players something to talk about back at the clubhouse.

---

| **DIRECTORY** |
| --- |

**GENERAL**

**Arizona Golf Association**
7226 N 16th St, St 200,
Phoenix, AZ 85020.
☎ (602) 944-3035.

**Golf Arizona**
☎ (800) 939-7998.
Ⓦ www.golfarizona.
com

**FLAGSTAFF & NORTHERN ARIZONA**

**Antelope Hills Golf Course**
1 Perkins Dr,
Prescott, AZ 86301.
☎ (800) 972-6818,
(928) 776-7888.
Ⓦ www.antelopehills
golf.com

**Sedona Golf Resort**
35 Ridge Trail Dr,
Sedona, AZ 86351.
☎ (877) 733-9885,
(928) 284-9355.
Ⓦ www.sedonagolf
resort.com

**Stoneridge Golf Course**
1601 N Bluff Top Rd,
Prescott Valley, AZ 86314.
☎ (928) 772-6500.
Ⓦ www.stoneridgegolf.
com

**PHOENIX & CENTRAL ARIZONA**

**The Boulders Club**
34831 N Tom Darlington,
PO Box 2090, Carefree,
AZ 85377.

☎ (480) 488-9028.
Ⓦ www.thebouldersclub.
com

**Gold Canyon Golf Resort**
6100 S Kings Ranch Rd,
Gold Canyon,
AZ 85219.
☎ (480) 982-9090.
Ⓦ www.gcgr.com

**Troon North Golf Club**
10320 E Dynamite Blvd,
Scottsdale,
AZ 85255.
☎ (480) 585-7700.
Ⓦ www.troonnorth.net

**Wildfire Golf Club**
5350 E Marriott Drive,
Phoenix, AZ 85054.
☎ (480) 473-0205,
(800) 324-8813.
Ⓦ www.wildfiregolf.com

**TUCSON & SOUTHERN ARIZONA**

**Randolph Park Golf Course**
600 S Alvernon Way,
Pima County,
Tucson, AZ 85711.
☎ (520) 791-5853.
Ⓦ www.tucsoncitygolf.
com/randolph.html

**Torres Blancas Golf Club**
3233 S Abrego Dr
Pima County,
Green Valley, AZ 85614.
☎ (520) 625-5200.

**Ventana Canyon Golf Resort**
6200 N Clubhouse
Lane, Tucson, AZ 85750.
☎ (520) 577-4015.
Ⓦ www.loewshotels.
com/hotels/tucson

# SURVIVAL
# GUIDE

# PRACTICAL INFORMATION

**Arizona State Parks' sign**

A VAST REGION OF fascinating and spectacular natural beauty, Arizona is dotted with dramatic rock formations, canyons, ancient archeological sites, and wild desert scenery that offers visitors a choice of pleasures, including a wide variety of outdoor activities.

Arizona's cities are famous for their combination of a laid-back Southwestern culture, and sophisticated urban pursuits such as excellent museums and great dining. In addition, unique attractions located on Native reservations provide a wonderful opportunity to observe American Indian cultures. Accommodations are excellent (*see pp122–31*), and visitor information centers are plentiful, even in the small towns.

The following pages contain useful information on planning a trip to this region. Personal Security (*see pp160–61*) recommends a number of precautions to visitors, while Travel (*see pp162–5*) provides information on travel by both public transportation and car.

## WHEN TO GO

A RIZONA IS A year-round destination, and its climate is dictated by elevation. The higher elevation areas have cold, snowy winters, making them a popular destination for skiing and other winter sports activities. In contrast, lower elevations in Southern Arizona are noted for the warm and sunny winter weather, with temperatures averaging a comfortable 70°F (21°C) in Phoenix. Be aware, however, that the average temperature in the summer months of July and August touches 100°F (37°C) in Phoenix, making it one of the hottest cities outside the Middle East. Spring and fall are ideal seasons to visit Arizona – there are fewer visitors, and the milder temperatures make outdoor activities a popular option. However, some services may be closed at these times: the North Rim of the Grand Canyon (*see p55*) is open only between May and October. Whatever the time of year, this is a region known for having a great deal of sun, with the northern areas averaging over 200 days of sunshine each year, and the southern parts famous for having more than 300 sunny days in a year.

## TOURIST INFORMATION

V ISITOR INFORMATION centers in Arizona offer everything from local maps to hotel and B&B bookings. Special tours,

such as guided history walks, ranger-led archeological tours, and wildlife expeditions, can also be arranged through these offices. In addition, the national and state parks have their own visitor centers that provide hiking maps, safety advice, and special licenses for hiking and camping out in the wilderness.

Arizona has a department of tourism, as do all the major towns and cities in the state. Contact the **Arizona Office of Tourism** when planning your trip and they will be pleased to send an information pack. Smaller urban centers and sights of special interest have offices that provide maps and guides. Information can also be obtained from the network of chambers of commerce in the region. Websites of the departments of tourism, as

**Ranger on a guided tour at Keet Seel, Navajo National Monument**

well as those of individual sights, also offer information and online booking services for accommodations.

Many tourist attractions, such as Canyon de Chelly (*see pp106–9*), are located on Native reservations and are managed by tribal councils. For advice on etiquette, opening times, and admission fees, contact the local **Bureau of Indian Affairs** or the **Navajo Tourism Department**.

## TIME ZONES

T HE STATE IS located in the Mountain Standard Time zone, but it does not follow Daylight Saving Time. From late spring to early fall, all of the neighboring states in the Mountain Standard Time zone (New Mexico, Colorado, and Utah) set their clocks forward by one hour, but not Arizona.

To confuse matters even more, it is important to be aware that the Navajo Nation (across Arizona and part of New Mexico) does use Daylight Saving Time, but the Hopi Indian Reservation (in the middle of the Navajo Reservation) does not.

## SENIOR TRAVELERS

A LTHOUGH THE AGE when you are considered a senior is 65, a multitude of discounts are available to people over 50. Reduced rates can apply to meals, accommodations, public transportation, and entrance fees, and are often

◁ **Highway to mesa, butte, and spire formations at Monument Valley National Monument** better than student discounts. The **National Park Service** offers Golden Age Passports that reduce the cost of park tours and services. **Elderhostel** arranges educational tours, which include inexpensive accommodations, lectures, and meals. The **American Association of Retired Persons (AARP)** offers good travel discounts.

## TRAVELERS WITH DISABILITIES

ARIZONA HAS excellent facilities to cater to the physically disabled traveler. All public places and buildings are legally required to be wheelchair-accessible, and to have suitably designed restrooms. However, call and check on the accessibility in smaller inns and B&Bs, and in small, local restaurants. Public transportation also comes under this law, and road crossings in city centers have dropped curbs to enable easier access. Service animals, such as guide dogs for the blind, are

the only animals allowed on public transportation.

Many national parks and archeological sights have paved walkways for wheelchairs. The National Park Service grants free entry, for one year, to those who are disabled or blind. The **Access-Able Travel Source** and the **Society for Accessible Travel & Hospitality** are two organizations that offer advice on traveling to the disabled, from how to rent specially adapted cars to qualifying for parking permits.

**Wheelchair access sign**

## STUDENT TRAVELERS

THE LARGEST provider of student travel products and services is **STA Travel**. It offers discounted accommodations, rail passes, phone cards, email options, travel packages, and cut-rate student airfares. The best deals are available at offices near colleges and universities. **Student Universe** offers similar services via the Internet. If you are planning to stay in youth hostels, you will need to join **Hosteling International/American Youth Hostels (HI/AYH)**.

**Water fountains in the courtyard of the Heard Museum in Phoenix**

## STATE & LOCAL OFFICES

**Arizona Office of Tourism**
1110 W Washington St,
Phoenix, AZ 85007.
☎ (866) 298-3795.
W www.arizonaguide.com

**Bureau of Indian Affairs**
PO Box 10, Phoenix.
☎ (602) 379-4511.

**Flagstaff Visitor Center**
One E Route 66,
Flagstaff, AZ 86001.
☎ (800) 842-7293.

**Greater Phoenix Convention & Visitors Bureau**
400 E Van Buren St, Suite 600, Phoenix, AZ 85004.
☎ (877) 225-5749.

**Metropolitan Tucson Visitors Bureau**
100 S Church Ave,
Tucson, AZ 85701.
☎ (800) 638-8350.
W www.visittucson.org

**Navajo Tourism Department**
PO Box 663, Window
Rock, AZ 86515.
☎ (928) 871-6436.

## SENIOR TRAVELERS

**American Asso. of Retired Persons**
3200 E Carson St,
Lakewood, CA 90712.
☎ (888) 687-2277.
W www.aarp.org

**Elderhostel**
11 Avenue de Lafayette,
Boston, MA 02111.
☎ (877) 426-8056.
W www.elderhostel.org

**National Park Service**
(see also under individual sights)
Intermountain Area,
PO Box 25287,
Denver, CO 80225.
W www.nps.gov

## DISABLED TRAVELERS

**Access-Able Travel Source**
PO Box 1796,
Wheat Ridge,
CO 80034.
☎ (303) 232-2979.
W www.access-able.com

**Society for Accessible Travel & Hospitality (SATH)**
347 Fifth Ave,
Suite 610,
New York, NY 10016.
☎ (212) 447-7284.
W www.sath.org

## STUDENT TRAVELERS

**Hostelling International/ American Youth Hostel (HI/AYH)**
733 15th St NW,
Suite 840, DC 20005.
☎ (202) 783-6161.
W www.hiusa.org.

**STA Travel**
5900 Wilshire Blvd,
Suite 900,
Los Angeles,
CA 90036.
☎ (800) 781-4040,
(800) 836-4115.
W www.statravel.com

**Student Universe**
100 Talcott Ave E,
Watertown,
MA 02472.
☎ (800) 272-9676,
(800) 351-3279.
W www.studentuniverse.com

# Personal Security & Health

**Fire Department badge, Sedona**

ARIZONA IS A relatively safe place as long as some general precautions are observed. Arizona's urban centers have lower crime rates in contrast to other US cities, but it is still wise to be cautious and to find out which parts are unsafe at night. When traveling across remote areas, take a reliable local map, and follow the advice of local rangers and visitor centers. These sources also offer invaluable information on survival in the wilderness and on safety procedures that should be followed during outdoor activities *(see pp58–61 & 150–55)*. It is also advisable to check the local media such as newspapers, television, and radio for current weather and safety conditions.

## PERSONAL SAFETY

MOST TOURIST AREAS in Arizona are friendly and non-threatening. However, to avoid being a victim of crime, it is wise to observe a few basic rules. Never carry large amounts of cash, wear obviously expensive jewelry, or keep your wallet in your back pocket. Wear handbags and cameras over one shoulder with the strap across your body. Keep your identification separate from your cash and traveler's checks. Most hotels have safety deposit boxes or safes in which you should store any valuables.

If you are driving, be sure to lock any valuables in the trunk where they are out-of-sight, and to park only in well-lit parking lots. Also, it is wise to have a roadside assistance service plan, such as AAA *(see p165)*, which sends licensed service representatives in case assistance is needed. Similarly, at night it is better to stay where there are other people and be aware of which areas could be unsafe. It is a good idea to carry a cell phone so that you can call 911 in an emergency. In tourist destinations, lock the car when stepping out.

**Police officer on horseback patrol in Nogales**

Parking areas in national parks, particularly overlooks and trailheads, are extremely popular targets for thieves.

## MEDICAL TREATMENT

FOR EMERGENCIES that require assistance from the medical, police, or fire services call 911. **Traveler's Aid Society**, a national organization, extends help to needy travelers. City hospitals with emergency rooms can be found in the directory, but they are often overcrowded. Private hospitals offer more personalized treatment and are listed in the Yellow Pages. Walk-in clinics offer basic medical services, and are usually less expensive and more efficient than hospitals for non-emergencies. You may be required to provide evidence of your ability to pay before a doctor will agree to treat you, hence the importance of adequate medical insurance. Hotels will usually call a doctor or recommend a local dentist.

## TRAVEL INSURANCE

ARIZONA HAS excellent medical services, but as in the rest of the US they are very expensive. Visitors are strongly advised to make sure they have comprehensive medical and dental coverage for the duration of their stay. Visitors planning to take part in outdoor activities in remote areas or stay on Native reservations should consider including medical air evacuation insurance as well.

## TRAVEL SAFETY

THERE ARE plenty of remote areas and lightly traveled roads in Arizona. Before you go, check that your car has a spare tire, and the tools required to change it, and that you know how to replace a flat tire. Carry a cell phone, blanket, and emergency food and water in case of a breakdown in a remote area.

**Lone truck on rough Arizona desert road**

Park ranger at the Petrified Forest National Park, Arizona

## OUTDOOR SAFETY

THE WEATHER in the Southwest can present a number of dangerous situations, especially in Southern Arizona, where sudden summer storms may cause flash floods. Weather information can be obtained from ranger stations, and through reports on radio and television. If you are planning a drive or hike in remote territory, always tell someone where you are going and when you expect to return.

The dry summer heat is often underestimated, and hikers are advised to carry at least a gallon (4 liters) of drinking water per person for each day of walking. Dry conditions also pose the risk of forest fires at higher elevations, and it is advisable to check with forest service rangers regarding fire danger before lighting any flame.

The sun is surprisingly strong at higher elevations, and an effective sunscreen and sunhat should always be worn. Temperatures can change rapidly in Arizona. It may be 80°F (26°C) during the day, and then drop to 30°F (-1°C) at night. Be prepared and dress accordingly.

Dangerous creatures are found in the wilderness (see p17), but these animals generally avoid humans and it

is unlikely you will be bitten if you avoid their habitats. Do not turn over rocks or reach up to touch rock ledges. Shake out clothes and shoes that have been on the ground before putting them on. Venomous stings and bites may hurt but are rarely fatal to adults with prompt medical attention. Always carry a first aid and snakebite kit if you are going into snake country.

## TRAVELING ON THE RESERVATIONS

VISITORS ARE welcome on reservations, and will generally find Natives to be friendly and helpful. However, take the same care as when traveling in any remote rural area of the US. Services such as restaurants, motels, gas stations, and ATMs are only located in towns and at major crossroads. Call 911 in case of an emergency. If a serious medical situation develops, you will be provided first-line treatment and then shifted to a hospital off the reservation. Most reservations also have their own highly trained police forces, which enforce the laws and assist lost tourists. It is illegal to bring alcohol onto reservations – even a bottle visible in a locked car will land you in trouble. Always ask before photographing anything, and

Navajo security personnel

be prepared that a fee may be requested. Do not wander off marked trails as this is forbidden. Dress respectfully – for example, the Hopi request that people do not wear shorts.

Speak softly when talking to Natives as loud voices are considered rude. Speak clearly and remember that English is a second language for many Native Americans.

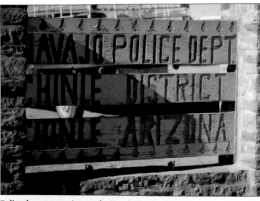

Police department sign on the Navajo Reservation

# TRAVEL INFORMATION

**P**HOENIX, followed by Tucson, is the main gateway for visitors arriving in Arizona by air. There are other major airports in neighboring states that also serve as entry points, including the cities of Las Vegas in Nevada, Salt Lake City in Utah, and Albuquerque in New Mexico. Visitors also arrive by long-distance bus or, less frequently, by Amtrak train. However, the automobile remains the preferred

**American Airlines**

mode of transport. Arizona has an excellent, well-maintained network of highways, service stations, and comfortable, air-conditioned cars for rent.

Public transportation options are increasing in major urban centers of the state – a light rail service has been implemented, and local bus systems have expanded their hours of operation. The downtown shuttle is used by visitors during weekday working hours.

An airplane flying over the Phoenix skyline at sunset

## ARRIVING BY AIR

**P**HOENIX'S SKY Harbor International is the largest airport in Arizona. It has three terminals and receives the bulk of domestic and international arrivals. Sky Harbor and Tucson International Airport are centers for major US airlines that offer both international and domestic routes; these include **American Airlines**, **Continental Airlines**, **Delta Airlines**, Frontier Airlines, **Northwest Airlines**, **Southwest Airlines**, and **United Airlines**. From Phoenix, **America West** flies

**Mesa Airlines logo**

to the cities of Tucson, Flagstaff, Sedona, and Yuma.

Unlike other American destinations, there are very few non-stop flights into Arizona from outside the United States. Most international visitors have to connect via one of the country's major airports, such as Los Angeles, San Francisco, Chicago, Atlanta, or Dallas. Travelers from Pacific countries generally change at Honolulu, Hawaii. Those foreign carriers that do have direct flights to Phoenix include **British Airways**, **Air Canada**, and **AeroMexico**.

## AIR FARES

**T**HERE IS AN array of fare types and prices available. The cheaper tickets are usually booked early, especially between June and September, as well as around the Christmas and Thanksgiving holidays.

Direct bookings can be done through an agent, travel website or through an airline. Agents are a good source of information on bargains and ticket restrictions. They may also offer special deals to those booking rental cars, accommodations, and flights. Fly-drive deals, where the cost of the ticket includes car rental, may also be a lower-priced option.

Although there are several websites offering bargains on last minute bookings, travel websites offer the convenience of price comparisons. Prices can change daily, so check at various times before buying tickets that impose penalties for changes. However, the travel websites may not always have the best prices on tickets or packages. Part of your comparison shopping should include visiting the websites, and calling up individual airlines, hotels, and rental car outfits. Also check the travel section of big city newspapers for special rates.

| AIRPORT |  INFORMATION | DISTANCE TO CITY CENTER | TRAVEL TIME BY ROAD |
|---------|-------------|------------------------|--------------------|
| Phoenix | (602) 273-3300 | 4 miles (6.4 km) | 15 minutes |
| Tucson | (520) 573-8000 | 8 miles (12.8 km) | 30 minutes |
| Flagstaff | (928) 556-1234 | 7 miles (11.3 km) | 10 minutes |

**A Grand Canyon Railway train on its way to Grand Canyon Village**

## TRAVELING BY TRAIN & BUS

TRAIN AND BUS travel in Arizona can be slower than the more popular car and plane travel, but it can also be an enjoyable means of exploring the region.

Long-distance **Greyhound** buses are the least expensive way to travel, and they also offer the widest choice of destinations. Some of the most useful bus links operate out of airports and train stations. There are 27 daily routes throughout Arizona, as well as eight daily trips direct to Tucson, from Phoenix's Sky Harbor airport. Greyhound and a number of other companies also offer package tours. Destinations include national parks, such as Grand Canyon, and casinos, as well as urban and historical tours on luxury, air-conditioned buses. The packages include meals and accommodations.

**Amtrak** offers two train routes through Arizona – Southwest Chief runs daily between Chicago and Los Angeles, through the Navajo and Hopi reservations, Winslow, Gallop, and Flagstaff, while the Sunset Limited travels three times a week

between Orlando and Los Angeles, passing through Tucson and Yuma. Both offer National Park Service cultural and natural heritage programs. The superliners have two-tier cars, a choice of sleeping accommodations, restaurant, lounge, and large windows.

For rail enthusiasts, the **Grand Canyon Railway** offers both diesel and steam rail trips from Williams *(see p29)* to the Grand Canyon. The two-hour trip offers packages with meals and overnight accommodations. Western entertainment – including a posse of bad guys staging an attack on the train – is also included.

## PUBLIC TRANSPORTATION IN CITIES

WITH THE EXCEPTION of Flagstaff, which can be explored on foot, the major cities in Arizona, such as Phoenix and Tucson, are large areas and are plagued by traffic problems. Visitors could use public transportation, such as local buses, to tour these. Booking a tour can often be the best way of seeing both major city sights and some of the more remote scenery.

Phoenix and Scottsdale *(see pp76–80)* are covered by the **Valley Metro** bus and light rail system, as well as by **Ollie the Trolley**, a bus service that runs between Scottsdale's resorts and its shopping districts. Downtown Phoenix also has the convenient **Downtown Dash**, which travels between the State Capitol, Arizona Center, and the Civic Plaza. Tucson *(see pp88–91)* has the **Sun Tran** bus system.

**Greyhound bus crossing Southwestern desert landscape**

---

# Traveling By Car & Four-Wheel Drive

**Sign for RV parking**

WHEN THE MOVIE characters Thelma and Louise, in the film of the same name, won a kind of freedom on the open roads of the Southwest, they promoted the pleasures of driving in this visually spectacular and dramatic region. However, for both residents and visitors, driving is a necessary part of life in Arizona, and a car is often the only means of reaching remote country areas. Tours of picturesque regions, such as the North Rim of the Grand Canyon *(see p55)*, Canyon de Chelly National Monument *(see pp106–9)*, or the Organ Pipe Cactus National Monument *(see p96)*, are best made by car. The entire state is served by a network of well-maintained roads, from multilane highways to winding, scenic routes that lead to even the remotest areas.

## RENTING A CAR

MOST OF THE major car rental businesses, such as **Alamo**, **Avis**, and **Hertz**, and some budget dealers, such as **Budget**, **Dollar Rent-A-Car**, and **Thrifty Auto**, have outlets at airports, and in towns and cities across Arizona. However, for those planning to fly into Phoenix, the least expensive option may be to arrange a fly-drive deal *(see p162)*.

There is a central computerized booking system for most of the car companies – use the toll-free number and the Internet to find the best rates. Bargains can also be found by booking in advance and for travel during the off-season.

*Hertz*

**Hertz car-rental logo**

## RENTING SUVs & 4WDs

VISITORS PLANNING to travel the back roads of Arizona to explore places like Chaco Canyon *(see pp112–3)* or Monument Valley *(see pp102–3)* may want to rent a sports utility vehicle (SUV) or a four-wheel drive (4WD) vehicle; such vehicles provide greater road clearance. Roads that require high clearance in Arizona are usually marked as such. In wet conditions, it is safest to travel by a 4WD on these roads, and it is also advisable to use 4WD vehicles on dirt roads. Most of the major car rental companies offer 4WD SUVs, but you must ask for guaranteed delivery, specify the 4WD

you want, and make sure you understand the usage restrictions, if any. Also, some car rental agreements do not allow travel on unpaved roads.

For serious off-road 4WD use, **Farabee** in Sedona rents modified jeeps for four to eight hours of use on designated trails.

## RENTING RVs

ONE OF THE most interesting and cost-effective ways of enjoying Arizona's vast and fascinating outdoors is in a recreational vehicle (RV). An RV gives you more freedom to explore on your own schedule, the ease of unpacking only once, and the convenience of cooking in your own kitchen.

Campgrounds are plentiful, and you can choose between the grounds of the National Park Service, Forest Service, Bureau of Land Management and private companies *(see pp150–53 & p159)*. The **Recreation Vehicle Rental Association (RVRA)** offers tips on selecting a rental RV, campground information, as well as rental agreement information. Make sure that the rental company provides roadside assistance if required, and that it explains the operations and usage of all the features of the RV. Also, plan to spend your first night near the dealer in case you require additional information after driving and sleeping in the RV.

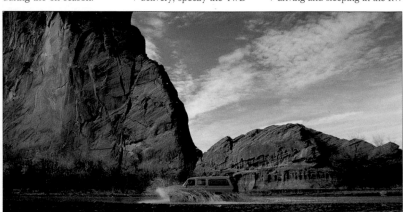

**Sports utility vehicle moving through Canyon de Chelly**

Recreational vehicle in Arizonan backcountry

## BACKCOUNTRY DRIVING

FOR ANY TRAVEL in the remote parts of Arizona, such as the desert regions and Native reservations, it is very important to check your route to see if a 4WD vehicle is required. Although many backcountry areas have graded dirt and gravel roads, which can be used by conventional cars, a 4WD is essential in some wild and remote areas. Monument Valley, for example, has a self-guided driving tour on dirt roads. Contact motoring organizations and tourist centers for information to assess your backcountry trip properly.

There are certain basic safety points that should be observed on any trip of this kind. Plan your route and carry up-to-date maps. When traveling between remote destinations, inform the police or National Park Service wardens of your departure and expected arrival times. Check weather and road conditions before you start, and be aware of seasonal dangers such as flash floods. Carry plenty of food and water, and a cell phone as an added precaution. If you run out of gas or break down, call for help and stay with your vehicle since it offers protection from the elements.

Native flora and fauna must not be removed or damaged. Also, visitors should not drive off-road unless they are in a specially designated area, and especially not on Native reservation land. If driving an RV, you must stop overnight in designated campgrounds.

## ROADSIDE SERVICES

ALTHOUGH ARIZONA has many remote destinations, service stations are usually located in towns and at the intersections of major highways. Most have small stores that offer drinks, snacks, and basic automotive parts. Seldom are they more than 60 miles (96 km) apart. Not all stations provide mechanical assistance, so visitors may want to join a roadside assistance organization, such as the **American Automobile Association (AAA)**, that will come to their aid at a call. In the Phoenix area, Freeway Safety Patrol vehicles assist stranded motorists by diagnosing minor vehicle problems, helping with repairs, and calling a tow truck.

Unimproved road sign

Gas service station on the legendary Route 66

# General Index

# Acknowledgments

**MAIN CONTRIBUTOR**
**Paul Franklin** is a travel writer and photographer specializing in the United States and Canada. He is the author of several guide books and magazine articles, and is based in Livingston, Texas.

**CONTRIBUTORS**
Nancy Mikula, Donna Dailey, Michelle de Larrabeiti, Philip Lee.

**FACTCHECKERS**
Paul Franklin and Nancy Mikula.

**PROOFREADER**
Sonia Malik.

**INDEXER**
Chumki Sen.

**DK LONDON**
**PUBLISHER**
Douglas Amrine.

**PUBLISHING MANAGERS**
Fay Franklin, Jane Ewart.

**EDITORIAL & DESIGN ASSISTANCE**
Brigitte Arora, Tessa Bindloss.

**ADDITIONAL PHOTOGRAPHY**
Paul Franklin, Steve Gorton, Dave King, Andrew McKinney, Neil Mersh, Tim Ridley, Clive Streeter.

**CARTOGRAPHY**
Uma Bhattacharya, Alok Pathak, Ben Bowles, Rob Clynes, Sam Johnston, James Macdonald (Colourmap Scanning Ltd).

**SENIOR DTP DESIGNER**
Jason Little.

**SENIOR CARTOGRAPHIC EDITOR**
Casper Morris.

**DK PICTURE LIBRARY**
Gemma Woodward, Hayley Smith, Romaine Werblow.

**PRODUCTION CONTROLLER**
Louise Daly.

**ADDITIONAL CONTRIBUTIONS**
Sonal Bhatt, Brett Steel, Ros Walford.

DORLING KINDERSLEY would like to thank the following people whose contributions and assistance have made the preparation of this book possible.

**SPECIAL ASSISTANCE**
Many thanks for the invaluable help of the following individuals: Juliet Martin, Heard Museum; Stacy Reading and Brett Brooks, Phoenix CVB; Barbara MacDonald and Hope Patterson, Tucson CVB; Leslie Connell and Ana Masterson, Flagstaff CVB; Michelle Mountain, Museum of Northern Arizona; Tom Pittinger, Grand Canyon National Park; Russ Bodner, Chaco Culture National Historic Park; and all the national park staff in the region.

**PHOTOGRAPHY PERMISSIONS**
Dorling Kindersley would like to thank all the cathedrals, churches, museums, hotels, restaurants, shops, galleries, national and state parks, and other sights for their assistance and kind permission to photograph at their establishments.

Placement Key – t=top; tl=top left; tlc=top left center; tc=top center; trc=top right center; tr=top right; cla=center left above; ca=center above; ca=center right above; cl=center left; c=center; cr=center right; clb=center left below; cb=center below; crb=center right below; bl=bottom left; b=bottom; bc=bottom center; bcl=bottom center left; br=bottom right; d=detail.

Works of art and images have been produced with the permission of the following copyright holders: Frank Lloyd Wright Foundation 21ca, 81b; University of Arizona Fine Arts Oasis Barbara Grygutis *Front Row Center* 88tl.

The publishers would like to thank the following individuals, companies, and picture libraries for their kind permission to reproduce their photographs:

AFP: Spaceimaging.com 9t; ALAMY: 72t, 161c; ARIZONA GAME & FISH DEPARTMENT: Pat O'Brien 12tc; ARIZONA OFFICE OF TOURISM: Chris Coe 28tr; ARIZONA STATE LIBRARY: Archive+Public Records, Archive Division, Phoenix no.99–0281 34; ARIZONA STATE PARKS: K. L. Day 99t; ASSOCIATED PRESS: Louisa Gauerke 29cl, Roy Dabner 148b; AURA/NOAO/National SCIENCE FOUNDATION: 94b.

BRANSON REYNOLDS: 23b; BRIDGEMAN ART LIBRARY: Christie's London Walter Ufer (1876–1936) *The Southwest* 6–7; Frederic Remington (1861–1909) *Aiding a Comrade* c.1890 24–5, *The Conversation, or Dubious Company* 24b.

CORBIS: 41t, 41clb, 41b; Art on File 21clb, 21br; Bettman *Cowboy on a Horse* Frederic Remington (1861–1909) 18cl, 24cb, 24tr, 38cb, 39bl, 43c, 109b, 162tc; Duomo/Jason Wise 154t; New Sport/Gark Newkirk 154b; James L. Amos 110t; Tom Bean 2–3, 12b, 17br, 26tr, 26b, 30cra, 33b, 37cr, 49b, 60b, 68bc, 142br, 151t, 151c, 152t; Patrick Bennett 68br; Yann Arthus-Bertrand 91b; Geoffrey Clements 147t; Richard A. Cooke 18b; Richard Cummins 13t, 68t, 68c, 73b; Owen Franken 165t; Marc Garanger 161b; Raymond Gehman 84cla, 85cb; Lowell Georgia 84bl, 84br; Mark E. Gibson 95b; Darrel Gulin 17tr, 17bc; Richard Hamilton 160b; Jan Butchofsky-Houser 27t, 164t; Dave G. Houser 85clb, 144b; George H. H. Huey 86–7, 96c; Liz Hymans 37t; Dewitt Jones 36tr; Catherine Karnow 22ca, 68clb, 68cb, 164b; Layne Kennedy 58c, 98b; Douglas Kirkland 120–21; Danny Lehman 59t, 142c; James Marshall 20tr; Joe McDonald 91t; David Muench 1c, 17cr, 36–7, 51c, 73t, 85t, 114–5; Marc Muench 58b; Pat O'Hara 52bl; Gabe Palmer 23c; Greg Probst 84cl; Carl & Ann Purcell 60t; Roger Ressmeyer 94c; Tony Roberts 154cl, 154cr, 155t; Joel W. Rogers 61t, 162c; Bob Rowan 3c, 22tl; Pete Saloutos 147crb; Phil Schermeister 30bl; Richard Hamilton Smith 143b; Scott T. Smith 17clb; Kennan Ward 16tr; Ron Watts 48cl; Nik Wheeler 122c; CORBIS SYGMA: Stone Les 160c.

DAVE G. HOUSER: 31b; © Mrs. Anna Marie Houser/The Allan Houser Foundation 19t; DIANA DICKER: 36b; DIGITAL CLARITY: Hayden Houser 83t, 83b.

GRAND CANYON CAVERNS: 28br; GREYHOUND LINES, INC.: 163b; GOULDINGS LODGE: 103b.

HEARD MUSEUM: Fred Harvey Collection/Daniel Namingha *Red-Tailed Hawk* 18–9, 79t; HOPI LEARNING CENTER: 18tr, 146cl; HOUSERSTOCK: Ellen Barone 32.

IMPACT PHOTOS: Jacquie Spector 28bl; INDEXSTOCK IMAGERY: Mark Gibson 144t; James Lemass 149b.

JOHN RUNNING: 22crb, 23t.

KERRICK JAMES PHOTOGRAPHY: 26–7; KOBAL COLLECTION, LONDON: Paramount Pictures 25b.

MASTERFILE: G.D.Gifford 148c; MESA AIRLINES: 162cb.

MUSEUM OF NEW MEXICO: Fray Orci *Portrait of Don Juan Bautista de Anza* 1774 neg. no. 50828 39br(d).

NHPA: 16br; John Shaw 16clb; courtesy of the NATIONAL PARK SERVICE, CHACO CULTURE NATIONAL HISTORIC PARK: 36cb, 37b, 112tl; NEW MEXICO TOURISM: 30tc.

PAUL FRANKLIN: 13c, 49cr, 50br, 55tr, 59b, 116 all, 117t, 117b, 143t; PETER NEWARK PICTURES: 24cla, 25tl, 35c, 39t, 40t, 40br; PRIVATE COLLECTION: 7c, 39cb, 157c.

RAMAN SRINIVASAN: 97t.

SHARLOT HALL MUSEUM: 31t; STONE: Tom Bean 33tc; Paul Chesley 100; Steve Lewis 29cr.

UNIVERSITY OF ARCHEOLOGY & ANTHROPOLOGY: 146bl; UNIVERSITY OF ARIZONA: 88tl.

YUMA CONVENTION AND VISITORS BUREAU: ©Robert Herko 1999 95t.

Front endpaper: all special photography except STONE: Paul Chesley cr.

Jacket photography: Front – CORBIS: Tom Bean Front t; DK IMAGES: Demetrio Carrasco cb; Alan Keohane bl, cr. Back – DK IMAGES: Demetrio Carrasco tl; Alan Keohane br. Spine – CORBIS: Tom Bean.

EYEWITNESS TRAVEL INSURANCE

# FOR PEACE OF MIND ABROAD,
## WE'VE GOT IT COVERED

 **DK INSURANCE** PROVIDES YOU WITH QUALITY WORLDWIDE INSURANCE COVER

**For an instant quote**
go to **www.dk.com/travel-insurance**

Organised by Columbus Travel Insurance Services Ltd, 17 Devonshire Square, London EC2M 4SQ, UK.
Underwritten by certain underwriters at Lloyd's and Professional Travel Insurance Company Ltd.